Low-fee Private Schooling:
aggravating equity or mitigating disadvantage?

Low-fee Private Schooling:
aggravating equity or mitigating disadvantage?

Edited by
Prachi Srivastava

Oxford Studies in Comparative Education
Series Editor: David Phillips

SYMPOSIUM
BOOKS

Symposium Books
PO Box 204, Didcot, Oxford OX11 9ZQ, United Kingdom
www.symposium-books.co.uk

Published in the United Kingdom, 2013

ISBN 978-1-873927-91-5

This publication is also available on a subscription basis
as Volume 22 Number 2 of *Oxford Studies in Comparative Education*
(ISSN 0961-2149)

Printed and bound in the United Kingdom by Hobbs the Printers, Southampton
www.hobbs.uk.com

Contents

Acknowledgements

Thanks are due to the following individuals. David Phillips, the series editor, Claire Noronha, Pauline Rose, Ricardo Sabates, Leon Tikly, and the anonymous reviewers who invested their time for the blind review of chapters and their astute commentary; and Lianna Baur and Paresh Soni for editorial assistance.

CHAPTER 1

Low-fee Private Schooling: issues and evidence

PRACHI SRIVASTAVA

Background and Aims

In 2001, when I first began studying low-fee private schooling, there were almost no published studies in the scholarly literature on the topic. Technical reports on the use of unrecognised or 'spontaneous' forms of private schooling by lower-income households had started to emerge (e.g. Majumdar & Vaidyanathan, 1995; Kim et al, 1999; Kitaev, 1999; Probe Team, 1999; Aggarwal, 2000; Alderman et al, 2001). An influential monograph by James Tooley (1999) based on a consultancy for the International Finance Corporation on emerging forms of private involvement in education across a range of developing countries captured the attention of policy elites. However, on the specific topic of low-fee private schooling, aside from a preliminary report of his first research project on this emerging form of provision (Tooley, 2001), there was little other than anecdotal reports and some news stories.

In international development and domestic policy circles, people spoke of 'budget schools', 'private schools for the poor', 'new types of private schools', or 'teaching shops' in amazed or derisory terms to describe this as yet undefined but seemingly tangibly different type of private schooling. However, until I was compelled to operationalise what seemed to me at the time a nebulous set of independently owned and operated private schools claiming to serve socially and economically disadvantaged groups, the term 'low-fee private schooling' did not exist.

One of my first experiences of reporting the results of my study on Lucknow District, Uttar Pradesh, India was at the World Congress of Comparative Education Societies (WCCES) in 2004, held that year in Havana. While the paper was well received, the broader proposal to the research community to expand the focus on emerging forms of private provision in education in developing countries for serious study was met, at best, with scepticism from academics, who were doubtful that these phenomena existed or were in sufficient volume to be of interest, particularly regarding the participation of poorer households; more often, however, they were apprehensive or unwilling to engage with them, given the Education for All mandate. I found this lack of scholarly engagement deeply disconcerting, feeling that the implications of increasing and emerging forms of private provision - and particularly low-fee private schooling - were potentially too great to leave a vacuum of rigorous academic and systematic analysis when there were serious equity considerations at stake, particularly in countries where even the most basic indicators of universal primary coverage and access were low. Similar to Belfield and Levin's (2005) experience of the discourse on vouchers in education, it seemed that 'ideology trumped evidence' emerging from the ground – that is, evidence of the real schooling choices that some (seemingly increasing numbers of) disadvantaged households were making to access low-fee private schools in the context of Education for All – and neither side of the camp, whether opponents or proponents of private sector involvement in education, had a monopoly on ideological persuasion.

However, it did not take long for the tide to turn. Technical reports showed that private provision increased during the span of Jomtien and Dakar Education for All commitments, and grew globally by 58% between 1991 and 2004 (Patrinos et al, 2009, p. 3). Internationally, the discourse on the role of private non-state actors in education quickly gained prominence with influential policy actors such as the World Bank, UNESCO and donor organisations (LaRocque, 2006; Rose, 2007; Genevois, 2008; Patrinos et al, 2009), causing a heated debate among scholars, practitioners and policy-makers. The 2009 UNESCO Education for All Global Monitoring Report addressed private non-state actors and provision for the first time in its analysis (a continued focus in subsequent reports), with a section devoted to low-fee private schooling (see UNESCO, 2008). Anecdotes of consulting, venture capital, and education companies investing in low-fee private schools emerged, the most recent example being the UK-based Pearson, reported as launching a £10 million fund to invest in 'affordable private schools' in Africa and Asia (Tran, 2012).

Among the first set of studies conducted on low-fee private schooling, there seemed to be a confluence of work on India (e.g. De et al, 2002; Tooley & Dixon, 2003; Srivastava, 2006), perhaps spurred by the number of earlier technical reports on the changing nature of private provision in the country. These studies used different methods, had different aims and scopes, and drew different conclusions. For example, De et al's (2002) household and school survey study of one district each in Haryana, Rajasthan and Uttar Pradesh found that while low-fee private schools were accessed in rural and urban areas, asset ownership confirmed that private-school children came from somewhat better-off families, and this choice was relatively more favourable for boys. The most disadvantaged accessed government schools which were of comparatively lower quality on basic indicators of facilities and teaching activity. On the basis of household data, the researchers concluded that the more newly established, low-fee private schools would probably cease to function if government schools were held up to the task of delivering good-quality schooling, as it would free disadvantaged households from the strain of sacrificing income and selecting which child to enrol to which type of school, or whether to enrol any child at all.

Tooley and Dixon's (2003) original work in India, funded by the Centre for British Teachers (CfBT), was based on a case study of 15 schools, 315 parents, 315 students and 244 teachers in Hyderabad, Andhra Pradesh. Based on the assumption of private sector superiority over the state, the project had four objectives for 'private schools for the poor': to create a sustainable business model for school capacity building; to explore appropriate pedagogy and curricula; to catalogue the regulatory framework; and to explore possibilities of creating a loan scheme for these schools and a private scholarship fund for the poorest students (p. 8). The researchers concluded that 'running a school even for low-income families was potentially a profitable undertaking, with estimated profits of about 25% in the year of recognition' (Tooley & Dixon, 2003, p. 19); many regulations were ignored or subject to the payment of bribes; and while these schools were not affordable to all, given state-sector dysfunctions, investment in them and establishing voucher or scholarship schemes offered the best chance for disadvantaged groups.

My in-depth qualitative work on Lucknow District, Uttar Pradesh showed that while low-fee private schools in that context certainly provided an alternative to state schools for a segment of the population, the exit of the mobilised poor from the state sector had the potential to contribute to a schooling arena increasingly segmented by social class, and further, that the set of corrupt practices and perverse incentives through which low-fee private schools operated and often gained recognition raised serious questions (see Srivastava, 2006, 2007a, 2008b). This range of conclusions signalled the quintessential debate that undergirds much of the broader discussion on the involvement of non-state actors in and privatisation of education in developing countries, underscoring the question: do low-fee private schools aggravate equity or mitigate disadvantage?

Almost a decade since those studies were conducted, there is now an emerging literature on low-fee private schooling in developing countries. As Walford (2011) notes, there remains a concentration of work on India (e.g. Shukla & Joshi, 2008; Baird 2009; Härmä, 2009; Tooley et al, 2010; Ohara, 2012), but there is also work on other countries, such as Ghana (Akyeampong, 2009; Akaguri, 2011), Malawi (Chimombo, 2009), Nigeria (Rose & Adelabu, 2007; Umar, 2008; Härmä, 2011), Pakistan (Alderman et al, 2003; Andrabi et al, 2008; Fennell & Malik, 2012), Uganda (Kisira, 2008), and others. Furthermore, numerous newer studies have documented the rise of different forms of private provision and private sector involvement (see collection of papers in Day Ashley & Caddell, 2006; Srivastava & Walford, 2007), including low-fee private schooling, but also private supplemental tutoring (e.g. Kenya and much of Asia) (e.g. Buchmann, 2002; Foondun, 2002; Bray, 2006); publicly and privately financed vouchers and targeted subsidies enabling private or government assisted private school choice (e.g. Chile, Colombia, India, Pakistan) (e.g. Gauri & Vawda 2004; Andrabi et al, 2008); public–private and multiple stakeholder partnership agreements (e.g. LaRocque, 2006; Genevois, 2008; Patrinos et al, 2009), including for-profit providers; and regulatory frameworks favouring increases in private schools (e.g. India, Madagascar, Malawi, Nigeria) (e.g. Rose & Adelabu 2007; Srivastava 2008b).

Thus, by the time the 2010 WCCES conference was held in Istanbul (the second after Havana), the topics of low-fee private schooling and, more broadly, non-state private sector involvement in the context of Education for All, while complex, ideological and problematic, were no longer on the fringe. The conference had a thematic group titled 'Privatization and Marketization in Education', with a number of illuminating presentations on private provision in different contexts around the world. I organised a research panel on low-fee private schooling under this theme to consolidate new field research evidence, from which some of the chapters in this volume are drawn (i.e. Akyeampong & Rolleston [Chapter 2]; Fennell [Chapter 3]; Härmä & Adefisayo [Chapter 6]), and which, to my surprise, attracted a standing-room-only audience.

This edited volume aims to add to the growing literature on low-fee private schooling by presenting seven empirically grounded studies in five countries (Ghana, India, Kenya, Nigeria and Pakistan), and begins and ends with an analysis of some of the evidence and debates on the topic thus far (Srivastava, Chapter 1; Walford, Chapter 9). The book aims to add to the literature in two ways. The first is by presenting research findings from studies across three levels of analysis that have proved relevant in the study of low-fee private schooling – the household, the school and the state. Chapters in this volume address household schooling choice behaviours regarding low-fee private and competing sectors (Akyeampong & Rolleston on Ghana [Chapter 2]; Fennell on Pakistan [Chapter 3]); the management, operation and relative quality of low-fee private schools (Dixon et al on Kenya [Chapter 4]; Härmä & Adefisayo on Nigeria [Chapter 6]); and changes to the regulatory frameworks governing low-fee private schools and the impact of low-fee private schools on those frameworks (Humayun et al on Pakistan [Chapter 8]; Ohara on India [Chapter 7]; Stern & Heyneman on Kenya [Chapter 5]).

The book does not seek to provide definitive answers since, as an emerging and evolving area of study, this would be premature. Instead, its second aim is to call attention to the need for further systematic research on low-fee private schooling, and to open up the debate by presenting studies that use a range of methods and, owing to the context specificity of the issue, draw different conclusions. The hope is that these studies may serve as springboards to further potential research.

Finally, the book does not aim to snuff out the political and sometimes heated debate surrounding low-fee private schooling (e.g. see Rose & Dyer, 2008; Sarangapani, 2009; Nambissan, 2010; Sarangapani & Winch, 2010; Walford, Chapter 9, this volume) and private provision more broadly, or to erase the complications that abound in conducting research in this area; rather, it seeks to engage with them. For example, in Chapter 9, Walford focuses on the debate and controversy that surrounded Tooley and his team's work when it was first published and that it still attracts (e,g., Rose & Dyer, 2008; Nambissan & Ball, 2010; Sarangapani & Winch 2010), providing a starting point towards this end. The remainder of this chapter will set out some of the salient issues that are at the heart of conducting research on low-fee private schooling as I see them, and will contextualise the chapters in this volume as relevant therein.

The Problem of Definition

Part of the problem in analysing low-fee private schooling is that much like the rest of the private sector, the low-fee private sector is heterogeneous. The heterogeneity of the private sector was perhaps most notably highlighted by Kitaev who, resulting from a large International Institute for Educational Planning (IIEP)-UNESCO study on private provision across Africa and Asia (Kitaev, 1999, 2007), supplied the following definition of private schools:

> An institution is classified as private if it is controlled and managed by a non-governmental organisation (e.g. church, trade union, business enterprise, etc.), or if its governing board consists mostly of members not selected by a public agency... The most common definition of a private school is one that is not managed by a state or public authority. (Kitaev, 2007, p. 92)

It is important to note that in this definition, the *management* arrangement assumes importance rather than the financing or regulatory arrangements, which, in addition to ownership, are also typically considered in classifying schools. Thus, a broader definition of 'private education is... all formal schools that are not public, and may be founded, owned, managed and financed by actors other than the state, even in cases when the state provides most of the funding and has considerable control over these schools' (Kitaev, 1999, p. 43).

The interest in low-fee private schools was initially sparked by their financing arrangements. Low-fee private schools were (and for the most part still are) usually characterised as being independently funded through comparatively lower tuition fees (relative to elite or higher-fee private schools), financially sustained through direct payments from poorer or relatively disadvantaged households (though not necessarily the poorest or most disadvantaged), and independently managed and owned by a single owner or team, usually comprising family members. Research on low-fee private schools thus far shows that they may be unrecognised or recognised; urban, peri-urban or rural; single operations or, as the sector has evolved, part of a chain; they may be run for different motives; they may provide instruction at a discrete level (usually primary) or at multiple levels (with or without recognition); and, as part of the private sector, they are likely to be governed by different regulations across countries (and in decentralised systems within countries). However, there is no standardised or universally agreed definition in the literature, complicating the collation of evidence across studies. Nonetheless, Phillipson (2008) attempts to provide one:

> Defining precisely what we mean by a 'low-cost private school' is easier to do in terms of what it is not rather than what it is. It is not a school run by a nongovernmental organisation [NGO] for charitable or development purposes. It is not a school run by a religious organisation for the furtherance of a particular set of moral values or beliefs. It is not a school offering an educational advantage to its pupils and charging a high price for the privilege of gaining access to it. Finally, it is not a school set up by the local community until the government agrees to take over ownership. In contrast to these distinctions, the low-cost private school is a school that has been set up and is owned by an individual or individuals for the purpose of making profit. (p. 1)

But Walford (2011) finds 'this definition unhelpful' and claims that it is

> not even consistently applied within [Phillipson's] book itself. Not only are these distinctions not clear, in that there may well be multiple reasons for starting and continuing to run a school for the poor, the exclusion of NGOs (especially small, local NGOs), religious organisations, and those who might eventually wish to obtain some state funding omits from consideration a considerable part of the growth in non-governmental low-fee schooling. It also restricts our understanding of why such schools might be started and how the schools themselves, and the motivations for their continued existence, may change in nature over a period of time. For example, even the idea that they must 'make a profit' collapses within the complexity of individuals and groups paying themselves salaries, or establishing schools so that they might gain employment. What is clear is that the vast majority of these new private schools are not the result of shareholders investing money in schools because they see that as the way to obtain the highest financial return. The reasons for starting and continuing with the schools are much more complex, and there is thus the need to consider the whole range of non-government-sector schools with

> low fees that are designed to serve some of the poorest families in each society. (pp. 402-403)

While one can certainly appreciate that the heterogeneity of private school types potentially falling into the low-fee sector necessitates a clarification on its scope, narrowing the focus too much may be as unhelpful as making it too broad. For example, implicit in part of Phillipson's (2008) definition that '[i]t is not a school offering an educational advantage to its pupils and charging a high price for the privilege of gaining access to it' (p. 1) is an assumption that low-fee private schools do not offer any educational advantage, with the further implication that poorer parents accessing these schools are 'duped'. While I agree that there are certainly many unanswered questions on the relative quality of these schools, and while my own work and that of others questions claims and assumptions of uniform 'better quality' when the baseline of the state sector in many contexts is so low as to be negligible (De et al, 2002; Srivastava, 2007b; Akaguri, 2011; Fennell & Malik, 2012; Fennell, Chapter 3, this volume), controversial as it may be, systematic research on the potential advantages of the low-fee private sector is mixed and in its infancy. It is premature to hold firm assumptions either way (see further discussion on quality below).

Second, work on low-fee private school choice shows complex motivations for accessing these schools, and for a range of reasons (Srivastava, 2006, 2008a; Härmä, 2009; Akaguri, 2011; Fennell, Chapter 3, this volume). While there is information asymmetry on the exact nature or quality of schooling provided, and relative inexperience with formal schooling of households that access them, some work nonetheless shows 'active choice' and engagement with these schools (Srivastava, 2006, 2007b, 2008a; Härmä, 2009; Fennell, Chapter 3, this volume), including actively seeking information about perceived quality. Further, while low-fee private schools may employ certain client retention strategies (e.g. raising school-based exam marks; passing students who did not master grade level, etc.) (Srivastava, 2007a), the relationship is more nuanced than 'dupers–duped'. Most studies on low-fee private schooling that analyse household perceptions and experiences report that they are aware that low-fee schools are not *the* absolute best choice, but may be preferred over other local schools (and are all they can afford) (De et al, 2002; Srivastava, 2006, 2008a; Härmä, 2009), though not necessarily in all instances (Noronha & Srivastava, 2012; Fennell, Chapter 3, this volume).

However, if the broader concern is with increased accountability to households - one of the key arguments of private schooling proponents - then this is a serious issue requiring further consideration and examination, as Phillipson (2008) rightly implies. There is no evidence in the low-fee private schooling literature thus far to suggest that the market-based engagement of households with these schools has translated into more equal power relationships between low-fee private schools owners - generally of higher social positioning than clients (and, in rural cases, deeply entrenched in historical class- and/or caste-based power relations) - and the households that access them, or of changed power structures within schools.

The third and final point in reassessing Phillipson's (2008) definition is that by excluding the possibility of government ownership, it is too static. It does not account for the way that the low-fee private sector may evolve, or for potential changes to regulatory frameworks that they may be subject to over time. Given that we are still at the beginning of our understanding of the way the low-fee private sector operates and may evolve, these possibilities cannot be ruled out a priori. For example, it may be that in certain contexts schools initially set up as independent low-fee operations evolve to a model in which the state takes them over, as was the case for private schools in many countries in the past.

Rose and Adelabu (2007) trace experiments with state take-over of private schools, including 'for-profit schools' in Nigeria over its history, as do Stern and Heyneman in this volume (Chapter 5) regarding *Harambee* schools in Kenya. Kitaev (2007) points to the nationalisation of private schools in transitional countries and formerly planned economies of Eastern Europe and the former USSR, and other countries such as Mongolia and Vietnam. In the current context, it is more likely that, as Walford (2011) notes in his assessment (quoted above), there may be some low-fee private schools that 'might eventually wish to obtain some state funding' (p. 402) similar to an aided model (e.g. India), primarily for the likely financial sustainability that state subsidisation would bring for the lowest fee-charging schools.

It may also be that individual governments decide to adopt low-fee schools into their fold to meet education targets beyond 2015, or institute greater attempts at regulating them. A relevant and topical example is the newly legislated Right of Children to Free and Compulsory Education Act, 2009 in India, effective as of April 2010 and de facto implemented in 2011, in which *all* private schools must provide 25% of their seats for free to socially and economically disadvantaged children until they complete elementary education (see Noronha & Srivastava [2012] for a report on initial implementation and the private sector). Schools are to be reimbursed the amount the state spends on education or the amount of the tuition fee charged at the school, whichever is less (Section 12, Government of India, 2009). Thus, under the Act, all private schools, even low-fee schools in Phillipson's (2008) strictest sense (i.e. independently established, self-financed and run by independent owners), will be subsidised by the state to an extent. This may be beneficial for private schools charging less than or close to the reimbursement amount, given the precarious nature of enrolment and fee collection at schools in this part of the spectrum, but it may be contested by others seeking greater autonomy from the state (Noronha & Srivastava, 2012; Ohara, 2012; Ohara, Chapter 7, this volume).

Walford (2011) is correct that the notion of 'profit' at these low-fee private schools is different from shareholders investing in a company as in a pure business model (particularly in family-run and -owned schools), and there is a range of schools beyond Phillipson's (2008) definition that charge lower fees, including religious and NGO schools. However, there is something qualitatively different about the latter set, not least because religious schools are governed by very different regulations in most contexts, and NGO schools by a very different set of procedural norms and structures. For example, Andrabi et al (2008) provide a glimpse of the difference between low-fee private and religious schools (*madrasas*), taking Pakistan as a case. Rose (2007) provides an analysis of different types of non-state private education provision, including NGO, faith-based, spontaneous community, and philanthropic, which may be helpful. In short, not only are the management arrangements of these types of provision different, but the regulatory environment under which they operate is usually distinct and separate. It is unhelpful to conflate them here.[1]

Moving forward, perhaps characterising the low-fee private sector along a continuum of management, financing, ownership and regulatory arrangements may more suitable. From this approach, Phillipson's (2008) definition may be conceptualised as a 'pure type' of low-fee private school, in which ownership, financing and management are independent of the state, and adding a specification for fees charged within a range that may be accessible by some among poorer groups may be also helpful. For my study, I operationalised low-fee private schools as that saw themselves targeting disadvantaged groups; that were entirely self-financing through fees; that were independently run; and that charged a monthly tuition fee not exceeding about one day's earnings of a daily wage labourer at primary and junior levels (up to grade 8), and two days' earnings at secondary and higher secondary levels (grades 9 through 12). As such, it was partial to the 'pure type'. However, given the need to interrogate the development of the low-fee private sector and the many questions that are as yet unanswered, it did not and does not presuppose the relative quality of these schools, the motivations of parents to access them or owners to start them, or the institutional path that may develop in particular contexts. As such, it enables a certain level of flexibility for analysis.

This leads us to a final note on operationalisation for future studies, and, indeed, for the studies in this book. As researchers studying low-fee private schooling do so in different contexts, it follows that what constitutes 'low fees' for particular groups, in particular contexts, and at particular points in time is relative. This complication is in addition to those embedded in the practice of research – namely, the different terms under which researchers conduct research, different disciplinary norms, different methodological approaches, and different arrangements or terms of reference for contract research teams, all of which may affect operationalisation across studies.

Since the authors in this volume conducted their own separate studies and were not part of a large, unified team project, unlike, for example, studies in Phillipson's (2008) edited volume (though operationalisation across the three countries there - India, Nigeria and Uganda - was relative to the context), what constituted 'low fees' and 'low-fee private schools' varied to suit the contexts and approaches of individual studies and, in some cases, the terms of reference for their projects. Some researchers operated as part of teams on research projects as part of a broader research agenda on low-fee private schooling (Dixon et al [Chapter 4]); others worked in large team projects in which low-fee private schooling was just one aspect of the research (Akyeampong & Rolleston [Chapter 2]; Fennell [Chapter 3]); others were contracted by agencies with set terms (Härmä & Adefisayo [Chapter 6]; Humayun et al [Chapter 8]; Stern & Heyneman [Chapter 5]); while others operated as single researchers with academic purposes in mind (Ohara [Chapter 7]). Some researchers used official government or agency distinctions where these existed and were relevant (Harma & Adefisayo [Chapter 6]; Humayun et al [Chapter 8]; Stern & Heyneman [Chapter 5]), while others operationalised low-fee private schools as relevant to the particular contexts.

Most have provided an estimate of fees charged at schools in their studies as proportions of official minimum wage rates and/or proportions of household incomes. There was also fee variation at schools within individual studies. Typical of the low-fee private sector, some sources of variation were: levels of schooling (with increasing fee levels as schooling levels increase); location (typically, lower fees in rural and less populated areas/districts); and registration/recognition status (typically, higher fees in registered/recognised schools). These complications are a genuine facet and part of the messiness of conducting research more generally and on low-fee private schooling and private provision; they are a feature of the literature, and part of the complexity of presenting research in an edited volume.

Hidden Schools: the problem with official data

According to the latest data available in the 2011 Education for All Global Monitoring Report statistical tables, primary-level enrolment in private schools as a proportion of total enrolment in countries covered in this volume was 5% in Nigeria, 11% in Kenya, 17% in Ghana, and 31% in Pakistan in 2007-2008 (UNESCO, 2011, pp. 306-308).[2] For India, it is estimated that the private unaided sector accounted for 18% of enrolment in primary education for the same year, according to national education management information system (EMIS) data (NUEPA, 2009, p. 10), and 21% according to latest estimates (2009-2010) (NUEPA, 2011, p. 21).[3] However, the above estimates may be more valid indications of the recognised private sector (as in most countries) than of the private sector in its entirety. This has implications for how we estimate enrolment in or other essential characteristics of the low-fee private sector.

Macro-level estimates of the low-fee private sector are rendered difficult owing to the fact that a number of these schools occupy a part of the private sector that is unrecognised, and hence unaccounted for in official administrative data. Moreover, administrative units rarely classify or disaggregate data by fee level even for recognised schools, making comparisons and longitudinal analyses of the low-fee private sector difficult, if not impossible. These shortcomings are reproduced in the collation of international administrative data (e.g. UNESCO data) which largely rely on official EMIS and national data collection systems.

Of course, it is likely that official attempts to collect data from unrecognised schools would be difficult even if an attempt were made to do so, particularly since in many contexts they operate in an amorphous policy space following a set of 'shadow institutions' comprised of informal norms and practices often in contravention of the official regulatory framework (see Srivastava, 2008b). For example, it was recently announced that India's next EMIS data collection phase will attempt to include data from unrecognised schools. However, the Right to Education Act prohibits the functioning of unrecognised schools within three years of its enactment (Section 18, Government of India, 2009); thus, it is unclear how forthcoming these schools will be. Based on her field study in Delhi, where the weight of the act has been most strongly felt in the initial stages of implementation, Ohara's chapter in this volume (Chapter 7) focuses on the potential implications for unrecognised low-fee private schools, which feel threatened by the possibility of closure.

Similarly, in their chapter, Härmä and Adefisayo (Chapter 6) provide an inside look at the operations of schools in two areas of Nigeria (Makoko and Iwaya). Their analysis of 34 schools includes ones that would be considered 'illegal' according to the government classification system (i.e. 'unapproved schools'). A particular contribution of Härmä and Adefisayo's chapter is the inclusion of 'lagoon schools' that serve communities living in houses on stilts on the Lagos Lagoon. The researchers found that these low-fee private lagoon schools were unknown to many officials in the education administration, and that they, like other unapproved schools, preferred to remain hidden from sight.

Thus, some low-fee private schools may not admit to their status to being a school, claiming instead to being pre-primary or private tuition centres, as the formal regulations governing these education providers in many countries tend to be more relaxed (e.g., Rose & Adelabu, 2007; Srivastava, 2007b, 2008a). Further, it is likely that there are and would be distortions in data (e.g. under-reporting fee levels and over-reporting teachers' salaries and qualifications) even for recognised low-fee and other private schools since there is pressure to comply on paper with official fee caps and other requirements. (Whether or not they comply in practice is a separate issue.) For these reasons, capturing trends within the low-fee private sector over time is rendered difficult, and is largely dependent on revisiting field sites by individual researchers where this is possible.

Affordability?

Perhaps one of the most contested points regarding the low-fee private sector is its presumed affordability. For a more nuanced understanding, the question is, *affordable for whom?* Research until now has shown that low-fee private schools are part of the non-state sector that is accessible to some segment of the population in developing countries that would be considered to be from among relatively poorer groups, and that would not normally have had access to private schooling in the more typical context where the sector is largely high-fee and catering to elite or privileged middle classes.

The evidence on low-fee private schooling suggests that it would not be incorrect to characterise many of these students as first-generation learners or as having parents with lower education levels relative to more advantaged and richer groups, and as tending, relative to these groups, to come from households that participate in the informal economy to a greater extent, that have lower-paid jobs, that make substantial sacrifices (economically and emotionally) to access the private sector, and that are more likely to be affected by migration (see Srivastava, 2006; Härmä, 2009; Akaguri, 2011; Akyeampong & Rolleston, Chapter 2, this volume; Fennell, Chapter 3, this volume). However, it is also evident by virtue of the fact that these schools charge tuition fees (in addition to other costs, such as books, transportation, activities, etc.) that households accessing low-fee private schools, while likely drawn from the lower-middle and working classes, are unlikely to be the *most disadvantaged* or the poorest of the poor from the bottom 20% (Lewin, 2007). This distinction is important and should be noted against totalising claims on the affordability of the sector (see Rose & Dyer, 2008, for critiques).

This is not surprising. There is ample literature confirming that tuition and other hidden schooling costs in state and private sectors are most prohibitive on the most disadvantaged and poorest (see Akyeampong & Rolleston, Chapter 2, this volume; Stern & Heyneman, Chapter 5, this volume for a review of the relevant literature). Siddhu's (2010) review of the literature confirmed that recent analyses of survey data and randomised trial studies in countries as diverse as Sri Lanka, Uganda, India and Kenya found participation in schooling 'to be more responsive to cost levels' (p. 3) than even previous studies had found. Akyeampong's (2009) analysis of Ghana's Free Compulsory Universal Basic Education policy showed that the richest made the most gain in terms of participation in basic education, noting incidents of over-age enrolment, child labour, and late entry all disproportionately related to poorer and disadvantaged households.

Akyeampong and Rolleston's analysis of Ghana Living Standards Survey data in this volume (Chapter 2) shows that private school attendance was notably more common among 'non-poor' households than it was among households falling in the 'poor' and 'extremely poor' consumption poverty categories. While private enrolment in all welfare deciles increased between 1991/1992 and 2005/2006, the highest incidences were in the highest welfare decile (i.e. the most advantaged). In a similar vein, Lewin's (2007) analysis of Demographic Health Survey household data from 23 countries in sub-Saharan Africa showed that participation in primary and secondary education was heavily skewed by household income, location and gender. In this context, he concludes: 'Where the growth of low-cost ... non-government providers reflects state failure to serve low/middle income households it is not ... likely to reach the ultra-poor and the "last 20%"' (Lewin, 2007, p. 59) who are excluded from schooling.

Similarly, Mehrotra and Panchamukhi's (2006) study based on household survey data in India, with a representative sample covering more than 120,000 households and 1000 schools spread over 91 districts in eight states, found that private unaided schools did not seem to favour gender- or caste-based equity in enrolment. Härmä (2009), in her study of low-fee private schooling in Uttar Pradesh, India, found low-fee private schools to be unaffordable to the most disadvantaged in her sample (i.e. low-caste groups, Muslim groups, and households falling in the last quintile of the poverty index), as well as aggravated gender equity concerns. Thus, while the sector has certainly expanded schooling options for a segment of the population (an important contribution), the literature nonetheless points to reassessing claims of the supposed affordability of low-fee private schools for poor and disadvantaged groups en masse.

Given the potentially negative equity concerns associated with fees, an early experiment in urban and rural areas of Balochistan, Pakistan was conducted between 1995 and 1999 to see if low-fee schools for poor girls created by subsidies supported by a World Bank credit could be self-sustained (Alderman et al, 2003). The results showed that only about half of the urban schools and one rural school could be self-sufficient without charging higher tuition fees, increasing class sizes, or paying teachers lower salaries.

Experiments aiming to expand the use of the low-fee private sector also exist in the current context. For example, the Centre for Civil Society, an Indian think tank campaigning for parental school choice, does so by aiming to institute state-funded voucher programmes and voucher-like measures, acknowledging that these schools would otherwise be inaccessible: 'Some low income parents spend up to 50% of their income on the education of their children. There are still poorer parents who, in spite of their aspirations, cannot afford to' (Centre for Civil Society, 2011, webpage). However, Noronha and Srivastava's (2012) recent analysis of the experiences of disadvantaged households accessing private schools in Delhi through the Right to Education Act's 25% free seats provision showed that it was the relatively more advantaged among this group who secured free places at private schools considered to be more prestigious or in middle-class areas, and once they did, they incurred significant schooling costs (i.e. transportation, private tuition, capitation fees, etc.) which were higher than even fee-paying households accessing local low-fee private schools closer to the slum area in the study.

On closer reading, Tooley and Dixon (2005b), widely known as proponents of low-fee schooling, also show that low-fee private school proprietors in Nigeria and India were themselves wise to the fact that the more disadvantaged among their clients, described typically as orphans, more financially unstable, or migrants, would be unable to pay the 'low' fees charged. Thus, 9% of places from their sample schools in Makoko and 17.7% of places in sample schools in Hyderabad were provided for free or at concessionary rates (Tooley & Dixon, 2005b). However, there is controversy surrounding the researchers' implications that these concessions were philanthropic (Sarangapani & Winch, 2010), with other research showing that such concessions are likely marketing ploys by low-fee private school owners to retain their clientele (see e.g. Rose, 2002; Rose & Adelabu, 2007).

Similarly, based on interview data from poor rural households in Mfantseman District (the fourth poorest region in Ghana), Akyeampong and Rolleston contend (Chapter 2, this volume) that private providers project an image of affordability through flexible fee policies to sustain demand in a low-income context, stating: 'To attract clients on low or fragile incomes it was important that the schools come across as "affordable" through their fees policy' (p. 7). In fact, the private schooling cost per child for households in their study was on average nearly 30% of the estimated household income, which was nearly double that of public schooling. In their chapter on Nigeria, Härmä and Adefisayo (Chapter 6, this volume) report that children were sometimes allowed to stay enrolled when parents experienced difficulty paying fees, not only because of philanthropy and care for their pupils, but also 'to keep enrolments up, project a positive image, and in the hope that parents will eventually pay' (p. 134).

My work in Lucknow District showed that the motivations of low-fee private school owners were complex, with some desire to help their communities (particularly in rural areas), but that they had to reconcile competing interests for philanthropy with profit-making (Srivastava, 2007a). Fee concessions were provided by setting fees at an inflated figure for the majority of households and reducing the amount charged for some households, on the basis of either need or household ability to negotiate lower amounts. Thus, 'free' places were in fact the result of parents' bargaining and/or of schools' unwillingness to expel students who were in arrears, retaining clientele in the hopes that they may pay in the future, similar to Härmä and Adefisayo's results (Chapter 6, this volume), rather than being due to a concerted scholarship scheme.

Finally, and perhaps most importantly for the future development of low-fee private schooling research, is the point that poverty is dynamic, relational, multi-dimensional, and characterised by multiple deprivations, where economic circumstances and household income are just one factor of disadvantage (Kabeer, 2000; Rose & Dyer, 2008; Chege & Arnot, 2012).

Economic slowdown, seasonal migration, malnutrition, deep social fissures and entrenched exclusion, among other factors, have all been shown to adversely affect schooling and aggravate gender and other inequities resulting in drop-out (e.g. Lewin, 2007; Cameron, 2010; Dyer, 2010; Nambissan 2010; Siddhu, 2010; Ananga, 2011; Buxton, 2011), particularly where fees are involved, at key transition points, and as schooling levels increase.

While the concept of 'affordability' focuses on the immediate economic ability of households to access to low-fee private schools, it does not sufficiently engage with how long they may be able to access them, or with the deeper and multidimensional aspects of potential exclusionary or 'push-out' factors. In other words, affordability may be just one criterion. The question is, how do we understand long-term meaningful access in the low-fee private sector regarding exclusion or deprivation? Conceptualising household ability to access low-fee private schools in this way has significant implications in assessing claims about the sector's role in increasing access en masse, even in cases where access to these and other private schools may be state subsidised (see, e.g., Noronha & Srivastava, 2012).

The Question of Quality

Evidence in the existing literature concerning the relative quality of the state and low-fee private sectors is inconclusive. While the relative malfunctioning of the state sector in many countries, including those covered in this volume, has been widely noted and generally accepted as the impetus for the growth of these schools, the question of whether the low-fee private sector is uniformly of superior quality in absolute terms as a whole is fraught with debate. This has to do with the variance in results among studies that attempt to compare relative quality, but also (and perhaps more so) it involves considerations about *what we mean by quality*, raising a number of related questions: is it mainly a concern with achievement? What about schooling experiences? Social justice? Equity? Rights? Social mobility? Social cohesion? Does the type of provision matter? Who decides what quality is, and how? Assuming we can agree on a definition, how is quality improved?

According to Sayed and Ahmed (2011), the following conceptualisation may be useful:

> quality is understood as encompassing the interaction between what learners bring to learning (learner characteristics), what happens in the learning space such as school/classroom setting (enabling inputs), what happens to individuals as a consequence of education (outcomes) and the context within which the activity takes place. However, deciding on *what constitutes quality is an intensely value laden activity and involves both what is, but also what should be.* (p. 105; emphasis added)

Tikly and Barrett (2011) take this further, and make an important contribution to the education-quality discourse, arguing for the integration of context-specific social justice approaches beyond the more common human capital and rights-based discourses that have permeated the education literature (see also Carney, 2003; Tikly, 2011). This has thus far been missing from general discussions of education quality more broadly, and certainly from the low-fee private schooling literature assessing relative quality. The latter discussion has been largely influenced by school-effectiveness-type studies assessing relative achievement levels in core subjects such as mathematics and language, or comparing facilities and teacher or classroom inputs across school types. The focus on *schooling processes and social outcomes* has largely been missing from such analyses, as have the long-term implications and impacts of low-fee private schooling in the context of uneven provision to the disadvantaged.

Inputs

Some studies have compared a range of inputs across private schools serving lower-income populations and government schools. In Nairobi, Ngware et al (2010) found government schools performed better on some attributes (i.e. teacher qualifications, building facilities and pupil textbook ratios) but worse on others (i.e. pupil–toilet ratios, pupil–teacher ratio). In relatively deprived Mfantseman District, Ghana, Akaguri (2011) found that public schools had more and better trained teachers than low-fee private schools, and pupil-teacher ratios were higher in primary and junior levels in public schools, but supply-wise, there were about three times as many public schools as low-fee private schools. Tooley and Dixon's (2006) earlier work in Hyderabad and Mahbubnagar districts in Andhra Pradesh, India showed that on a range of input indicators (classrooms, toilets, drinking water, etc.), and in some observation of 'teaching activity', low-fee private schools seemed to perform better.

De et al's (2002) study in Haryana, Rajasthan and Uttar Pradesh, India found that low levels of school income in low-fee private schools led to poorly qualified and poorly paid teaching staff, with high turnover. The most disadvantaged groups accessed government schools which were comparatively of even lower quality on basic indicators of facilities and teaching activity. In her study of recognised and unrecognised private unaided low-fee primary schools in 10 villages in Uttar Pradesh, Härmä (2009) found that none of the teachers were trained, that only 34% had secondary schooling, and that they received salaries only up to one-tenth of those in government schools. Muralidharan and Kremer's (2007) results from a nationally representative survey of rural private primary schools in India found no significant difference between private and public school infrastructure, and 'the results with state and with village fixed effects suggest that conditional on being in the same village, private schools have poorer facilities and infrastructure than the public schools' (pp. 10-11). The mean teachers' salary at these schools was less than at government schools, being typically one-fifth of the amount at the latter.

Similarly, Andrabi et al's (2008) study in Pakistan showed that low-fee private schools could only keep their fees at comparatively lower rates by reducing recurrent costs, mainly by paying low teachers' salaries. This finding has been confirmed in all of the studies in this volume where this was examined, as well as by others (e.g. Rose & Adelabu, 2007; Phillipson, 2008; Härmä, 2009; Ohara, 2012). Interestingly, and perhaps controversially, however, Andrabi et al (2008) suggest that at the primary level, the use of unqualified, lesser-paid teachers in these schools, but who are local, predominantly female, have secondary education, and are accountable (and thus less absent), may not necessarily compromise quality: 'If what really matters for primary schooling is that the teacher puts in effort, the more consistent presence of female teachers at private schools may more than compensate for their lower qualifications since a primary school teacher who has a higher level of formal education will have less impact if she shows up for work less often' (p. 352). They warn that results are preliminary, and not necessarily replicable to other contexts and to higher levels of education, even in Pakistan.

However, Nambissan (2010) asserts that there has been a general acceptance of less skilled and poorly paid teachers as suitable alternatives in order to expand education to disadvantaged children: 'the advocacy of budget schools for the poor and for "para skilling" to cut costs and maximise profits is a travesty of social justice and the right to education for their children' (p. 735) (see also Sarangapani, 2009). Furthermore, the overwhelming use of female teachers by low-fee private schools because of their positioning 'as the cheapest source of labor' (Andrabi et al, 2008, p. 331) is disconcerting. Approaching quality education from an integrated social justice approach would have to ensure that not only are children from disadvantaged backgrounds provided with equitable basic resources, a key component of which consists of teachers, but also that teachers' basic rights of fair wages are protected. In this vein, there have been reports, for example, that the Coalition of Uganda Private Teachers Association and the Ministry of Education are to establish a framework for the government to regulate fees in the private sector and take over teachers' welfare concerns. The impact of such emerging discourse and regulations concerning the low-fee private sector in Uganda, and more generally, remains to be seen.

Achievement

Some studies have attempted to assess relative achievement of state and private schools serving disadvantaged groups. Akaguri's (2011) results in Ghana showed that the question 'cannot be answered in a way that suggests low-fee private schools perform consistently better than their public school counterparts' (p. 27). The evidence from his analysis of low-fee private and public school Basic Education Certificate Examination (BECE) results showed that differences were not significantly different or consistent. In some communities low-fee private schools performed better, in others they performed as poorly as public schools, and in still others, some public schools performed as well as low-fee private schools. Though not specifically focusing on low-fee private schools, Muralidharan and Kremer (2007) found that in rural Indian private schools, controlling for family and other characteristics reduced the private-school advantage that Class 4 students had on a standardised mathematics and language test (weighted in favour of mathematics), but that results remained 'strongly significant and of considerable magnitude (0.4 standard deviations on the test)' (p. 15).

Pratham's (2010) extensive national rural 2009 ASER survey covering 30 villages each in every district in India showed that once characteristics other than the type of school were controlled for (e.g. mother's education, father's education, private tuition, etc.), the learning differential between government and private school students fell dramatically from 8.6 percentage points to 2.9 percentage points overall (p. 7). Furthermore, in some states (i.e. Andhra Pradesh, Madhya Pradesh and Tamil Nadu) the controlled difference showed a negative relationship between private school attendance and local language achievement. This led the team to conclude that, at least in the case of reading in the local language, rural private schools generally performed only marginally better than government schools, and in some cases, no better. Closer readings of the work of Tooley and his colleagues also reveal variation. In later analyses of Indian data, while the researchers found a private school advantage in mathematics and English (to be expected, since many private schools were purportedly English-medium), this achievement gap narrowed when background variables were controlled for, and disappeared in the case of Urdu (Tooley et al, 2010).

Dixon et al's chapter in this volume (Chapter 4) presents a fresh analysis of original data gathered in slum areas of Nairobi. Using multi-level modelling techniques, it assesses the relative quality of public and private schools for low-income families regarding the achievement of students at both school types, controlling for background variables. Taking all other factors into account, the researchers found a significant positive relationship between private school attendance and test scores in mathematics and Kiswahili, but no statistically significant difference in English. In all tests, boys fared less well than girls. When pupil characteristics (i.e. IQ, family income, sex, age) were taken into account, the private school effect was reduced for English and Kiswahili for boys, also reducing also the attainment gap with girls.

The significance of Dixon et al's results presented in this volume, as well as others in the broader literature, lies in the need for *nuanced interpretation* when speaking of relative quality in terms of achievement to avoid blanket assessments about the superiority of the low-fee private sector over the state sector, or vice versa. For example, results in the studies above show variance in language achievement (local or English), though in mathematics, private school students in those studies seemed to perform better. The role of individual background characteristics also seems important, but there may also be other characteristics that are contextual and that have yet to be explored. Thus, low-fee private schools may be better in some areas and under certain conditions than state schools, but not in others. The question then becomes not whether low-fee private schools are uniformly better, but *in what instances, under which circumstances, and owing to which background characteristics do students in different school types achieve higher results?*

Recognition/Registration

Quality assessment is complicated further, since official external signifiers such as recognition or registration status (as the case may be), meant to confer certain minimal standards in terms of basic infrastructure, teacher qualifications, and curricula, are not always accurate markers. Tooley and Dixon's (2005a) work in Andhra Pradesh, my study in Uttar Pradesh (Srivastava, 2008b), and Ohara's study in Delhi (Chapter 7, this volume) found that low-fee private schools in these contexts often gained recognition through informal practices and bribery, not meeting set norms (see Rose & Adelabu, 2007; Härmä & Adefisayo, Chapter 6, this volume, for similar results in Nigeria). As mentioned above, this encourages the development of a shadow system of rules and practices which undermine the formal regulatory framework, weakening the recognition system as an enforcement mechanism to maintain basic quality standards.

Härmä and Adefisayo (Chapter 6, this volume) describe the challenges that schools in Makoko and Iwaya, Nigeria face in upgrading their facilities and expanding operations, forcing many to operate underground and without having met set norms. Ohara's chapter (Chapter 7, this volume) presents an analysis of the potential implications for low-fee private schools operating in Delhi under the Right to Education Act, in which unrecognised schools are compelled to obtain recognition or face closure. Her study reveals the strong contestation mounted by private school lobbies against changes in the regulatory environment. Results showed that, feeling threatened, unrecognised low-fee private schools made an effort to affiliate themselves with recognised schools and other organisations considered more powerful to increase their legitimacy. Furthermore, larger and more profitable recognised schools also opposed the regulations because some of them simultaneously ran unrecognised schools, seeking later to expand their operations by 'chaining' or 'branching'. Similar to Ohara's findings, research evidence from the other studies above suggests that many low-fee private schools thus operate through informal arrangements with other private schools or with the state, or usurp the process entirely.

Among Stern and Heyneman's analysis of Kenya (Chapter 5, this volume) is a detailed description of the registration process for low-fee and other private schools in the country, comprising a complex set of procedures. In particular, the arrangements for land ownership were tricky and complex, representing a barrier for private and even government schools, particularly in slum areas. They further found that delayed inspections, lost forms, postponed committee meetings, or cumbersome paperwork led to significant delays for registration. This prompted many private school owners to pre-emptively open their schools without registration, well aware that insufficient monitoring by central authorities, with their lack of manpower, would ward off immediate consequences (see also Chimombo, 2009 for similar results in Malawi).

Humayun et al's chapter (Chapter 8, this volume) provides an interesting analysis of the impact of Pakistan's attempt at regulating private schools by establishing a self-financed body, the Private Educational Institutions Regulatory Authority (PEIRA) for Islamabad Capital Territory, in order to exert some quality control. The logic behind PEIRA's creation was that promoting private sector development and regulating schools in accordance with established norms would lead to improved quality of the private education sector - in particular, low-fee private schools. However, the study found that PEIRA had failed to provide quality service standards for schools, and further, since its financing partly relied on fee payments received by private schools for inspection and registration, its credibility as a regulating authority was called into question. Finally, for the lowest fee schools, the financing structure created an additional financial burden, and those with the tightest revenue margins likely passed inspection and registration costs on to parents.

Quality Perceptions and Recuperation

Finally, school choice, leading some households to access low-fee private or other private schools, may be a marker of perceived quality in certain instances, but it may not in others. This is not to say that state sector dysfunctions do not exist, but that low-fee private school choice *may also* be related to perceived social status, prestige, gender norms, parental aspirations, or concerns with social closure. Akaguri (2011) found that household perceptions about the better quality of low-fee private schools in Mfantseman District, Ghana were 'based on beliefs rather than realities' (p. vii) and did not match actual examination results, but were deeply held. In their chapter on Ghana (Chapter 2, this volume), Akyeampong and Rolleston find that 'the power of image and marketing in shaping attitudes towards low-fee private schooling' (p. 57) was key, reflecting a bias and reinforcing peer group effects, rather than superior provision. My study showed that motivations to access low-fee private schools in Lucknow District, India were complex and sometimes ideological, and reflected such concerns as presumed better quality (without necessarily having information of performance on achievement or other quality indicators), prestige, marriage or labour market aspirations, peer pressure, and a desire on the part of some parents to distance themselves from more 'backward' or 'less educationally aware' parents in their communities (Srivastava, 2006, 2008a).

In this vein, some household aspirations, if set against discursive gendered, classist and casteist contexts, may not simply reinforce a desire to access 'better schools', but may also reproduce existing social inequities (Stash & Hannum, 2001; Carney, 2003; Jeffrey et al, 2005; Rao, 2010). The low-fee and more recent private schooling literature indicates a preference for accessing the private sector (including private tuition) to a greater extent for boys because of institutional factors including assumed labour market returns, patrilineal marriage customs, and cost constraints, particularly in Asian and African contexts (De et al, 2002; Härmä, 2009; Cameron, 2010; Kamwendo, 2010; Rao, 2010; Siddhu, 2010; Noronha & Srivastava, 2012). Even Tooley and Dixon's (2006) analysis of low-fee private schooling in Andhra Pradesh indicated potential gender bias, with the authors stating that 'in Hyderabad, boys, if they are in school, are more likely to go to private unaided school [than government schools]' (p. 451), and private unaided schools in Mahbubnagar had slightly more boys than girls, representative of the schooling situation more generally. While my analysis was an exception, showing as many girls in low-fee private schools as boys, the reasons behind this choice were often gendered, though there was evidence that the mental models affecting that choice attempted to challenge dominant perceptions, and sometimes vehemently so (Srivastava, 2006).[4]

Much of this literature also reveals significant class, caste and other socio-economic factors in accessing low-fee and other private schools (De et al, 2002; Härmä, 2009; Rao, 2010; Siddhu, 2010; Noronha & Srivastava, 2012). However, the confluence of low-fee and other private schooling work on India on the topic of household schooling decisions and the need for more fine-grained analyses on these issues indicates a need for future research to diversify the methods used in favour of in-depth analyses, as well as the need to revisit existing work and expand such work to other contexts.

Assessing the accuracy of low-fee private school choice and schooling decisions as markers of quality is crucial since the classical literature (stemming primarily from western contexts) espoused school choice as a lever for enhancing competition between public and private schools, thus increasing the quality of the education sector as a whole (e.g. Chubb & Moe, 1990; Hoxby, 2003). A suitable application in this regard is Hirschman's (1970) framework of exit, voice and loyalty in response to the low quality of a service. Exiting to a competitor is meant to provide a clear signal for the organisation to correct deficiencies, whereas voice is meant to express dissatisfaction with the service, but is predicated on a notion of loyalty to the organisation. The limited work on the low-fee private sector in this regard (see Srivastava, 2007b, for India; Fennell & Malik, 2012, and Fennell,

Chapter 3, this volume, for Pakistan) has concluded that the exit of the mobilised poor to the low-fee private sector did not seem to have the recuperative effect of increasing the quality of local state schools because incentives were not tied to these mechanisms (Srivastava, 2007b), and there is a substantive time lag before effects are felt (Fennell & Malik, 2012).

Fennell's chapter in this volume (Chapter 3) on quality discernment in rural and urban areas of two districts in Pakistan - Sargodha (Punjab province) and Charsadda (Khyber Pakhtunkhwa province) - makes a further important contribution, problematising the straightforward notion of the supposed superior quality of the private sector and inferior quality of the government sector, and its perception. Using Hirschman's framework to determine whether exit and voice mechanisms seemed to exert a potential recuperative effect on local schools, the presentation of qualitative focus group and interview data relating to youths' and parents' perceptions of low-fee private and other local schools provides interesting insights. For many participants, quality was a central consideration, but they were not necessarily convinced that it was better in low-fee private schools in all cases, and felt that, at times, this choice was made by relatively better-off households as a sign of social status. Fennell concludes that differences in perception and in levels of experience with the low-fee private sector imply that low-quality schooling will not receive adequate pressure to improve in the short run.

Looking Ahead

As post-2015 education aims and targets are being contemplated and set, we see continued debate not only on the potential role that the non-state private sector, comprising myriad different actors and arrangements, may play in achieving basic indicators of initial entry and access, but also on its impacts on the quality of basic (and, increasingly, secondary) education and longer-term social equity goals. In this debate, the existence of the low-fee private sector is no longer seen as an anomaly, as it was at the beginning of the Education for All movement, but is taken as a de facto given in many developing countries.

However, as I hope this chapter and the studies in this volume show, there is much work to be done in understanding the full impact of the low-fee private sector. A number of interests, ideological, political, academic and commercial, are at play. Furthermore, initial understandings of the low-fee private sector in the literature thus far are tentative, and should be interpreted with caution and nuance, attuned to the changing contexts in specific countries over time, and to the potential interests shaping future activities of and in the sector.

Regarding future research, there is an urgent need to broaden the focus on the relative quality of the low-fee and state sectors beyond inputs and achievement analyses, to include the sector's impact on relative schooling experiences, schooling processes and social outcomes, and to seriously consider the dynamic aspects of 'disadvantage' and how groups thus defined are positioned within and against these sectors. This is, of course, a call to much longer programmes of study, but goes, I believe, to the heart of potentially answering the question of whether the low-fee private sector aggravates equity or mitigates disadvantage.

Notes

[1] Of course, it may be that in certain contexts the regulatory environments for NGO, religious, independent/individual, and other non-state schools are not separate or distinct. Where it is contextually relevant to include them in analyses of the low-fee private sector, it should be done. See, for example, Härmä & Adefisayo, Chapter 6, this volume, for Nigeria.

[2] The data for Ghana are reported as being based on UNESCO Institute for Statistics estimates.

[3] Private sector enrolment data were not available for India in the 2011 Education for All Global Monitoring Report (UNESCO, 2011).

[4] Though not specifically focusing on private schooling, Arnot et al (2012) report similar micro-changes in rural Ghana and India regarding the impact of education on gender roles/constructions and transitions.

References

Aggarwal, Y. (2000) *Public and Private Partnership in Primary Education in India: a study of unrecognised schools in Haryana.* New Delhi: National Institute for Educational Planning and Administration.

Akaguri, L. (2011) Low-fee Private Schools for the Rural Poor: perception or reality? Evidence from southern Ghana. CREATE Pathways to Access Research Monographs, No. 69. Brighton: Centre for International Education, University of Sussex. http://www.create-rpc.org/pdf_documents/PTA69.pdf

Akyeampong, K. (2009) Public–private Partnership in the Provision of Basic Education in Ghana: challenges and choices, *Compare*, 39(2), 135-149.

Alderman, H., Kim, J. & Orazem, P.F. (2003) Design, Evaluation, and Sustainability of Private Schools for the Poor: the Pakistan urban and rural fellowship school experiments, *Economics of Education Review*, 22(3), 265-274.

Alderman, H., Orazem, P.F. & Paterno, E.M. (2001) School Quality, School Cost, and the Public/Private School Choices of Low-income Households in Pakistan, *Journal of Human Resources*, 36(2), 304-326.

Ananga, E. (2011) Dropping out of School in Southern Ghana: the push-out and pull-out factors. CREATE Pathways to Access Research Monograph, No. 55. Brighton: Centre for International Education, University of Sussex. http://www.create-rpc.org/pdf_documents/PTA55.pdf

Andrabi, T., Das, J. & Khwaja, A.I. (2008) A Dime a Day: the possibilities and limits of private schooling in Pakistan, *Comparative Education Review*, 52(1), 329-355.

Arnot, M., Jeffery, R., Casely-Hayford, L. & Noronha, C. (2012) Schooling and Domestic Transitions: shifting gender relations and female agency in rural Ghana and India, *Comparative Education*, 48(2), 181-194.

Baird, R. (2009) Private Schools for the Poor: development, provision, and choice in India. A report for Gray Matters Capital. http://www.dise.in/Downloads/Use%20of%20Dise%20Data/Ross%20Baird.pdf

Belfield, C. & Levin, H.M. (2005) Vouchers and Public Policy: when ideology trumps evidence, *American Journal of Education*, 111(4), 548-567.

Bray, M. (2006) Private Supplementary Tutoring: comparative perspectives on patterns and implications, *Compare*, 36(4), 515-530.

Buchmann, C. (2002) Getting Ahead in Kenya: social capital, shadow education, and achievement, in B. Fuller & E. Hannum (Eds) *Schooling and Social Capital in Diverse Cultures*. Amsterdam: JAI Press.

Buxton, C. (2011) The Impact of Malnutrition on Access to Primary Education: case studies from Ghana. CREATE Pathways to Access Research Monograph, No.68. http://www.Create-rpc.org/pdf_documents/PTA68.pdf

Cameron, S. (2010) Access to and Exclusion from Primary Education in Slums of Dhaka, Bangladesh. CREATE Pathways to Access Research Monograph No. 45. Brighton: Centre for International Education, University of Sussex. http://www.Create-rpc.org/pdf_documents/PTA45.pdf

Carney, S. (2003) Globalisation, Neo-liberalism and the Limitations of School Effectiveness Research in Developing Countries: the case of Nepal, *Globalisation, Societies and Education*, 1(1), 87-101.

Centre for Civil Society (2011) What is School Choice? In *School Choice: frequently asked questions*. New Delhi: Centre for Civil Society. http://schoolchoice.in/faq.php

Chege, F.N. & Arnot, M. (2012) The Gender–Education–Poverty Nexus: Kenyan youths' perspective on being young, gendered and poor, *Comparative Education*, 48(2), 195-209.

Chimombo, J. (2009) Expanding Post-primary Education in Malawi: are private schools the answer? *Compare*, 39(2), 167-184.

Chubb, J.E. & Moe, T.M. (1990) *Politics, Markets and America's Schools*. Washington, DC: The Brookings Institution.

Day Ashley, L. & Caddell, M. (Eds) (2006) The Private Education Sector: towards a reconceptualization. *Compare*, 36(4) (Special Issue).

De, A., Noronha, C. & Samson, M. (2002) Private Schools for Less Privileged: some insights from a case study, *Economic and Political Weekly*, 37(52), 5230-5236.

Dyer, C. (2010) Education and Social (In)justice for Mobile Groups: re-framing rights and educational inclusion for Indian pastoralist children, *Educational Review*, 62(3), 301-313.

Fennell, S. & Malik, R. (2012) Between a Rock and a Hard Place: the emerging educational market for the poor in Pakistan, *Comparative Education*, 48(2), 249-261.

Foondun, A.R. (2002) The Issue of Private Tuition: an analysis of the practice in Mauritius and selected South-East Asian countries, *International Review of Education*, 48(6), 485-515.

Gauri, V. & Vawda, A. (2004) Vouchers for Basic Education in Developing Economies: an accountability perspective, *World Bank Research Observer*, 19(2), 259-280.

Genevois, I. (2008) Can and Should Public Private Partnerships Play a Role in Education? Working Document. Paris: UNESCO-IIEP. http://www.iiep.unesco.org/fileadmin/user_upload/Research_Challenges_and_Trends/pdf/symposium/IGenevois.pdf

Government of India (2009) *The Right of Children to Free and Compulsory Education Act, 2009*. No. 35 of 2009, 26 August. New Delhi.

Härmä, J. (2009) Can Choice Promote Education for All? Evidence from Growth in Private Primary Schooling in India, *Compare*, 39(2), 151-165.

Härmä, J. (2011) *Study of Private Schools in Lagos*. Education Sector Support Programme in Nigeria Assignment Report, Report No. LG: 303. Lagos: ESSPIN/UKAID.

Hirschman, A. (1970) *Exit, Voice and Loyalty: responses to decline in firms, organisations and states*. Cambridge, MA: Harvard University Press.

Hoxby, C.M. (2003) School Choice and School Productivity: could school choice be a tide that lifts all boats?, in C.M. Hoxby (Ed.) *The Economics of School Choice*, pp. 287-341. Chicago: University of Chicago Press.

Jeffrey, C., Jeffery, P. & Jeffery, R. (2005) Reproducing Difference? Schooling, Jobs, and Empowerment in Uttar Pradesh, India, *World Development*, 33(12), 2085-2101.

Kabeer, N. (2000) Social Exclusion, Poverty and Discrimination: towards an analytical framework, *IDS Bulletin*, 31(4), 83-97.

Kamwendo, M. (2010) A Comparison of Students' Achievement in Private and Conventional Public Secondary Schools in Malawi from a Gender Perspective, *Research in Education*, 83(1), 17-25.

Kim, J., Alderman, H. & Orazem, P.F. (1999) Can Private School Subsidies Increase Enrollment for the Poor? The Quetta Urban Fellowship Program, *World Bank Economic Review*, 13(3), 443-465.

Kisira, S. (2008) Uganda, in B. Phillipson (Ed.) *Low-cost Private Education: impacts on achieving universal primary education*. London: Commonwealth Secretariat.

Kitaev, I. (1999) *Private Education in Sub-Saharan Africa: a re-examination of theories and concepts related to its development and finance*. Paris: UNESCO-IIEP.

Kitaev, I. (2007) Education for All and Private Education in Developing and Transitional Countries, in P. Srivastava & G. Walford (Eds) *Private Schooling in Less Economically Developed Countries: Asian and African perspectives*, pp. 89-109. Oxford: Symposium Books.

LaRocque, N. (2006) *Contracting for the Delivery of Education Services: a typology and international examples*. Wellington: Education Forum. http://www.educationforum.org.nz/documents/publications/contracting_education.pdf

Lewin, K. (2007) The Limits of Growth to Non-government Private Schooling in Sub-Saharan Africa, in P. Srivastava & G. Walford (Eds) *Private Schooling in Less Economically Developed Countries: Asian and African perspectives*, pp. 41-65. Oxford: Symposium Books.

Majumdar, M. & Vaidyanathan, A. (1995) *The Role of Private Sector Education in India: current trends and new priorities*. Trivandrum, Kerala: Centre for Development Studies.

Mehrotra, S. & Panchamukhi, P. (2006) Private Provision of Elementary Education in India: findings of a survey in eight states, *Compare*, 36(4), 421-442.

Muralidharan, K. & Kremer, M. (2007) Public and Private Schools in Rural India. Working paper. Cambridge, MA: Harvard University. http://www.economics.harvard.edu/faculty/kremer/files/Public%20and%20private%20schools%20in%20rural%20india%20(Final%20pre-publication).pdf

Nambissan, G.B. (2010) The Global Economic Crisis, Poverty and Education: a perspective from India, *Journal of Education Policy*, 25(6), 729-737.

Nambissan, G. & Ball, S.J. (2010) Advocacy Networks, Choice and Private Schooling of the Poor in India, *Global Networks*, 10(3), 324-343.

National University of Educational Planning and Administration (NUEPA) (2009) *Elementary Education in India: progress towards UEE. Flash statistics DISE 2007-2008*. New Delhi: National University of Educational Planning and Administration and Department of School Education and Literacy, Ministry of Human Resource Development, Government of India. http://dise.in/Downloads/Publications/Publications%202007-08/Flash%20statistics2007-08.pdf

National University of Educational Planning and Administration (NUEPA) (2011) *Elementary Education in India: progress towards UEE. Flash statistics DISE 2009-2010*. New Delhi: National University of Educational Planning and Administration and Department of School Education and Literacy, Ministry of Human Resource Development, Government of India. http://www.dise.in/Downloads/Publications/Publications%202009-10/Flash%20Statistics%202009-10.pdf

Ngware, M.W., Oketch, M. & Ezeh, A.C. (2010) Quality of Primary Education Inputs in Urban Schools: evidence from Nairobi, *Education and Urban Society*, 43(1), 91-116.

Noronha, C. & Srivastava, P. (2012) *The Right to Education Act in India: focuses on early implementation issues and the private sector*. Report submitted to the Privatisation in Education Research Initiative (PERI), Open Society Foundation. Ottawa/New Delhi: University of Ottawa/CORD.

Ohara, Y. (2012) Examining the Legitimacy of Unrecognised Low-fee Private Schools in India: comparing different perspectives, *Compare*, 42(1), 69-90.

Patrinos, H.A., Barrera-Osorio, F. & Guaqueta, J. (2009) *The Role and Impact of Public–Private Partnerships in Education*. Washington, DC: World Bank.

Phillipson, B. (Ed.) (2008) *Low-cost Private Education: impacts on achieving universal primary education*. London: Commonwealth Secretariat.

Pratham. (2010) Annual Status of Education Report (Rural) 2009. Provisional, 15 January 2010. New Delhi: Pratham. http://images2.asercentre.org/aserreports/Aser_2009_Report.pdf

Probe Team (1999) *Public Report on Basic Education in India*. New Delhi: Oxford University Press.

Rao, N. (2010) Aspiring for Distinction: gendered educational choices in an Indian village, *Compare*, 40(2), 167-183.

Rose, P. (2002) Is the Non-state Education Sector Serving the Needs of the Poor? Evidence from East and Southern Africa. Paper presented at the 'Making Services Work for Poor People' World Development Report (WDR) 2003/04 Workshop. Eynsham Hall, Oxford, UK, 4-5 November 2002. http://siteresources.worldbank.org/INTWDR2004/Resources/22485_roseWDR.pdf

Rose, P. (2007) *Supporting Non-state Providers in Basic Education Service Delivery*. CREATE Pathways to Access Research Monograph No. 4. Brighton: Centre for International Education, University of Sussex. http://www.Create-rpc.org/pdf_documents/PTA4.pdf

Rose, P. & Adelabu, M. (2007) Private-sector Contributions to Education for All in Nigeria, in P. Srivastava & G. Walford (Eds) *Private Schooling in Less Economically Developed Countries: Asian and African perspectives*, pp. 67-88. Oxford: Symposium Books.

Rose, P. & Dyer, C. (2008) Chronic Poverty and Education: a review of the literature. Working Paper No. 131. Manchester: Chronic Poverty Research Centre. http://www.chronicpoverty.org/uploads/publication_files/WP131_Rose_and_Dyer.pdf

Sarangapani, P.M. (2009) Quality, Feasibility and Desirability of Low-cost Private Schooling, *Economic and Political Weekly*, 44(43), 43-67.

Sarangapani, P.M. & Winch, C. (2010) Tooley, Dixon and Gomathi on Private Education in Hyderabad: a reply, *Oxford Review of Education*, 36(4), 499-515.

Sayed, Y. & Ahmed, R. (2011) Education Quality in Post-apartheid South African Policy: balancing equity, diversity, rights and participation, *Comparative Education*, 47(1), 103-118.

Shukla, S., & Joshi, P. (2008) India, in B. Phillipson (Ed.) *Low-cost Private Education: impacts on achieving universal primary education*. London: Commonwealth Secretariat.

Siddhu, G. (2010) Can Families in Rural India Bear the Additional Burden of Secondary Education? Investigating the determinants of transition. CREATE Pathways to Access Research Monograph Series, No. 50. Brighton: Centre for International Education, University of Sussex. http://www.Create-rpc.org/pdf_documents/PTA50.pdf

Srivastava, P. (2006) Private Schooling and Mental Models about Girls' Schooling in India, *Compare*, 36(4), 497-514.

Srivastava, P. (2007a) For Philanthropy or Profit? The Management and Operation of Low-fee Private Schools in India, in P. Srivastava & G. Walford (Eds) *Private*

Schooling in Less Economically Developed Countries: Asian and African perspectives, pp. 153-186. Oxford: Symposium Books.

Srivastava, P. (2007b) Neither Voice nor Loyalty: school choice and the low-fee private sector in India. Research Publications Series, Occasional Paper No. 134. New York: National Center for the Study of Privatization in Education, Columbia University.

Srivastava, P. (2008a) School Choice in India: disadvantaged groups and low-fee private schools, in M. Forsey, S. Davies & G. Walford (Eds) *The Globalisation of School Choice?*, pp. 185-208. Oxford: Symposium Books.

Srivastava, P. (2008b) The Shadow Institutional Framework: towards a new institutional understanding of an emerging private school sector in India, *Research Papers in Education*, 23(4), 451-475.

Srivastava, P. & Walford, G. (Eds) (2007) *Private Schooling in Less Economically Developed Countries: Asian and African perspectives*. Oxford: Symposium Books.

Stash, S., & Hannum, E. (2001) Gender, Caste, and Ethnicity in Nepal, *Comparative Education Review*, 45(3), 354-378.

Tikly, L. (2011) Towards a Framework for Researching the Quality of Education in Low-income Countries, *Comparative Education*, 47(1), 1-23.

Tikly, L. & Barrett, A.M. (2011) Social Justice, Capabilities and the Quality of Education in Low-income Countries, *International Journal of Educational Development*, 31(1), 3-14.

Tooley, J. (1999) *The Global Education Industry: lessons from private education in developing countries*. London: Institute of Economic Affairs.

Tooley, J. (2001) The Enterprise of Education: opportunities and challenges for India. Liberty Institute Occasional Paper 6. New Delhi: Liberty Institute. http://www.libertyindia.org/pdfs/tooley_education.pdf

Tooley, J. & Dixon, P. (2003) *Private Schools for the Poor: a case study from India*. Reading: CfBT. http://www.isfc.in/tooley_hyderabad_study.pdf

Tooley, J. & Dixon, P. (2005a) An Inspector Calls: the regulation of 'budget' private schools in Hyderabad, Andhra Pradesh, India, *International Journal of Educational Development*, 25(3), 269-285.

Tooley, J. & Dixon, P. (2005b) Is There a Conflict between Commercial Gain and Concern for the Poor? Evidence from Private Schools for the Poor in India and Nigeria. *Economic Affairs*, 25(2), pp. 20-26.

Tooley, J. & Dixon, P. (2006) 'De Facto' Privatisation of Education and the Poor: implications of a study from Sub-Saharan Africa and India, *Compare*, 36(4), 443-462.

Tooley, J., Dixon, P., Shamsan, Y. & Schagen, I. (2010) The Relative Quality and Cost-effectiveness of Private and Public Schools for Low-income Families: a case study in a developing country, *School Effectiveness and School Improvement*, 21(2), 117-144.

Tran, M. (2012) Pearson to Invest in Low-cost Private Education in Africa and Asia, *Guardian*, 3 July. http://www.guardian.co.uk/Global-development/2012/jul/03/Pearson-Invest-Private-Education-Africa-asia

Umar, A. (2008) Nigeria, in B. Phillipson (Ed.) *Low-cost Private Education: impacts on achieving universal primary education*. London: Commonwealth Secretariat.

UNESCO (2008) *2009 Education for All Global Monitoring Report. Overcoming Inequality: why governance matters*. Paris/Oxford: IIEP-UNESCO/Oxford University Press.

UNESCO (2011) *2011 Education for All Global Monitoring Report. The Hidden Crisis: armed conflict in education*. Paris: UNESCO.

Walford, G. (2011) Low-fee Private Schools in England and in Less Economically Developed Countries: what can be learnt from a comparison? *Compare*, 41(3), 401-413.

CHAPTER 2

Low-fee Private Schooling in Ghana: is growing demand improving equitable and affordable access for the poor?

KWAME AKYEAMPONG & CAINE ROLLESTON

Introduction

The Millennium Development Goal of universal basic education for all the world's children faces some of its most serious challenges in the region of sub-Saharan Africa, owing partly to continuing inadequate schooling supply, as well as to deficiencies in demand. Nonetheless, as progress towards basic access is slowly being improved in the region, focus is turning to the issue of ensuring 'good quality'. Important recent studies have attested to the role not only of schooling per se, but of quality education and consequent cognitive development as key to the economic well-being of both individual and nation (e.g. Hanushek & Woessmann, 2007). Basic education in many parts of sub-Saharan Africa is of poor quality in comparative terms, while its cost to the national budget remains high.

In comparison with the sub-region, Ghana has the highest average unit cost for primary education as a share of gross domestic product (GDP) per capita (19%, compared with the sub-Saharan African average of 11%) (World Bank, 2010). The education sector accounts for 7.57% of annual GDP, and 30% of the annual government budget is spent on education, figures which are both high by international norms for education investment (World Bank 2010). Although spending on public basic education in Ghana has increased substantially, compared with the rich, the poorest in society appear to have made the smallest gains in terms of participation in basic education (Akyeampong, 2009). Two decades of education reforms have resulted in more children from poor households gaining access to public basic education (World Bank, 2004), but at the same time, more poor households are patronising private education, as the analysis in this chapter reveals. This raises questions about the allocation of public spending on education, and about whether recent reforms have done enough to target the needs of the poor regarding access.

The phenomenon of growing private school enrolment in Ghana is not simply an urban trend, and is present both in rural areas and among the poor (Akaguri, 2011). It is also notable that the trend has been little affected by the introduction of substantial initiatives to reduce the costs of public schooling to households. Some argue that this growth in private basic education is in part a response to perceptions of poor quality in the state sector. Some work suggests that private provision produces better quality, and is able to do so at lower costs (e.g. Patrinos et al, 2009). But such claims should be interpreted cautiously, given the variations in the types of private provision and the different contexts within which they operate.

Part of the conventional justification for state provision of basic schooling, in addition to the fulfilment of a basic human right, lies in the extensive external benefits that arise from public education and the consequent failure of markets in the sector to make socially optimal provision. Conversely, the prevalence of 'government failure' in the education sector in respect of socially sub-optimal resource allocation, along with issues of inefficiency, must, nonetheless, be set against that of market failure in a consistent approach to the issue of equity and social justice outcomes of education delivery mechanisms.

Over the years, efforts to improve equitable access to basic education in Ghana have been pursued relentlessly, starting with the accelerated development plan (ADP) in 1951 which abolished tuition fees in public schools. After independence, the 1960 Education Act made fee-free primary and middle schools a constitutional right. Both the 1960 Education Act and the ADP laid the foundation for rapid expansion of access and contributed to narrowing the inequalities associated with earlier patterns of access. But by the mid-1970s, setbacks in Ghana's economy had led to a widening participation gap in education between the poor and non-poor (World Bank, 2004; Akyeampong et al, 2007).

However, major education reforms launched in 1987 and, later, the 1995 Free Compulsory Universal Basic Education (FCUBE) programme with financial assistance from the World Bank and other bilateral organisations narrowed the participation gap (World Bank, 2004). FCUBE identified quality as key to its success and focused on school reforms to improve pupils' learning and achievement. Although both reforms improved access, they did not result in a significant improvement in the pattern of school attendance and completion (Akyeampong, 2011). In 2005, Ghana introduced the Capitation Grant Scheme for public schools as a further step to achieve universal access.

Essentially, capitation was introduced as a strategy to eliminate school fees associated with public basic education. Each public school received about US$6 per child per year (Ministry of Education, Science and Sports [MOESS], 2009). Capitation was intended to motivate demand for schooling, narrow the access gap between poor and non-poor households, and improve quality of education provision in basic schools. During this time, the country was seeing a rise in low-fee private schools serving mostly populations among the rural and urban poor, prompting questions about whether the trend represented growing demand from households dissatisfied with public basic education and, further, what this may mean in terms of equitable access to quality education for the poor. Some asked questions about whether this was a message to policy makers that once the poor had choice, they would seek private education even if it meant making significant financial sacrifices, and if this was the case, to what extent this choice would promote equitable access to quality basic education.

In this chapter, we analyse trends in access to both public and private schools in mostly rural contexts where the majority of poor Ghanaians reside, providing insights into how equitable the access has been, and on the structure of costs associated with poor household access to predominantly low-fee private schools. Populations in rural areas of Ghana are considered relatively poor. An analysis of household incomes by the Ghana Statistical Service (2005b) indicates that 'poverty continues to be most prevalent in rural communities, especially in rural forest and rural savannah, where 46% of the population live below the lower poverty line' (p. 266). In fact, according to the Ghana Living Standards Survey Round 5 (GLSS 5), poverty is a substantially rural phenomenon in Ghana, with up to two-thirds of rural households living below the poverty line. By basing the analysis on data from rural areas, we have assumed that private schools in these areas are predominantly in the low-fee category.[1] We also examine access trend data for the effect that capitation might have had on school choice, and investigate the behaviour of rural households towards public and private provision in some communities of southern Ghana.

Using GLSS large-scale survey data and Ghana Education Management Information System (EMIS) data, we identify the factors associated with low-fee private school choice and other key indicators for education. The analysis examines trends in expenditure on private education between welfare groups, assesses the overall trend in inequality in terms of access to schooling, and examines what patterns of spending and enrolment may indicate in terms of access to quality schooling vis-à-vis public and private schooling in rural settings.

Finally, we use Consortium for Research on Educational Access, Transitions and Equity (CREATE) qualitative case study data, gathered in rural/peri-urban communities in southern Ghana, to discuss the perspective of poor households on their schooling choices and, in particular, the factors that influenced their choice of low-fee private basic education for their children.

A Review of the Literature on School Choice

Modelling the determinants of schooling participation and schooling choice needs to account for features of the full range of constraints and influences on the household decision to send a child to school, and to which kind of school. This decision may be considered as part of a household's long-term utility or welfare maximisation strategy, and hence may be analysed within the cost-benefit analysis framework of Becker's (1964) household production function. This framework conceptualises the household's decision in terms of an attempt to compare the direct and opportunity costs of schooling - and of a particular kind of schooling - on the one hand, and the future economic benefits to the household, including income returns, on the other.

The household costs and benefits of sending a child to school may also be understood in terms of the supply and demand for education. Household demand for education reflects the net benefits of education which depend on features of the particular child, her/his parents and household, the school (particularly the quality of education provided), and the wider location and context, especially the local community. The supply of public education is, of course, largely determined by local and national education policy and provision. The provision of private schooling may be considered a response to demand.

At the level of the individual child, gender and age affect the true and perceived net benefits of education through differences in the opportunity costs of schooling in terms of lost current earnings, and in terms of differences in the returns to education, and hence in future earnings (UNESCO Institute for Statistics, 2005; Kingdon & Theopold, 2006). The opportunity cost of schooling is largely determined by the rewards to and availability of child labour. But work is not necessarily antithetical to schooling, and, indeed, wages from work may even be required to afford schooling, particularly prior to the implementation of free education policies. Further, poverty is not necessarily the main reason for child labour, and the poorest households may be those whose children neither work nor attend school (Siddiqi & Patrinos 1995; Canagarajah & Coulombe, 1997; Ravallion & Wodon, 2000; Bhalotra & Heady, 2003; Bhalotra & Tzannatos, 2003).

A child's birth order and relationship to the household head have been found to affect school participation in economically poor countries, including Ghana, partly because households may be constrained from educating all children to the same level (Glewwe & Jacoby, 1994). Parents' education is also found to be an important determinant of children's school participation in sub-Saharan countries, including Ghana (UNESCO Institute for Statistics, 2005; Sackey, 2007; Kazeem et al, 2010). Where these effects are separated from income, parental education may serve as an indicator of 'preferences for education' developed through parents' own educational experiences. Socio-economic and occupational groupings are also associated with school participation (Drèze & Kingdon, 2001). In the case of those in formal employment, the increase in preference for education may be linked to the positive effect of education in selection into more lucrative occupations – an effect which is strong in Ghana.

Cultural and religious differences may offer an additional explanation with regards to household decisions regarding private schooling. Household assets and income/consumption levels are unsurprisingly found to be closely associated with children's participation in schooling, especially private schooling, and clearly affect the affordability of education, particularly of private education. These effects might be expected to rise with the level of education, given that direct and opportunity costs are often much greater at the secondary level than they are at the primary level (Checchi, 2001).

Household size and composition, including the nature and extent of dependency among household members, may be expected to impact on the affordability of schooling decisions. Outside the household and immediate locale, the panoply of regional and contextual factors affects both supply and demand for schooling. These factors include urban/rural location, dominant forms of agriculture, and the overall level of development, including employment opportunities (Drèze & Kingdon, 2001; Baschieri & Falkingham, 2006). Perhaps the most striking feature of the Ghanaian context overall is the North/South divide, which affects almost all indicators, including school participation generally (Fentiman et al, 1999; Akyeampong et al, 2007) and private education.

On the supply side, availability, accessibility and quality of schooling are clearly important factors. Moreover, the availability of opportunities for progression to higher levels of education has been found to affect enrolment earlier on in a child's school career (Glewwe & Jacoby, 1994; Lavy, 1996). Distances to school have been found to be significant with regard to participation in Ghana, although their effects in general appear to be declining, perhaps as a result of school building and infrastructure development (World Bank, 2004; Filmer, 2007). School quality, while difficult to measure, may be expected to influence participation. Limited work in Ghana has established positive effects of higher-quality indicators (Lavy, 1996; Fentiman et al., 1999).

Educational costs can create a disincentive for the poor to access schooling. For example, before the introduction of fee-free primary education in Zambia and Uganda, about a third of all households' expenditure was spent on education. Removal of school fees reduced the cost burden considerably and improved access significantly, especially for poor households (UNESCO, 2007). In Ghana, direct and opportunity costs have acted together to prevent many poor children from accessing basic education (Oduro, 2000; Boateng, 2005; GNECC, 2005; Sackey, 2007). But other related costs of education can equally act as a disincentive for enrolling in school, even when school fees have been abolished. For example, costs related to books, food, clothing (uniforms) and transport have been shown to act as barriers to access.

Thus, school fees may not be the major obstacle to access, and in fact may, in some contexts, constitute a relatively smaller element of education costs that households have to shoulder. In Tanzania, for example, one study found that school fees constituted only a fifth of total costs of primary schooling (Mason & Khandker, 1997). Thus, in terms of cost burden, school fees may represent a relatively small element relative to other costs (see Colclough et al, 2003), meaning that if the difference in household education costs between public and low-fee private schooling is not great, this may tip choice in favour of the latter, especially if it is perceived to offer better value for money.

Abolishing school fees in public schools may also shift the cost-benefit calculus in favour of the low-fee private option for those who believe that it offers better quality and improves chances in selection examinations. In effect, households' decisions to access low-fee private schools could depend on affordability, trade-offs, and perceived value in relation to the investment. Among the poor who seek education as a way out of inter-generational poverty, that desire, in combination with other enabling factors, may make low-fee private schools attractive and worth the effort of making a small investment.

Methodology

The analysis begins with descriptive analysis of private schooling enrolment at the basic level using GLSS and EMIS data. It proceeds to examine the determination of private school supply in rural Ghana using 2005/2006 GLSS household and community data addressing the factors that are associated with the location of private schools in rural Ghana. It examines the determination of private school choice in rural locations using GLSS 5 community and household data. This is according to a two-stage procedure involving: (1) modelling the determination of the decision to (currently) enrol a child in school; and (2) conditional upon the decision to enrol a child in school, modelling the determination of the decision to opt for private schooling. Approaches are employed to model individual- and village-level effects.

The GLSS collects nationally representative data with the aim of measuring levels and changes in standards of living useful for evaluating and informing policy decisions. Clusters or 'primary sampling units' are census enumeration areas (from the 2000 census) - typically villages where rural areas are concerned. In addition to the household survey, a community survey is conducted for each rural community in the GLSS sample. This contains information on the schools located in each community and their funding status – public or private. Most enumeration areas contain one community, but a number contain more than one. Where there is more than one community, the community survey contains data identifying the households sampled in the household survey for each community.

A total of 371 rural communities were surveyed in the GLSS 5 Community Survey. The sample of rural communities which may be considered for the purposes of this paper is reduced to 355 communities in which it is possible to match communities and households. Among these, 54 communities were found to contain both a private and a public primary school; 286 contained only public school(s); 14 had only private school(s); and one community had no schools of either type. Clearly, some households chose to send their children outside the community, either for public or private basic schooling.

CREATE gathered qualitative data on educational access in the Mfantseman District of Ghana. Mfantseman is located in the Central Region of Ghana, and is classified as the fourth poorest out of 12 regions. The district's population represented about 7% of the total population of the region (Ghana Statistical Service, 2005a). About 60% of its inhabitants lived below the one-dollar-a-day level (Ghana Statistical Service, 2000; Mfantseman District Assembly, 2006), indicating wide poverty levels among its population. Interview data presented here were conducted between June and August 2008 with household heads in the lowest income quintile with an estimated annual income of GH¢208.[2] The mean private school cost per child was GH¢62, compared with GH¢33 for public schools (see also Akaguri, 2011).[3]

The main economic activities were farming and fishing, with nearly half of the adult population (49.4%) engaged in agricultural, animal-keeping and forestry activities (Ghana Statistical Service, 2005a). Farming activities are rain fed. Given the perennial erratic rainfall patterns and labour-intensive nature of farming in the area, many farmers can only produce at the subsistence level. About a third of the population had never enrolled in school, and about 17% of these were of school age (i.e. 6 to 14 years). Compared with the other districts in the Central Region, Mfantseman District had the highest proportion (about a fifth) of school-age children who had never enrolled in school (Ghana Statistical Service, 2005a), and yet there were low-fee private providers operating alongside public schools.

An interest for this chapter is the factors which motivate relatively poor households in this district to choose low-fee private education when capitation has been introduced into public schools to effectively abolish fees. Before delving into the case study evidence about school choice, the next section presents the analysis of two datasets (GLSS and EMIS) on patterns of growth in private schooling relative to public basic education in rural areas where low-fee private providers exist.

The Growth of Private Schooling in Ghana

The GLSS Rounds 3 and 5, completed in 1992 and 2006, contained questions on private basic schooling both at household and community levels in rural areas, providing relatively rich data on both supply and demand conditions. Alongside the Ghana EMIS data, these provide useful descriptive data on recent trends in private schooling.

GLSS Data

Tables I-IV show the numbers and proportions of children aged 6-17 years who were, at the time of GLSS 3 and 5, either not attending school, attending a public school, or attending a private school, tabulated according to household poverty status. In total, just about 30% of children were not attending school in 1991/1992, compared with around 23% in 2005/2006. In rural areas, the corresponding figures were 33% and 28%. In 1991/1992, just less than 7% of all children (including those not attending any school) were attending a private school overall, with a figure of around 2.5% for rural areas. These figures had increased dramatically by 2005/2006, when almost 17% (all Ghana) and 10% (rural Ghana) of children were in private schools. When examined by household poverty status, the figures show that, unsurprisingly perhaps, private school attendance was notably more common among non-poor households than among households in either Ghana Statistical Service (GSS) consumption poverty category.

Poverty status	Schooling type			
	No school	Public	Private	Total
Extremely poor	1042	1741	73	2856
%	36.48	60.96	2.56	100.00
Poor	328	742	39	1109
%	29.58	66.91	3.52	100.00
Non-poor	651	1904	347	2902
%	22.43	65.61	11.96	100.00
Total	2021	4387	459	6867
%	29.43	63.89	6.68	100.00

Table I. School type attended, by household poverty status – all Ghana 1991/92 (aged 6-17).
Source: Computed from GLSS 3.

In 1991/1992 between 0.5% and 1.61% of children in extremely poor and poor households in rural Ghana were in private school. But by 2005/2006 these almost negligibly low figures had risen to between 4.76% and 10.39% respectively. Notably, more than 10% of rural poor children were in private schools in 2005/2006. Among the non-poor, growth in private school attendance was very strong, rising from 5.32% in rural areas and 11.96% overall, to 16.93% and 26.68% respectively (see Tables I to IV). This was despite the fact that, according to the GLSS 5 Community Survey, most rural communities and most rural census enumeration areas did not contain a private school.

Poverty status	Schooling type			
	No school	Public	Private	Total
Extremely poor	915	1473	39	2427
%	37.70	60.69	1.61	100.00
Poor	246	545	4	795
%	30.94	68.55	0.50	100.00
Non-poor	356	962	74	1392
%	25.57	69.11	5.32	100.00
Total	1517	2980	117	4614
%	32.88	64.59	2.54	100.00

Table II. School type attended, by household poverty status – rural Ghana 1991/92 (aged 6-17). Source: Computed from GLSS 3.

Poverty status	Schooling type			
	No school	Public	Private	Total
Extremely poor	1596	2563	223	4382
%	36.42	58.49	5.09	100.00
Poor	265	910	144	1319
%	20.09	68.99	10.92	100.00
Non-poor	801	3660	1623	6084
%	13.17	60.16	26.68	100.00
Total	2662	7133	1990	11785
%	22.59	60.53	16.89	100.00

Table III. School type attended, by household poverty status – all Ghana 2005/06 (aged 6-17). Source: Computed from GLSS 5.

Poverty status	Schooling type			
	No school	Public	Private	Total
Extremely Poor	1519	2324	192	4035
%	37.65	57.60	4.76	100.0
Poor	232	743	113	1088
%	21.32	68.29	10.39	100.0
Non-Poor	454	1896	479	2829
%	16.05	67.02	16.93	100.0
Total	2205	4963	784	7592
%	27.73	62.41	9.86	100.0

Table IV. School type attended, by household poverty status – rural Ghana 2005/06 (aged 6-17). Source: Computed from GLSS 5.

It may be that children were being sent to other parts of rural areas where low-fee private schools existed, or were moving in with relatives living in areas where they could find such schools. According to Srivastava's (2006, 2008) work, these strategies were quite commonly employed by poorer households in India. It must also be noted that population growth among school-age pupils in the period from 1991 to 2006 was very rapid, indicating a large rise in absolute pupil numbers in private schools.

EMIS Data

The EMIS school census collects information from both public and private basic schools annually. Not every school reports its data, however, although for public schools the EMIS estimates that data from more than 95% of schools are included. Estimates are between 70% and 90% coverage for private schools. The EMIS included a figure for the percentage of schools reporting data between 2001 and 2005, but thereafter these data were not available. Because of differences in reporting, figures taken directly from EMIS would likely under-represent private schools in comparison with public schools unless a correction is made. In the figures that follow (see Figures 1 through 5), data have been corrected to estimate the population of schools.[4]

Figure 1 shows the pattern of growth in the primary school-aged population and in enrolment in both public and private schools.

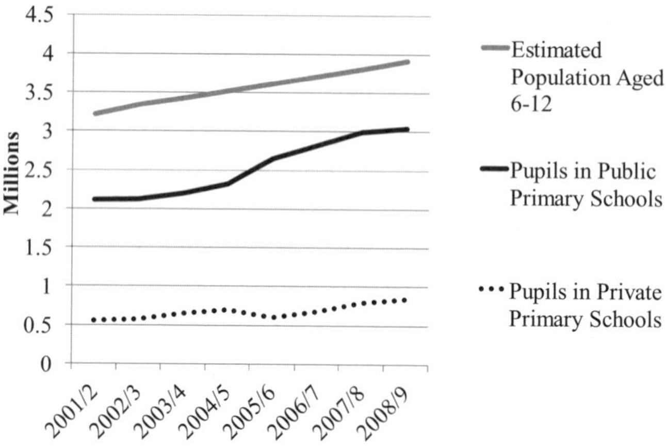

Figure 1. Enrolment in public and private primary schools 2001-2009.
Source: Authors' calculations from EMIS.

The population is estimated using the 2000 census, and growth is projected using a national average annual population growth rate of 2.7%. It is apparent that while the gap between the numbers of children of school age and of those enrolled were fairly static between 2001/2002 and 2004/2005, a steep increase in enrolment growth is observed between 2004/2005 and 2005/2006, corresponding to the period when the Capitation Grant Scheme was introduced, effectively removing direct costs of basic education. In the years between 2004/2005 and 2007/2008, growth in enrolment outstripped population growth, although it appears to have slowed in 2008/2009. In private primary schools, enrolments increased steadily until 2004/2005, when they dropped. Since this also coincides with the introduction of the capitation grant, it appears that some families opted for public schooling in place of private in that year, owing to reductions in cost. From 2005/2006, private primary school enrolments again began to increase steadily, and at a faster rate than between 2001/2002 and 2004/2005.

Figure 2 illustrates comparable data for junior secondary school (JSS) enrolment. A distinctly similar pattern emerges.

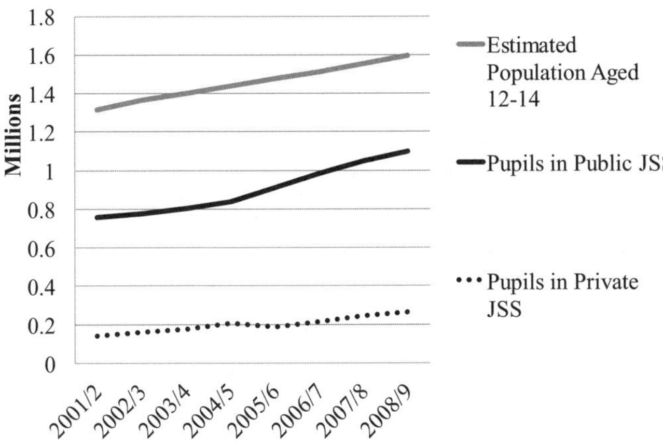

Figure 2. Enrolment in public and private JSS 2001-2009.
Source: Authors' calculations from EMIS.

Figure 3 shows the trend in the total number of private schools. Over the period, the number of private JSSs doubled and the number of private primary schools increased by two thirds. Both trends follow the same pattern, albeit exaggerated, in that the general increase in school numbers over time is interrupted between 2004/2005 and 2005/2006, when school numbers declined sharply. However, the numbers recovered to their 2004/2005 levels by 2007/2008. The data for teacher numbers in private schools show a corresponding pattern, as shown in Figure 4.

When examining trends in the shares of all children and all pupils in public and private schools, again the pattern persists. In relation to the share of pupils in private primary schools, shown in Figure 5, the drop between 2004/2005 and 2005/2006 is particularly dramatic. Indeed, by 2008/2009 the share had not yet returned to its 2004/2005 levels. The same was true in relation to the trend in private JSS enrolment. These patterns are indicative of the very large increase in public school enrolments following the introduction of the capitation grant. Nonetheless, the share of pupils enrolled in private schools had been increasing steadily since 2005/2006, indicating a faster rate of growth in private than in public school enrolment in the years following the introduction of the capitation grant.

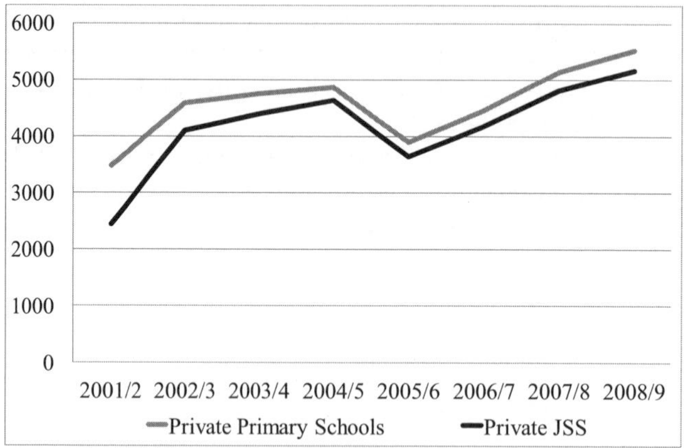

Figure 3. Private primary school numbers 2001-2009.
Source: Authors' calculations from EMIS.

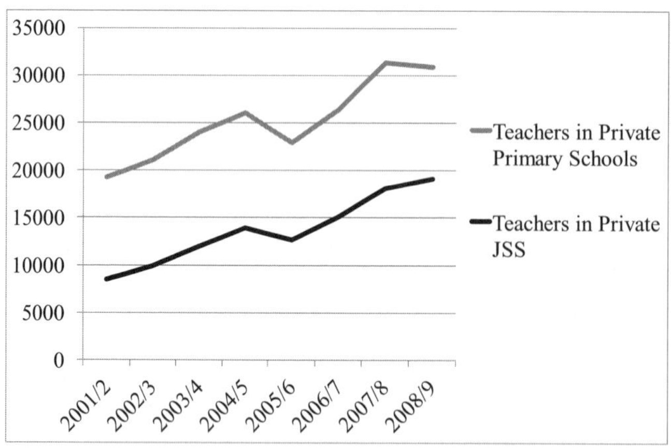

Figure 4. Teacher numbers in private schools 2001-2009.
Source: Authors' calculations from EMIS.

These patterns illustrate a longer-term trend of increasing enrolment in private schools, both in absolute terms and relative to public school enrolments. The uncharacteristic reversal between 2004/2005 and 2005/2006 may be taken to indicate the importance to households of schooling costs in determining school choice. It appears that the introduction of capitation grants, effectively eliminating public school fees, caused a supply-side shock which altered the calculus of relative costs and benefits facing households so that public schooling became relatively better value for money, persuading households on the margins to select public schools for new enrolments. It also seems that this perception did not endure, given the rate of increase since 2005-2006. A plausible explanation might be that parents reassessed the quality provided in public schools and no longer saw them as better value for money, exiting the public sector for private schools.

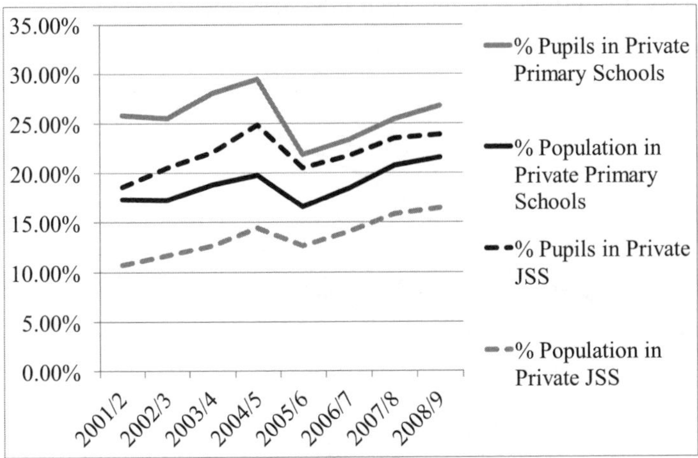

Figure 5. Enrolment shares in private schools 2001-2009.
Source: Authors' calculations from EMIS.

According to the Ghana Ministry of Education's own assessment, the surge in enrolments that accompanied the introduction of capitation created conditions that worsened quality as they put pressure on infrastructure needs and worsened the pupil-teacher ratio (MOESS, 2006). It also appears that some families removed their children from private schools to send them instead to public school between 2004/2005 and 2005/2006. Numbers of pupils in private primary schools between those years were reduced by an estimated 97,352, and in private JSSs, by an estimated 21,206. These numbers amount respectively to 25.7% and 28.5% of the increased intake in public schools between the same academic years. At mean public school sizes, these pupils would have required an additional 450 public primary schools and 174 public JSSs. This analysis shows the pressure that the introduction of capitation grants exerted on public schools in terms of increased enrolments in limited space, but also the contribution that private providers made towards alleviating this pressure by absorbing pupils who otherwise would be in overcrowded public schools.

Figure 6 shows the incidence of private school enrolment in Ghana by household economic welfare in 1991/1992 and in 2005/2006 using data from

GLSS 3 and GLSS 5.[5] Welfare is shown in deciles and is defined in terms of the money-metric value of household consumption per equivalent adult, corrected for relative prices. In 1991/1992, the pattern of the incidence of private school enrolment is consistently and almost negligibly low and below the mean level (decile 5). It then begins to rise fairly sharply by decile, with the steepest rise occurring in the highest welfare decile. Around 28% of children in the highest welfare decile (decile 10) were attending private schools. The pattern in 2005/2006 is somewhat different. The incidence rises across all deciles at a steeper rate and is markedly higher overall than in 1991/1992, reaching around 50% in the highest welfare decile.

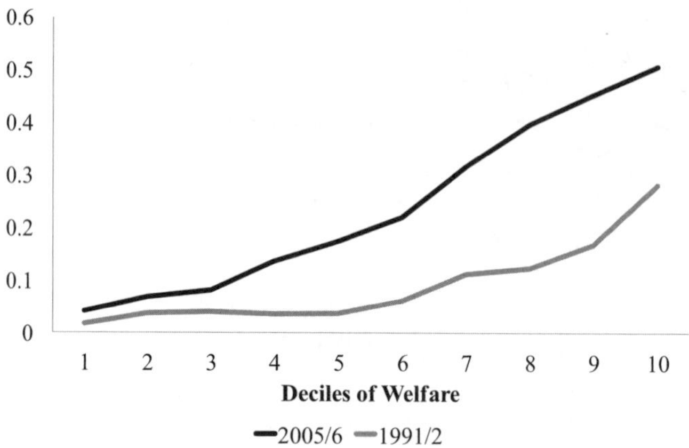

Figure 6. Incidence of private school enrolment (at age 6-12) by household economic welfare.
Source: Authors' calculations from GLSS 3 and GLSS 5.

Figure 7 shows how household expenditure per child in private school varies with economic welfare. Real expenditure on school fees was similar in 1991/1992 and 2005/2006 for the first four welfare quintiles, rising only gradually by quintile, although the fees paid in 2005/2006 by households in the highest quintile showed a sharp rise when compared with lower welfare quintiles or with 1991/1992. Total expenditure on schooling was considerably greater than the level of fees, and also rose more sharply with welfare. Most notably, the gradient is much steeper in 2005/2006 than in 1991/1992. Total real spending in the highest welfare quintile is more than three times higher. Owing to economic growth, among other factors, household welfare increased over this period, with larger increases for the higher income quintiles. Hence it is useful to examine the share of expenditure at the household level that is going to private schooling.

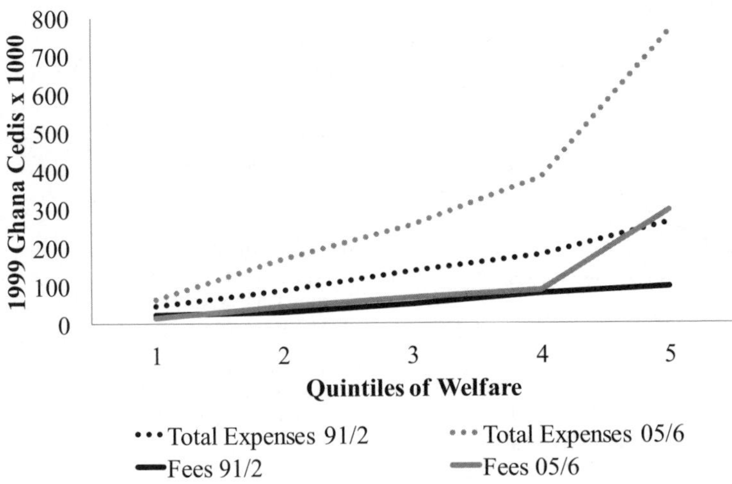

Figure 7. Real expenditure on private schooling (at age 6-12) by household economic welfare.
Source: Authors' calculations from GLSS 3 and GLSS 5.

Figure 8 illustrates the data used in Figure 7 in terms of the shares of household expenditure spent on private schooling per child. Fees per child typically amounted to between 1% and 2% of total household expenditure in both 1991/1992 and 2005/2006, and across welfare distribution. In relation to all expenses, however, these were found to rise sharply between the first and second or third quintiles as a proportion of all spending. We also note that proportionate spending on all expenses rose markedly between 1991/1992 and 2005/2006. Except in the two lowest quintiles, spending on private schooling per child amounted to around 5% of all household expenditure in 2005/2006, and to 3% in 1991/1992.

Table V reports the mean levels of parental education in terms of years of schooling for children in the three school-attendance categories (i.e. no school, public school, private school). It shows that average parental education is very low among children not attending school. It increases for those in public school, and increases again for those in private school, especially where the father's education is concerned. Evidently, as parental education improves, particularly that of the father, the more likely it is that households will consider the private option. It may be that as the household decision about schooling increasingly shifts to fathers who are more educated, so preference for private schooling increases. This is consistent with the literature on the determinants on school choice which suggests that demand improves with rising parental education, and more so for private education.

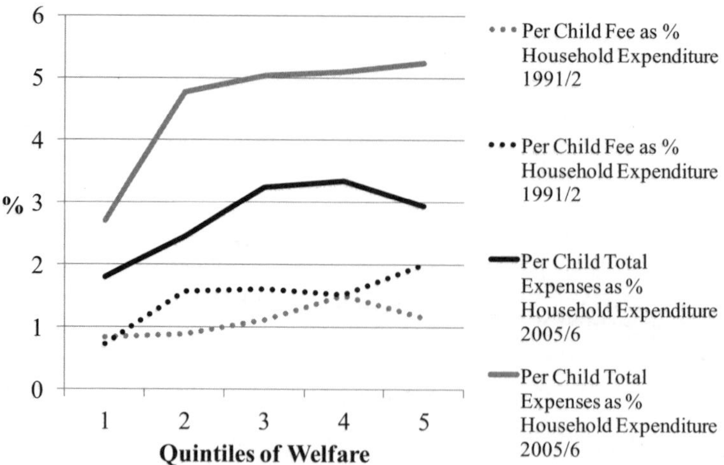

Figure 8. Expenditure on private schooling per child as a percentage of all household spending, by household economic welfare. Source: Authors' calculations from GLSS 3 and GLSS 5.

	No school	Public school	Private school
Mother's education (years)	0.97	2.49	4.23
Father's education (years)	1.78	4.75	6.44

Table V. Parents' education and child's school attendance. Source: Computed from GLSS 5.

Modelling Results: school choice

Table VI reports the results of a logistic regression model for current attendance at school for children in the primary school age range (ages 6-12). Table VII reports the results of a logistic regression model for attendance at private compared with public school, conditional on school attendance for the same age group. The analysis shows that compared with farming communities, children in fishing communities were notably more likely to attend school. Although both communities are known to experience barriers to access because of children's involvement in casual labour, children engaged in activities around fishing may have spent less time working than those engaged in farming as the latter is more labour intensive and, therefore, more time-consuming. Unsurprisingly, in villages where there was a school, the odds of attendance were substantially raised. Compared with the savannah (northern Ghana), coastal and forest villages were associated with higher attendance. These ecological zones are associated with economic and educational advantage generally in Ghana.

	Village level only	Individual and village level	Village fixed effects
Village population	1.449	1.361	
	(2.39)**	(1.96)**	
Fishing community	13.129	9.944	
	(1.86)*	(1.72)*	
School in village	14.938	15.906	
	(10.57)***	(11.11)***	
Community welfare	1.639	0.889	
	(2.21)**	(-0.50)	
Coastal	3.593	2.735	
	(3.53)***	(2.63)***	
Forest	4.503	2.963	
	(5.87)***	(4.69)***	
Sex of child (male)		0.997	0.987
		(-0.03)	(-0.14)
Age of child		1.885	3.922
		(2.91)***	(5.75)***
Age of child squared		0.969	0.933
		(-2.62)***	(-5.24)***
Sex of head (male)		0.710	0.991
		(-1.60)	(-0.05)
Other relative of head		0.639	0.444
		(-2.03)**	(-4.48)***
Non-relative of head		0.639	0.472
		(-1.16)	(-2.28)**
Mother's years of schooling		1.040	1.037
		(1.72)*	(1.86)*
Father's years of schooling		1.098	1.043
		(5.73)***	(2.82)***
Age of household head		0.996	0.993
		(-0.82)	(-1.54)
Log of household welfare		1.584	2.060
		(4.02)***	(6.13)***
Observations	3242	3170	3017
pseudo R-squared	0.148	0.181	0.0623
Number of villages			207

***$p < .01$, **$p < .05$, *$p < .1$.

Table VI. Logit for current attendance at school: odds ratios (age 6-12).
Note: Robust z-statistics in parentheses.

Compared with a son or daughter of the household head, children who were 'fostered' were less likely to attend, while, again unsurprisingly, those in higher-welfare households were more likely to attend. When comparing within villages only, an additional year of the mother's education increased the odds of a child attending by around 4%, and an additional year of the father's schooling did so by a similar amount. These results provide background for the examination of private school choice, since it is considered that parents' decision to opt for private schooling is conditional on their first choosing to enrol a child in school at all.

	Village level only	Individual and village level	Village fixed effects
Village population	1.117	1.088	
	(1.05)	(0.80)	
Ethnic group: Akan	4.439	3.613	
	(2.77)***	(2.33)**	
Ethnic group: Nzema	5.415	5.181	
	(2.59)***	(2.49)**	
Ethnic group: Maprusi	4.147	4.007	
	(1.79)*	(1.77)*	
Ethnic group: Guan	2.986	2.131	
	(1.82)*	(1.26)	
Ethnic group: Kassena/Nankani	11.614	10.182	
	(3.56)***	(3.36)***	
Ethnic group: Konkomba	8.075	8.151	
	(2.66)***	(2.70)***	
Ethnic group: Other	4.044	3.963	
	(2.04)**	(2.03)**	
Private school in community	3.156	3.375	
	(3.85)***	(3.97)***	
Community welfare	2.249	1.195	
	(2.61)***	(0.53)	
Sex of child (male)		1.056	0.969
		(0.38)	(-0.24)
Age of Child		0.834	0.733
		(-0.58)	(-0.95)
Age of Child Squared		1.009	1.014
		(0.49)	(0.79)
Sex of Head (male)		1.147	0.933
		(0.67)	(-0.38)
Other relative of head		1.177	0.822
		(0.57)	(-0.64)
Non-relative of head		1.037	1.180
		(0.07)	(0.39)

Mother's years of schooling		1.063	1.057
		(3.32)***	(3.29)***
Father's years of schooling		1.008	1.005
		(0.45)	(0.32)
Log of household welfare		1.836	1.997
		(2.60)***	(4.35)***
Observations	2375	2323	1671
pseudo R-squared	0.0993	0.121	0.0481
Number of villages			155

***$p < .01$, **$p < .05$, *$p < .1$.

Table VII. Logit for attendance at private school: odds ratios (age 6-12).
Note: Robust *z*-statistics in parentheses.

Table VII shows that, given that a household decided to send a child to school at all, village-level factors associated with private as opposed to public schooling included ethnic differences (using the dominant group in the village) and the availability of a private school within the village. Ethnicity indicators were highly collinear with variables for the dominant religion at the village level. When religion indicators were included in the absence of variables for ethnicity, Christian villages were associated with notably higher levels of private school than Muslim villages. There was, however, also collinearity between ethnicity, religion and geographic location, so that these effects are difficult to disentangle.

Since village and household welfare are included alongside the availability of a private school, it may be argued that at least part of the 'effect' of ethnicity and religion may be due to differences in preferences for private schooling. The reference group for religion was the Gonja, a predominantly Muslim group with low attendance rates at private school, and who typically live in northern districts with low education indicators. Groups associated with higher odds of attending private school included the dominant Akan group, typically located in southern regions, but, interestingly, also some northern ethnic groups. While samples by ethnic groups are relatively small, descriptive analysis found that in the 6-18 age group, attendance at private school varied from 3% in villages dominated by the Wali ethnic group to as high as 20% in villages dominated by the Nzema, and as high as 18% with respect to Konkomba villages.

Within villages, an additional year of the mother's education was found to increase the odds of private school attendance by almost 6%, while the effect of the father's schooling was not significant. Increasing household welfare was found to be strongly associated with increased odds of private school attendance. It is notable that a child's gender was not found to be significantly associated either with the odds of being in school at all or with the odds of attending private school.

Reasons Households Give for Choosing Particular Schools: evidence from CREATE

To understand household school choices further, we turn our attention to a small sample of interview data of 38 poor household heads in the Mfantesman case study community where CREATE work in the south was located. Generally, household heads saw the introduction of capitation as a factor in reducing the education cost burden, but they raised the issue of quality and standards as important in considering school choice. Some household heads with children in low-fee private schools were of the view that these schools demonstrated a stronger sense of purpose in terms of their management of instructional time and the good examination results they achieved. They spoke about the interest shown by proprietors of low-fee private schools and head teachers in their children's educational welfare through regular home visits and feedback about their progress.

Teacher and pupil discipline were also qualities that interviewees felt distinguished low-fee private schools from the public schools they were familiar with. But clearly the most important reason these households gave for choosing low-fee private schools was simply a belief that they delivered better academic results in terms of the final junior secondary terminal examinations (a belief which was not necessarily accurate). For them, this was an indication that these low-fee private schools were more goal oriented, as they focused on securing improvements in children's learning and achievement, which many felt was lacking in the public schools.

Generally, the households were quite critical of public schools, citing poor teacher attendance, high absenteeism, poor pupil performance, teacher indiscipline, corporal punishment, and the use of child labour in these schools as the main reasons. When asked how households with low earnings and unstable jobs could afford the low-fee schools, about a third of the respondents pointed to credit purchasing either from friends or from the school, or to the occasional sale of personal assets to meet costs.

In her study of households in rural India, Härmä (2009) found that households which used low-fee private schools had to reduce expenditure on other household needs. The desire to access quality education, it seems, motivated demand even though it meant making financial sacrifices or seeking assistance from social networks of friends, relatives or older siblings engaged in fishing, petty trading or casual labour. Others said that though they found it hard paying the fees, because the schools were open to spreading the costs over a period of time this gave them time to raise the amount through a variety of means (e.g. borrowing from relatives, income generated from farming/fishing).

It was clear that the schools themselves adopted marketing strategies to induce demand through their flexible fees policy, similar to findings in India by Srivastava (2007). Low-fee private schools in Mfantseman District had introduced flexible fee payments to ease the burden on households. According to the household heads, some schools allowed households to spread fees over the term or year, and others were prepared to reduce fees for every additional child enrolled. Others had introduced 'fee-free' pre-schools which enrolled children between the ages of three to five. This ensured that the low-fee private schools had a stock of children ready to enter the fee-paying stream. Some household heads cited cases where paying fees promptly had been 'rewarded' with a discount ranging from between 10% and 15%. Thus, household demand for quality education was being met with 'fee-friendly' strategies that made the low-fee private option attractive for some poor households.

What also emerged from household-head interviews was the willingness of relatively poor households to make small fee payments as the price for accessing what they saw as quality education, which, as mentioned above, centred mainly on positive perceptions of examination results, school discipline and teacher professionalism, in contrast to their negative perception of teacher attendance and academic results in public schools. This led to household heads being more optimistic about children's chances of passing the final JSS leaving examinations from low-fee private schools, though reference to children at these schools being more capable of communicating fluently in English - seen as an additional quality indicator - was also made.

What emerges from the interviews is the power of image and marketing in shaping attitudes towards low-fee private schooling. It appeared that private providers were projecting an image of affordability through flexible fee policies as well as one of being goal-oriented in terms of managing teachers and pupils to achieve good examination results. One could argue that low-fee private schools' survival depended on their ability to motivate and sustain demand in a low-income context. To attract clients on low or fragile incomes, it was important that the schools come across as 'affordable' through their fees policy, but also that they show that they were offering something different and better than what was available at public schools. In this context, the incentive to be successful is strong, whereas it can be argued that public schools lacked an incentive to operate in ways which would sustain demand and increase accountability to their communities. Essuman and Akyeampong (2011) argue that Ghanaian public schools feel more responsible to the education bureaucracy than to their school communities. This may explain why they are less likely to take the initiative through their own volition to increase demand from the communities they serve.

Discussion and Conclusion

Overall, the analysis shows that, somewhat surprisingly, even households falling into the GSS 'extremely poor' category in per capita economic welfare made use of private schools. Strong associations were found on the supply side between private school choice and the level of fees, and between private school choice and household welfare levels on the demand side. Nonetheless, key factors associated with preferences for quality education are found to exert effects which may be considered to some extent independent of the household's economic status. These included the household head's age and sex, and parental education levels. This suggests that although fees may be a factor in determining who goes to low-fee private schools, gender, age and education level probably exert a stronger influence. Further, if, as the CREATE evidence suggests, low-fee private schools operate fee policies that lessen the cost burden for their clients, the choice to access these schools is made somewhat easier even for those who may be characterised as 'extremely poor'.

Compared with the 1990s, many more households in rural areas (10%) were accessing private schools. In about a span of fifteen years (1991-2005), private spending per child among the lowest welfare quintile increased by just about 2%, whereas for those in the highest welfare quintile, the increase to about three times was more appreciable. The small increase in private spending for the poorest group may reflect just how difficult it is for this group to access private schooling because of the costs. But it also indicates the limits of expansion as far as this group is concerned.

The evidence also indicates that household spending on education comprises considerably more than the level of fees. While school fees are an important barrier to accessing schooling, they may not necessarily be the final determinant when considering rural households' decisions to enrol a child in the first place. It is conceivable that the practices of low-fee private providers in rural areas, in particular their flexible fees system, induce and sustain demand from some poor households.

Further, it should not be assumed that the mere introduction of fee-free education will simply increase demand and lead to high participation and completion rates, which appeared to be the belief enshrined in public policy, with the introduction of capitation seen as the main incentive for the poor to enrol. To be effective, such a policy must do more – induce and reward efficiency in order for schools to achieve high enrolment, participation and completion. At the moment, regardless of whether pupils enrol and complete, there is no risk to the survival of public schools. In the case of low-fee private schools, their incomes and operation are dependent on how their clients judge their worth.

The qualitative CREATE data suggest that the poor households formed strong opinions about what low-fee private and public schools offered, and although costs mattered, perceptions about quality influenced their behaviour. The introduction of capitation grants appeared to have caused a wave of exit from private to public schools, but it is also clear that this represented a supply-side shock that was not sustained. In fact, the surge appears to have undermined quality provision in the public sector and caused a negative backwash effect resulting in greater demand for low-fee and other private schools, and, as we saw, the rate of growth in the private sector was higher post-capitation.

Capitation may not eliminate the cost burden associated with education. Households still have to pay for food, uniforms and expenses associated with other school logistics. Nevertheless, the interest shown by households in the lowest welfare quintile for private schools suggests that the state may need to entertain the possibility of supporting these schools to keep their costs low, especially if there is evidence of growing demand from this group. In practical terms, this may mean initiatives such as supplying them with instructional materials (e.g. textbooks) and extending free-school-meal programmes to areas where low-fee private schools recruit a large proportion of school-age children. However, this should also mean that private providers open their doors for inspection of their facilities and operations to ensure accountability of public investment. This ultimately raises the question of whether public funds should go towards improving the quality in public schools that are failing. Indeed, that may be a first priority. However, unless increased public funding to improve quality in public schools also promotes greater internal efficiency and accountability, quality may still become elusive, and the initial demand unsustainable.

Low-fee private schools necessarily have to operate in ways that lower their costs. However, these costs are borne mostly by households; thus, the sector's expansion would only be pro-equity if outcomes are considerably better than those in public schools, at an affordable cost. CREATE interview data suggest that some households believed quite strongly that low-fee private schools offered value for money. Nonetheless, the effects of school type in rural areas on achievement and completion of basic education need to be thoroughly investigated, as quality perceptions may be over-claimed. Regardless of this, the interview data indicate that public schools in rural areas have an image problem that can be associated with some negative practices (e.g. corporal punishment) and unprofessional behaviour (e.g. teacher absenteeism). This contrasts with an image of low-fee private schools as better managed and outcomes-oriented. If the presence of private schools in rural areas offers a real choice for poorer households wishing to access better-quality education, then it might be worth considering the conditions under which they can receive state assistance.

However, any initiative that puts public funds into private schools in low-income rural contexts has to be based on whether similar investments in nearby public schools accessible to the poor can achieve similar or better outcomes. Judging from the capitation experience, simply giving public schools direct funds without linking them to some performance-related target is not the answer. In the case of private schools, we must be satisfied that such investments will not, in the long run, increase educational inequality. As our analysis shows, among the poorest group, some may be able to access low-fee private schools, but there still remains a sizeable proportion, including ethnic and religious minorities, for whom the public sector may be still be the only option. Thus, if learning outcomes are better in some low-fee private schools and parents who use them receive no subsidy, their expansion is likely to be anti-equity, although this depends on the size of the group for whom they are unaffordable and on the difference in outcomes between private and public schools.

These questions depend very much on whether the issue is addressed from the household point of view under the existing system (in which case, private school expansion is probably anti-equity). From the point of view of the state system, however, expansion of low-fee private schools with fees met by the state may, in some contexts and under some conditions, seem a more efficient and equitable way to reach Education for All. The state has some responsibility to alleviate the cost burden of accessing low-fee private schools among the poor, *if* such schools can demonstrate that they actually provide better-quality education at relatively lower costs, *and* if there is evidence of growing demand. Similarly, investments in the public sector to improve access should be linked to a system of accountability that is lined to indicators of quality outcomes. As we have argued, the critical question is: what are the long-term consequences of achieving equitable access?

Notes

[1] The term 'low-fee private school' as used here refers to tuition fees charged by private providers operating in the rural sector. In a case study of school choice among poor households, Akaguri (2011) found that households which pay private school fees spent around 30% of household income on such on fees.

[2] Exchange rate US$1 = GH¢1.43.

[3] These household data were further used and analysed in Akaguri, 2011.

[4] EMIS data are inflated on the assumption that non-reporting schools contain the same numbers of pupils and teachers as reporting schools of the same type (e.g. private junior secondary school). For 2001-2005 the actual reporting rate is used. For 2005-2009 the mean reporting rate for 2001-2005 is used. While it is not possible to confirm this assumption, the approach is considered preferable to using the raw data when reporting rates are known to differ substantially by school type.

[5] No data on private schooling were collected in GLSS 4.

References

Akaguri, L. (2011) Household Choice of Schools in Rural Ghana: exploring the contribution and limits of low-fee private schools to Education for All. Unpublished doctoral thesis, University of Sussex, Brighton.

Akyeampong, K. (2009) Revisiting Free Compulsory Universal Basic Education (FCUBE) in Ghana, *Comparative Education*, 45(2), 175-195.

Akyeampong, K. (2011) (Re)assessing the Impact of School Capitation Grants on Education Access in Ghana. CREATE Pathways to Access Series, Research Monograph No. 71. Brighton: Centre for International Education, University of Sussex. http://www.create-rpc.org/pdf_documents/PTA71.pdf

Akyeampong, K., Djangmah, J., Oduro, A., Seidu, A. & Hunt, F. (2007) Access to Basic Education in Ghana: the evidence and the issues. CREATE Country Analytic Report. Brighton: Centre for International Education, University of Sussex. http://sro.sussex.ac.uk/1872/1/Ghana_CAR.pdf

Baschieri, A. & Falkingham, J. (2006) Staying in School: assessing the role of access, availability and opportunity cost. S3RI Applications & Policy Working Paper, A07/02. Southampton: University of Southampton. http://eprints.soton.ac.uk/45358/1/45358-01.pdf

Becker, G. (1964) *Human Capital: a theoretical and empirical analysis, with special reference to education.* New York: National Bureau of Economic Research.

Bhalotra, S. & Heady, C. (2003) Child Farm Labor: the wealth paradox, *World Bank Economic Review*, 17(2), 197-227.

Bhalotra, S.R. & Tzannatos, Z. (2003) Child Labor: what have we learnt? Social Protection Discussion Paper Series, No. 0317. Social Protection Unit, Human Development Network. Washington, DC: World Bank. http://info.worldbank.org/etools/docs/library/135857/child%20labor%20-%20what%20have%20we%20learnt-bhalotra%20%26%20tzannatos.pdf

Boateng, A. (2005) Causes of Drop out: a case study of the Awutu Senya District. Unpublished master's thesis, University of Education, Winneba, Ghana.

Canagarajah, S. & Coulombe, H. (1997) Child Labor and Schooling in Ghana. Background paper, World Bank Economic and Sector Work (ESW) on Ghana: Labor Markets and Poverty. Washington, DC: World Bank.

Checchi, D. (2001) Education, Inequality and Income Inequality. Discussion Paper, No. DARP 52. Distributional Analysis Research Programme, Toyota Centre, Suntory and Toyota International Centres for Economics and Related Disciplines. London: London School of Economics. http://sticerd.lse.ac.uk/dps/darp/DARP52.pdf

Colclough, C., Al-Samarrai, S., Rose, P. & Tembon, M. (2003) *Achieving Schooling for All in Africa: costs, commitment and gender.* Ashgate: Aldershot.

Drèze, J. & Kingdon, G.G. (2001) School Participation in Rural India, *Review of Development Economics*, 5(1), 1-24.

Essuman, A. & Akyeampong, A. (2011) Decentralisation Policy and Practice in Ghana: the promise and reality of community participation in education in rural communities, *Journal of Education Policy*, 26(4), 513-527.

Fentiman, A., Hall, A. & Bundy, D. (1999) School Enrolment Patterns in Rural Ghana: a comparative study of the impact of location, gender, age and health on children's access to basic schooling, *Comparative Education*, 35(3), 331-349.

Filmer, D. (2007) If You Build it Will They Come? School Availability and School Enrolment in 21 Poor Countries, *Journal of Development Studies*, 43(5), 901-928.

Ghana National Education Coalition Campaign (GNECC) (2005) Report on Education. Accra: GNECC.

Ghana Statistical Service (2000) *Poverty Trends in the 1990s.* Accra: Ghana Statistical Service.

Ghana Statistical Service (GSS) (2005a) *Ghana 2000 Population and Housing Census.* Central Regional Analysis of District Data and Implications for Planning, GSS. Accra: Ghana Statistical Service.

Ghana Statistical Service (GSS) (2005b) *Population Data Analysis Report: policy implications of population trends, vol. 2.* Accra: Ghana Statistical Service.

Glewwe, P. & Jacoby, H. (1994) Student Achievement and Schooling Choice in Low-income Countries, *Journal of Human Resources*, 29(3), 843-864.

Hanushek, E. & Woessmann, L. (2007) The Role of Cognitive Skills in Economic Development, *Journal of Economic Literature*, 46(3), 607-668.

Härmä, J. (2009) Can Choice Promote Education for All? Evidence from Growth in Private Primary Schooling in India, *Compare*, 39(2), 151-165.

Kazeem, A., Jensen, L. & Stokes, C. (2010) School Attendance in Nigeria: understanding the impact and intersection of gender, urban-rural residence, and socioeconomic status, *Comparative Education Review*, 54(2), 295-319.

Kingdon, G., & Theopold, N. (2006) Do Returns to Education Matter to Schooling Participation? Global Poverty Research Group Working Paper, GPRG-WPS-052. Oxford: University of Oxford. http://economics.ouls.ox.ac.uk/14031/1/gprg-wps-052.pdf

Lavy, V. (1996) School Supply Constraints and Children's Educational Outcomes in Rural Ghana, *Journal of Development Economics*, 51(2), 291-314.

Mason, A.D. & Khandker, S.R. (1997) *Household Schooling Decisions in Tanzania.* Washington, DC: World Bank.

Mfantseman District Assembly (2006) 2006-2009 District Medium Term Development Plan. District Planning Coordinating Planning Unit, Saltpond, Ghana.

Ministry of Education, Science and Sports (MOESS) (2006) *Preliminary Education Sector Performance Report.* Accra: Ministry of Education.

Ministry of Education, Science and Sports (MOESS) (2009) *Education Sector Performance Report.* Accra: Ministry of Education.

Oduro, A.D. (2000) *Basic Education in Ghana in the Post-reform Period.* Accra: Centre for Economic Policy Analysis.

Patrinos, H.A., Barrera-Osorio, F. & Guaqueta, J. (2009) *The Role and Impact of Public–Private Partnership in Education.* Washington, DC: The International Bank for Reconstruction and Development/World Bank.

Ravallion, M. & Wodon, Q. (2000) Does Child Labour Displace Schooling? Evidence on Behavioural Responses to an Enrollment Subsidy, *Economic Journal,* 110(462), 158-175.

Sackey, H.A. (2007) The Determinants of School Attendance and Attainment in Ghana: a gender perspective. AERC Research Paper, 173. Nairobi: African Economic Research Consortium. http://www.aercafrica.org/documents/RP173.pdf

Siddiqi, F. & Patrinos, H.A. (1995) Child Labor: issues, causes and interventions. Human Capital Developmental and Operations Policy Working Paper, No. HCOWP 56. Washington, DC: Human Resources and Operations Policy Department and Education and Social Policy Department, World Bank.

Srivastava, P. (2006) Private Schooling and Mental Models about Girls' Schooling in India, *Compare*, 36(4), 497-514.

Srivastava, P. (2007) For Philanthropy or Profit? The Management and Operation of Low-fee Private Schools, in P. Srivastava & G. Walford (Eds) *Private Schooling in Less Economically Developed Countries: Asian and African perspectives*, pp. 153-186. Oxford: Symposium Books.

Srivastava, P. (2008) School Choice in India: disadvantaged groups and low-fee private schools, in M. Forsey, S. Davies & G. Walford (Eds) *The Globalization of School Choice?*, pp. 185-208. Oxford: Symposium Books.

UNESCO (2007) *2008 Education for All Global Monitoring Report. Education for All by 2015: will we make it?* Oxford: UNESCO-Oxford University Press.

UNESCO Institute for Statistics (2005) *Children out of School: measuring exclusion from primary education*. Montreal: UNESCO Institute for Statistics. http://www.ungei.org/resources/files/unesco_children_out_of_school.pdf

World Bank (2004) *Books, Buildings, and Learning Outcomes: an impact evaluation of World Bank support to basic education in Ghana*. Washington, DC: World Bank.

World Bank (2010) Education in Ghana: improving equity, efficiency and accountability of education service delivery. Report No. 59755-GH. AFTED, Africa Region. Washington, DC: World Bank. https://openknowledge.worldbank.org/handle/10986/3012

CHAPTER 3

Low-fee Private Schools in Pakistan: a blessing or a bane?

SHAILAJA FENNELL

Introduction

Low-fee private schools have emerged as a new player in education markets in developing countries. These schools are regarded as an important form of provision that permits households in poor communities to choose an education provider rather than being relegated to a failing state sector, or to taking the worse option of removing their children out of education altogether. The additional potential value of these schools is that they are seen to provide better education at a lower cost than state schools, though cost savings seem to come from paying lower teachers' salaries and often employing less-qualified teachers.

The low-fee private schooling phenomenon occurs at a juncture when the provision of education by providers other than the state is being encouraged, particularly by using the form of public–private partnerships (PPP). The use of PPPs through partnerships for the financing and provision of school education is seen a method of ensuring education access and quality within the education system (Patrinos, 2005). However, it is also argued that while these partnerships have the positive result of increasing the number of schools, they provide a low-quality alternative to the failing government school (LaRocque, 2008). Early partnership models focused on the gains from private corporate financing, due to greater perceived efficiency and the superior ability of the sector to raise resources. More recent models have encouraged the introduction of social and political dimensions of education provision.

The evidence provided in this chapter on low-fee private schooling in Pakistan is from a larger project on PPPs, which was part of the Research Consortium on Educational Outcomes and Poverty (RECOUP). RECOUP, a five-year research programme (from 2005 to 2010) funded by the British government's Department for International Development, was led by the

University of Cambridge in collaboration with six other research institutions in the UK, South Asia and Africa. The PPP project examined the impact of PPPs on the supply and demand for schooling in Ghana, India, Kenya and Pakistan. The focus was on the obstacles that the poorest households faced in relation to access and learning outcomes (see Fennell [2010] for the conceptual and methodological basis for the larger project).

The focus of this chapter is on the perceptions and quality assessments of youth (young men and women) and parents about local low-fee private and government schools, particularly on teacher attributes and quality and perceived learning outcomes. Participants were from rural and urban communities in two districts, Sargodha (Punjab province) and Charsadda (Khyber Pakhtunkhwa province). By using Hirschman's (1970) model of exit, voice and loyalty, the broader aim is to conceptually link their levels of discernment to understanding potential impacts on activating improvements in schooling provision in the local context.

This chapter begins with a brief introduction to the current education marketplace in Pakistan, followed by the conceptual framing for this study and a review of the relevance of Hirschman's original exit, voice and loyalty model for examining the impact of newly introduced private schools in poor communities. The methodology and sampling design of the study is then presented, before turning in the final two sections to the data on youth and parental perceptions of low-fee private schools.

The Education Marketplace in Pakistan: positioning low-fee private schools

Pakistan has witnessed rapid growth in small-scale, low-fee private schools over the past decade. This sector is distinct from the top-quality, high-cost, elite private schools in urban areas and caters predominantly to peri-urban and rural areas. Literature on Pakistan indicates that the average low-fee private school charges a monthly fee of Rs. 60 (< £1) and tends to employ teachers who have less training than and earn half the salary of government school teachers (Andrabi et al, 2002; Aslam, 2007).

Education at the primary level in government schools in Pakistan is free of school fees and school books are also free of charge. In addition to tuition fees in private schools, considerable non-fee expenditure is incurred. Nonetheless, in Pakistan, the low quality of public schooling has contributed to falling education returns and growing dissatisfaction with public schooling provision among poor households (Andrabi et al., 2002; Aslam, 2007), which has contributed to the growth of low-fee private schools (Naseer et al, 2010).

There is evidence to suggest that the private sector is growing rapidly in urban and rural areas, catering to urban elite and middle- and lower-income groups, though rural/urban and socio-economic gaps remain (Andrabi et al, 2002; Khan et al, 2003). The total number of private schools increased from 32,000 to 47,000 between 2000 and 2005 (Andrabi et al, 2007). The latest education census data estimate the share of private sector enrolment in relation to total enrolments to be 35% (Government of Pakistan, 2005), which is attributed to the growth in low-fee private schools in the country (Andrabi et al, 2007). The view is that these private schools are emerging as substitutes for the government sector at the primary level and as they increase their share of the private sector, they have started to account for a larger share of enrolments at the national level (Aslam, 2007).

The recent growth in private sector schools is explained in part by the chronically dismal performance of the public sector and its inability to address low standards of education. There is a significant gap in learning achievements between public and private school students in Pakistan (Arif & Saqib, 2003). The current literature observes that this could be due to less teacher absenteeism and higher teacher commitment in the private sector (Andrabi et al, 2007).

Other studies indicate that there are significant differences in learning outcomes, not directly due to school type, but attributable to household socio-economic status. For example, in a sample of schools in urban Pakistan, Aslam (2007) found that primary school students with higher scores on standardised tests also had a supportive educational environment, with parents who were wealthier, more educated and more likely to be professionally employed. Thus, there is concern that the poorest households do not have the financial means or social networks to make low-fee schools a realistic option for them (Aslam & Kingdon, 2008; Muzaffar, 2010). Such studies seem to indicate that although low-fee private schools are becoming relatively more available to poorer households, they are only accessible to the better-off sections among this group.

Conceptual Framing

The earliest literature on PPPs focused on improving the supply and demand aspects of education provision by introducing economic incentives that would bring about a closer approximation to market conditions (Burchardt, 1997). The ushering in of market forces was regarded as sufficient to ensure that there was both expansion and improvement in the provision of education. From this perspective, demand-side improvements are seen to be achieved by introducing competition, thus allowing parents to choose between school providers. On the supply side, perceived benefits are meant to occur through improved management and the greater availability of finances so that more teaching and better facilities can be made available.

More recent literature on schooling indicates that successfully providing education is also dependent on the larger social and political terrain (Akerlof & Kranton, 2002; Di John, 2007) and the manner in which state and non-state players engage with each other (i.e. the type of contract and the nature of the financing arrangement) when establishing additional schools. If competition is to eventuate, it requires both types of providers in the partnership to be willing to work with each other in creating an expanded education market where providers are responsive to the demands of poor households (Fennell, 2007). If there is little or no incentive to improve responsiveness to households, competition will not be an achievable objective.

While competition is desirable in the conceptualisation of PPP models, it has not always been achievable when new educational hierarchies have emerged, particularly where 'cream-skimming' (i.e. the process of selecting more academically able students for enrolment) occurs (Smith, 1994). Bringing in private contracts as a mechanism to introduce competitive forces can also have the negative consequences of reducing public accountability and increasing consumer prices in the education market without accompanying improvement in provision (Ellman, 2006).

Furthermore, the market framework assumes perfect or at least complete information where consumers can indicate their dissatisfaction with existing provision by exiting from the services of a particular provider. Such a perfectly competitive marketplace in education is difficult to realise in countries that do not have mass state education systems covering the entire school-aged population. One major challenge in this regard is the lack of information facing both consumers and suppliers/producers of education services on how to use mechanisms to signal dissatisfaction or demand remedy in this context (Banerjee et al, 2006).

Exit, Voice and Loyalty: revisiting Hirschman

Conceptually, we frame the decisions regarding school choice among poor households from concepts set out by Hirschman's (1970) exit, voice and loyalty model, in which these three strategies were seen as 'recuperation mechanisms' to redress deterioration in firms, public services and other organisations (Hirschman, 1980, p. 431). In the context of schooling, exit in this model is an economic response to deteriorating education quality whereby parents take their children out of a poorly performing school and transfer them to a better school. The implication is that exit can alter the number of students in a set of schools by increases in favoured schools and reductions in poorly performing schools.

Voice in this model is a political response from within the school that can work to improve the quality of provision. The presence of loyalty is a feature that would lessen exit by increasing the affinity an individual felt for a particular school, thus inducing a greater propensity to political action and personal motivation for demanding improvements from within. These three mechanisms provide a useful framework for mapping how households in poor countries may signal their satisfaction with schooling choices in situations where new providers - in this case, low-fee private schools - are entering the education environment.

Hirschman's original formulation was with a view to examining how each one of these mechanisms might operate as a recuperative mechanism to rectify deteriorating quality of provision within an organisation or service. There has been a tendency to regard exit as the simpler mechanism as it does not require interaction with others, but Hirschman (1970) maintains that 'in a whole gamut of human institutions, from the state to the family, voice, however "cumbrous", is all their members have to work with' (p. 17).

The importance of these mechanisms is evident in the manner in which parental choice is exercised in relation to schooling choices. In a situation where both private and state schools exist and where the former are considered the better option, parents are who are quality conscious can choose to exit from a failing state school and opt for a private school. From this perspective, those who do not leave the state education system would be seen as either price conscious and/or less quality conscious. In this situation, there is likely to be asymmetry regarding the proportion of households by socio-economic group who exit the state school system – that is, with a greater proportion of better-off households leaving a deteriorating state education system and those remaining in the system less able to exercise voice (Hirschman, 1970).

The case of households choosing between providers who have differing degrees of quality consciousness must also be considered. This is the situation where the demand for a service increases and a particular service is offered to a new group of households that previously did not have access to such a service. In the specific case of education provision, this can be applied to circumstances where education is extended to populations that were difficult to reach and that previously did not have access. While Hirschman's model has not readily been applied to a context where mass education has not been achieved, there is much to be gained by undertaking such an exercise. This case closely corresponds to the situation in many developing countries that have been unable to expand mass education systems in elementary education and where particular disadvantaged groups, such as the chronically poor, have fallen outside the public sector.

The literature on PPPs has tended to regard education providers as being responsive to quality discernment by households, as the latter would show their dissatisfaction by voting with their feet (i.e. by exiting from a poor quality provider). The view is that competition breaks the public school monopoly on service provision and puts pressure on schools to alter their behaviour. The threat of exit from schools by parents is seen to be strong enough to compel school administrators to respond to parental demands for improvements in education provision, be these quality or other considerations. The changing environment brought about by the entry of new providers should affect both household schooling choices and the manner in which schools provide education. In relation to the household, it should create the possibility of exit as a way for individuals to leave failing state schools and the possibility for these schools to respond by improving quality in order to increase their ability to compete with other preferred schools (van Zanten, 2005). Thus, by enabling household school choice, private schools are seen to bring improved competition and responsiveness within the school system, though public schools are further disadvantaged against private schools as they cannot change location or vary price in order to increase market share (Gibbons & Silva, 2006).

However, according to Hirschman's model, discerning quality is aggravated if communities have not had prior experience of a particular public good. For example, since these communiteies have often not had earlier experience with the formal education system, it is assumed that they would find it difficult to discern the difference between high and low quality education, with major consequences. As Hirschman (1980) explains:

> Consumers are poorly informed about the quality of the expanded services of an educational system, and have few alternatives to choose from. Nevertheless, if the newly offered services are in fact defective the result will eventually be widespread disappointment and discontent. The damage inflicted by having received a poor education is not easily undone: unlike apples, education is not bought recurrently in small quantities. (p. 115)

Additionally, it is also possible that providers of new services do not have sufficient prior knowledge of how to provide that service, thus resulting in rather poor delivery in the early stages of provision. The lack of previous experience in providing education, for example, could end up with a service being offered that merely has the outward appearance of 'good' quality but is found to be wanting at closer scrutiny. Hirschman (1982) indicates the consequences of such a case:

> There is a class of services for which a strong demand may arise in advance of real knowledge of how to satisfy them… What happens in these situations is that there is response to an effective market demand, some members of society come forward proclaiming like any good hustler, 'We can handle this for you', but actually only begin to learn 'on the job', in the process of rendering these newly popular services as best they can. (p. 42)

The provision by these 'hustlers' is not likely to result in adequate education service delivery, as 'learning on the job' will take time. Additionally, if the ability of clients to discern quality is also the result of a learning process, then households will only express anger and/or disappointment in response to partial or inadequate provision after a considerable time lag (Hirschman, 1982, p. 44). By showing that public demand for goods can nonetheless result in low quality provision given the above conditions, and where responses to inadequate provision are delayed, Hirschman opens up the distinct possibility that school choice can take place in conditions that are far removed from perfect competition. In such circumstances where neither producers nor consumers are in possession of full information about the good, the successful use of exit and voice in bringing about competition and improved quality seems highly unlikely [1], calling into question the perspective that private schools readily encourage competition in the education market (Jimenez et al, 1991).

Research Methods and Sampling

The larger RECOUP project on PPPs, on which this chapter is based, focused on the impact of new PPPs on the education outcomes of the poor in Ghana, India, Kenya and Pakistan. The research in Pakistan was conducted in rural and urban communities in two districts, Sargodha (Punjab province) and Charsadda (Khyber Pakhtunkhwa province). An urban community was defined as one urban block as specified by the sampling frames set out by the Federal Bureau of Statistics. The urban community comprised 216 households in Sargodha and 300 households in Charsadda. The rural community refers to one village in each district. The village in Sargodha had 477 households, while that in Charsadda had 418.

Sample Design and Criteria

Research was conducted in one rural and one urban community in both Sargodha and Charsadda districts. The communities were selected to ensure that they had access to both public and private providers within a short distance (see Table I). While government schools outnumbered private schools in each community, at least three private schools were available for 300 to 400 households.[2] Primary schools, both private and public, were located within a 1-km radius of the community, while the middle and high schools were within a 2-km radius.

Fees charged in the private schools ranged from Rs. 100 to 500 a month. Non-fee expenditure incurred by parents in these private schools amounted to Rs. 200-400 a month. Reported fees in Table I represent 1.42% to 7.1% (Charsadda) and 2.3% to 7.1% (Sargodha) of the minimum wage rate (Rs. 7000/month) as specified in Pakistan's 2010 Labor Policy and the 2010-2011 Federal Budget. The sample of schools included registered and unregistered private schools in the communities, all of which, with one exception, were unaided.[3] The RECOUP qualitative research began with a household census of each community mapping households by socio-economic and education background. This was an important source of baseline data for selecting respondents from varying backgrounds for focus group discussions. Semi-structured interviews and focus group discussions with parents and youth provided the qualitative data from which voice and exit mechanisms in these communities were identified and classified. The sample of respondents included 50 parents and 50 school-going youth (between the ages of 14 and 18) enrolled at the secondary level (grade 8 and above). Half the parents and youth in focus groups and individual interviews came from the lowest socio-economic groups in each community. Separate focus group discussions for fathers, mothers, girls and boys were organised. Detailed individual interviews were conducted with selected respondents from among the focus group discussants.[4]

	Charsadda		Sargodha	
	Urban	Rural	Urban	Rural
Number of households	300	418	213	477
Population	2163	2985	1276	3348
% of *kachcha* houses[a]	26.6	30.7	2.4	3.8
% of houses with flush toilets	87.6	56.6	82.2	64.6
Emigrants per 100 population	3	5	12	13
% adults doing unskilled labour	22.7	15.7	14.6	20.6
Number of private schools	4	3	4	4
Number of government schools	5	6	3	6
Private school fees	Rs. 100-500 a month		Rs. 160-500 a month	
Private non-fee expenditure	Rs. 250-400		Rs. 200-400	
Private school size	139-455	168-726	72-110	70-159
Public school size	103-972	123-725	445-1159	151-473

[a]*Kachcha* houses refer to dwellings that are made of mud or other traditional material, and not of kiln-fired bricks.

Table I. Rural and urban communities in Charsadda and Sargodha.

All communities in the study were serviced by private and public schools. Private schools were predominantly primary schools, while public schools were a mix of primary, middle and high schools. It is important to note that the research design of the PPP study focused on understanding how the combined presence of both government schools and newly introduced private schools, under an umbrella of provincial promotion of partnerships in education, impacted on poor communities. The schools operating in our communities can be regarded as low-fee private schools as these schools were specifically designed to service the education demands of these poor communities and charged relatively low fees. Some private schools were registered, while others were not.

The responsibility to register private primary schools belonged to the Assistant Education Officers, while for private middle and high schools it lay with the District Education Officer. Many low-fee private schools start providing education as unregistered bodies, though officials interviewed in both districts felt that as all pupils, whether enrolled in private or government schools, are obliged to sit board exams it would only be a matter of time before all schools were registered.

While the research design used in both sites was identical, the richness of data obtained from each research technique varied across the sites. The analysis of data from Charsadda indicated far richer data obtained from focus group discussions than from individual semi-structured interviews, while in the case of Sargodha, there was far more depth in the individual semi-structured interviews. The respondents at the former site felt that their collective view (obtained from focus-group research methods) was a more accurate representation, as it was voiced in the presence of community members. This could be on account of the more communitarian and less commercialised nature of local interactions in hilly regions of Khyber Pakhtunkhwa, compared with the more industrialised region of Punjab (see Fennell & Malik [2012] for a discussion on the difference between collective and individual voice). The different results in both districts could be on account of the fact that participatory methods which permit more 'organic' responses from the community (Chambers, 2007) elicit different responses to those obtained from a single research method. We now turn to results from the study.

Youth Perceptions of Low-fee Private Schools

Evidence from focus groups conducted with youth in urban Charsadda indicates that they distinguished between government and private schools with regard to the perceived quality of education. Focus group discussions with young men revealed that they were particularly concerned with learning outcomes in each school type, how these might relate to teacher qualifications and ability, and whether or not good teachers would stay at private schools. For example:

> In private schools there is little certainty that the teacher will be there for the entire school year. What happens, if I take admission in a school where there are brilliant teachers with good qualifications, but they leave the next day and go somewhere else? It is not the contribution of the teacher that should be the measure of a good school but the school results.
> (Young man, Respondent 6)

> People see how good a teacher is because it is the teacher's ability that [affects] how good the result of that school is.
> (Young man, Respondent 8)

Interestingly, responses of male youth from poorer households indicated that they did not necessarily regard private schools as providing better quality education. Rather, they saw the act of choosing private schools as a way for better-off households to gain a new type of social status. There was also a sense among some of the youth that they were compelled to go the school that was closest to them because of financial constraints. This resulted in any quality discernment being meaningless, as they were unable to follow up on assessments or distinctions on account of their financial straits.

> A person who is well off, they choose to go to a private school. Such people do not care about the quality of the teachers [or the teaching] as they are only interested in achieving social status from going to a private school. (Young man, Respondent 5)
>
> We go to the school that is nearest to us. If there is a good government school which is further away we cannot go there as we cannot pay for the transport, so we go for the school that is near to us. (Young man, Respondent 7)

The importance of teachers in school and the relationship to learning outcomes also emerged as an important point of discussion in the focus group discussions with young women in urban Charsadda. Private school teachers were not considered to be necessarily better or responsible for better learning outcomes, and as it was for the young men, the rapid turnover of private school teachers was a matter of concern:

> The students in almost any private school are relatively few [compared with government schools] so it is very manageable for any teacher to give attention to these students. Moreover, tuition fees are collected which mean that these teachers need to teach really effectively [to keep the fees coming in]. The teachers in any private school are likely to change [during the course of the academic year] or move to another school. This practice has devastating effects on the studies of a student. Why? Simply because every teacher has a different way of teaching and any student will find it really difficult to keep up with their studies if the methods keep changing. (Young woman, Respondent 4)

The ability of urban youth in Charsadda to discern the quality of individual teachers on the basis of their teaching ability and teacher turnover rather than to regard this as an automatic feature associated with a particular type of school was strongly evident from the focus group data. In fact, the young women had rather favourable views of teachers in government schools, with particularly complimentary views on their teaching qualifications and lack of teacher turnover.

> The teachers of government schools have good qualifications and are well trained, and thus, quite good at teaching.
> (Young woman, Respondent 5)

> Government schools have a special edge over private schools because the teachers in any government school are permanent. They are not likely to be suspended or get transferred. Any school where teachers are frequently changed has a bad impact on the studies of the students as these students get time to get along with the teaching methods of the new teacher as these teaching methods vary from teacher to teacher.
> (Young woman, Respondent 6)

Focus group discussions conducted in rural Charsadda indicated that the rural youth were aware of the existence of both low-fee private and state schools; however, there was less evidence of discernment about the potential relationship between learning outcomes and teacher commitment or turnover. Among this group, there was a tendency to regard private schools as producing better learning outcomes because better-off parents were able to choose these schools, or because they demanded more of their children since they were paying fees. In contrast to the participants from urban Charsadda, these participants did not distinguish between teacher abilities and school type as much.

> In private schools, the teachers take good care of their students and they work hard with them, while in the government, the teachers work hard but the students are lazy. The teachers are hard workers in both, but in private schools the parents also ask their children to study, as the parents themselves are educated. So they admit their child to schools where the future of their children could be bright. The parents of the child studying in government schools are not educated. They just hand their children their schoolbag and ask their child to go to school.
> (Young man, Respondent 3, rural)

> Those who have money go for private schools because the educational level is better there while in government schools it is not that good. (Young man, Respondent 6, rural)

Others were of the opinion that while better-off households choose low-fee private schools, it was not the case that government schools were failing or were filled with poor quality teachers and high degrees of teacher absenteeism.

> There are good learning outcomes and very intelligent teachers in government schools. There are no problems in the government school. (Young man, Respondent 1, rural)

> We are poorer so we go to government schools while those (households) who are well off send their children to private ones. Both schools are similar with regard to educational standards. The only difference is with regard to the fees paid for private school. What is taught is the same and the quality of teachers is the same in both types of school. (Young man, Respondent 2, rural)

In the case of youth in Sargodha, detailed data on teachers and learning outcomes were based on individual interviews. Once again, the data indicated that youth had considered the role that teachers and teaching played in determining learning outcomes reflected in the schools that were chosen. The key areas of complaint were with regard to the rapid turnover of teachers who were not qualified, and who were not available throughout the academic year. The lack of knowledge among the new education providers was also the subject of discussion among the young men. The following is an example of the experience of one male rural youth in Sargodha; he attended a private school that he felt was run as a 'business':

> In Class 9, I moved to a private school. The school was close to the village. I joined because my uncle recommended the school and advised me to take admission there. The school was a new enterprise for the school owners. In fact, they said that they had started the school as their new business. The way they ran the school was exactly that. The school owners had a dodgy set-up where sometimes there was one particular teacher and sometimes another. If a second teacher joined the school, another one in the school would leave. The teachers in the private school were mostly university students reading for a M.Sc. or B.Sc. degree. When they had completed their university degree and they got employment or links with another sector, they would leave. They completed their own education but left our education incomplete. This situation continued throughout my time there. The students had to study the entire syllabus on their own.
> (Young man, Respondent 2, rural)

In some instances, their description of providers accessible to them closely resembled the 'hustlers' referred to by Hirschman (1982), as described above. For example, one young rural man described the characteristics of local political patrons who had recently started running private schools:

> You know that there are local political patronage and networks in our area. There is no one in the local political set-up who regards children's education as a high priority. Each one is concerned with keeping their political office, and each one is worried about the possibility of infighting and political battles that might emerge.
> (Young man, Respondent 3, rural)

The ability to evaluate teaching quality in relation to other features of school type was evident among young women. For example, and perhaps surprisingly, a girls' *madrasa* was the preferred choice over private schools. This was because the private school was co-educational, and girls had to behave in a religiously conservative manner in the presence of boys. As one rural female student explained:

> I chose my school myself. At first I went to a private school and teaching was good, and so was the lady teacher. However, my mother said that it would be good for me to move to another school, that I would gain confidence from making such a change. She said that there were more girls in the new school and I could make more friends. In my earlier school there were boys, so we only sat around and did not have a lot of activities. I asked around about what activities or functions they had at this other school, and I was told that there were many activities and I would have many opportunities to take part and this was the reason that I changed schools.
>
> I now study in a *madrasa* and a lot of my friends go to that school as well. We have a lot of opportunities to participate in school events. In my previous school there were boys there and there was a strict rule about keeping ourselves covered [heads and upper body with a *dupatta* [shawl)].We were not allowed out of the school and it was very boring.
>
> (Young woman, Respondent 3, rural)

The ability of young men and women to analyse schooling choices in reference to teaching attributes, teacher turnover, and perceived learning outcomes indicates that quality discernment was present among this generation of participants. These participants were aware of certain defects in provision, in both government and private schools, but also they did not regard parental knowledge of education quality or of the providers themselves as being complete, nor did they see parents as discerning. (See Fennell et al, 2010, for further discussion on the difference between youth and parental perceptions.) We now present data on parental perceptions and quality discernment.

Parental Perceptions of Low-fee Private Schools

The level of discernment expressed by parents regarding learning outcomes and their relation to teaching quality and teacher absenteeism was comparatively less than that expressed by the youth in each community. This could be due to lower levels of knowledge among parents on the new private providers, since low-fee private schools were only recent entrants to the educational terrain in local communities. Data indicated that this is similar to Hirschman's (1982) model where there may be a strong demand for education but little sense of exact quality attributes. However, parents did have perceptions of certain teaching attributes. For example, data from individual interviews with parents in Sargodha indicate that teachers' ability to manage classes was regarded as an indicator for improved learning outcomes, though the unnecessary use of force was looked upon negatively. One rural father stated:

> If you think about it, the more children there are in a class the more difficult it is for the teacher to pay attention to each one. So instead of giving individual attention they just teach the entire class. It also matters if the teachers scold or discipline the children. If they do, the next day the child says that they do not want to go to school ... In addition, scolding and beating affects the child's health, thinking, and ability to learn.
> (Rural father, Punjab, matric educated)

The ability of parents to discern private school quality seemed to improve when they had personal experience of low-fee private schools. For example, comments of the urban mother below showed how her own schooling experiences of having attending such schools gave her a better sense when judging the quality of teaching and facilities in different local private schools. She claimed:

> Another bad point of private schools is that they don't have good laboratories or libraries. I myself was in private school. They would take us to the government school for the practicals just because the private schools did not have all the facilities, so we would go for our science practicals to a government school that was nearby. (Urban mother, Focus group Respondent 6, Charsadda)

One rural mother pointed out that she was able to acquire knowledge about new private providers only after her children had been enrolled in a low-fee private school. Once the school was accessed, she realised that the quality of teaching was poor and there was high teacher turnover, features which were not evident at the time of enrolment.

> The negative feature of a private school is that they only have a reputation for being better. People would say that the school is very good, but when you get in there yourself, it's not worth studying there. The other thing is that the salaries of the teachers in private school are pretty low, because of which the teachers don't spend much time there. They just come for a short period, and after a couple of months they leave because of the salary issue, which is quite a big problem. The other thing is that the teachers keep on changing in private schools which has a negative impact on the children because they get used to one teacher, and when that teacher leaves and another comes who has her own way of

> teaching, this affects the child a lot. (Rural mother, Respondent 4, Charsadda)

Comparatively, there was greater awareness in Sargodha and in urban Charsadda than in rural Charsadda. As the Charsadda site was located in a less developed and more tribal part of Pakistan, it might be presumed that parents would be less informed about education provision and quality, which may be particularly relevant to rural and other underserved areas where low-fee private schools are a relatively new phenomenon. However, the ability of parents in this study to become more discerning about the consequences of school choice over time in relation to perceived learning outcomes indicates that they were concerned about the relative quality and limited infrastructure in the low-fee private sector. However, they took more time in becoming responsive than the younger generation (youth respondents), as most did not have any prior direct experience of these schools, or of formal schooling in some cases.

Conclusions

Data on youth and parental perceptions of local government and low-fee private schools indicated that the youth were more attuned to teacher attributes and perceived teacher quality than were the parents, as well as to the context surrounding the entry and operation of low-fee private schools in their local communities. This seemed to be related to their and their peers' direct personal experiences of schools on which to base their assessment. In the case of most parents, this baseline experience was absent, and thus they appeared to postpone judgement and action until their children had gone through the experience of schooling. Thus, the consequence of provision by new private providers in these contexts (i.e. low-fee private schools) appears to be more akin to that of the non-competitive state that Hirschman (1970) highlighted where there are low levels of knowledge on new providers of a service, rather than that approximating a perfectly competitive market where clients have full information.

Some concerns were raised that the new provision offered by low-fee private schools can be cornered by 'hustlers' who may also lack knowledge of what constitutes high quality education in an environment where parents are slow to respond to poor quality. Furthermore, many respondents stated that the poorest sections of the community were not able to access low-fee schools as such schools appeared to be beyond their financial ability. As a result, even though a number of poor youth showed discernment with regard to school quality, they felt resigned to sometimes poorer quality schooling due to severe financial constraints.

Finally, the lower level of perception among parents who did not have prior experience of low-fee private schools will likely result in a delay to activate exit and/or voice, limiting the pressure on new providers (hustlers or otherwise) to immediately improve in the short run. Therefore, it is likely that competition will not emerge rapidly in areas where low-fee private schooling has only recently been introduced. The educational marketplace for the poor in Pakistan is, therefore, not an unmitigated boon, and the bane of poor quality education will likely persist until the next generation of parents (with personal, peer and their own children's experience of low-fee private schooling) has the necessary knowledge base to use exit and voice effectively and force improved competition.

Notes

[1] Hastings and Weinstein (2007) analyse the effect of providing transparent information to parents (on school-level academic achievement) on their school choices and their child's subsequent academic outcomes. They find that full information disclosure helps parents to make substantially better choices in terms of choosing higher performing schools. However, in our case, the lack of full and transparent information results in households being unable to discern which schools provide better learning outcomes.

[2] It is important to note that urban communities represent urban blocks within cities in Sargodha and Charsadda as per official divisions of urban areas. The number of private schools jumps significantly as the boundaries are relaxed to include surrounding urban blocks which often are separated by a small street. Hence, the actual number of schools in the choice bundle available for parents in urban areas will be higher than the numbers shown in Table I.

[3] One school in Charsadda was identified as a charity school. This was set up and run by a prominent family and did not charge fees. It was unaided by the government. There was no evidence of community financing. No religious schools (*madrasas*) were identified in the sample communities.

[4] The interviews in Sargodha were conducted in Urdu and Punjabi. In Charsadda, they were predominantly in Pashto. Interviews for Sargodha communities were transcribed in Punjabi and Urdu, and the relevant quotes translated as required. Those for communities in Charsadda were transcribed directly into English.

References

Arif, G.M. & Saqib, N.U. (2003) Production of Cognitive and Life Skills in Public, Private, and NGO Schools in Pakistan, *Pakistan Development Review,* 42(1), 1-28.

Akerlof, G. & Kranton, R. (2002) Identity and Schooling: some lessons for the economics of education, *Journal of Economic Literature*, 40(4), 1167-1201.

Andrabi, T., Das, J., Khwaja, A.I., Vishwanath, T., Zajonc. T. & LEAPS Team (2007) Pakistan Learning and Educational Achievement in Punjab Schools (LEAPS): insights to inform the education policy debate. http://leapsproject.org/assets/publications/LEAPS_report.pdf

Andrabi, T., Das, J. & Khwaja, A. (2002) *The Rise of Private Schooling in Pakistan: catering to the urban elite or educating the rural poor?* Pomona College Economics Department Report. http://economics-files.pomona.edu/Andrabi/Research/Pakschool%20March29.pdf

Aslam, M. (2007) The Relative Effectiveness of Government and Private Schools in Pakistan: are girls worse off? RECOUP Working Paper No. 4. Cambridge: RECOUP-University of Cambridge. http://recoup.educ.cam.ac.uk/publications/WP4-MAs.pdf

Aslam, M. & Kingdon, G. (2008) What Can Teachers Do to Raise Pupil Achievement? RECOUP Working Paper No. 19. Cambridge: RECOUP-University of Cambridge. http://recoup.educ.cam.ac.uk/publications/WP19-Whatcanteachersdofinal.pdf

Banerjee, A., Banerji, R., Duflo, E., Glennerster, R. & Khemani, S. (2006) Can Information Campaigns Spark Local Participation and Improve Outcomes? A Study of Primary Education in Uttar Pradesh, India. World Bank Policy Research Working Paper No. 3967. Washington, DC: World Bank. http://siteresources.worldbank.org/DEC/Resources/Khemani_CanInformationCampaignsRaise.pdf

Burchardt, T. (1997) Boundaries between Public and Private Welfare: a typology and map of services. Case Paper No. 2. London: Centre for Analysis of Social Exclusion, London School of Economics. http://eprints.lse.ac.uk/6534/1/Boundaries_between_Public_and_Private_Welfare_a_typology_and_map_of_services.pdf

Chambers, R. (2007) Who Counts? The Quiet Revolution of Participation and Numbers. Working Paper No. 296. Brighton: Institute of Development Studies. http://www.ids.ac.uk/files/Wp296.pdf

Di John, J. (2007) Albert Hirschman's Exit-voice Framework and its Relevance to Problems of Public Education Performance in Latin America, *Oxford Development Studies*, 35(3), 295-327.

Ellman, M. (2006) Does Privatising Public Service Reduce Public Accountability? Mimeo. http://www.recercat.net/bitstream/handle/2072/3791/997.pdf?sequence=1

Fennell, S. (2007) Tilting at Windmills: public private partnerships in Indian education today. RECOUP Working Paper No. 5, University of Cambridge.

Fennell, S. (2010) Public-Private Partnerships and Educational Outcomes: new conceptual and methodological approaches. RECOUP Working Paper No. 37. Cambridge: Recoup-University of Cambridge. http://recoup.educ.cam.ac.uk/publications/Wp37-ppp_and_Educational_Outcomes.pdf

Fennell, S., Agbley, G. & Irfan, S. (2010) Perspectives on Types of Schools from Ghana and Pakistan: revisiting the relationship between intergenerational poverty and education. RECOUP Policy Brief, No. 18. Cambridge: Recoup-University of Cambridge. http://recoup.educ.cam.ac.uk/publications/Pb18-perspectives_types_schools_Ghana_Pakistan.pdf

Fennell, S. & Malik, R. (2012) Between a Rock and a Hard Place: the emerging educational market for the poor in Pakistan, *Comparative Education*, 48(2), 249-261.

Gibbons, S. & Silva, O. (2006) Competition and Accessibility in School Markets: empirical analysis using boundary discontinuities, in Timothy J. Gronberg & Dennis W. Jansen (Eds) *Improving School Accountability: check-ups or choice*, pp. 157-184. Oxford: Elsevier.

Government of Pakistan (2005) *National Education Census*. Islamabad: Government of Pakistan. http://www.statpak.gov.pk/fbs/content/national-education-census-2005-pakistan

Hastings, J.S. & Weinstein, J.M. (2007) Information, School Choice, and Academic Achievement: evidence from two experiments. NBER Working Paper No. 13623. Cambridge, MA: National Bureau of Economic Research. http://www.nber.org/papers/w13623

Hirschman, A.O. (1970) *Exit, Voice, and Loyalty: responses to decline in firms, organizations, and states*. Cambridge, MA: Harvard University Press.

Hirschman, A.O. (1980) Exit, Voice, Loyalty: further reflections and a survey of recent contributions, *Milbank Memorial Fund Quarterly: Health and Society*, 58(3), 430-453.

Hirschman, A.O. (1982) *Shifting Involvements: private interest and public action*. Princeton, NJ: Princeton University Press.

Jiminez, E., Lockheed, M. & Paqueo, V. (1991) The Relative Efficiency of Public and Private Schools in Developing Countries, *The World Bank Research Observer*, 6(2), 205-218.

Khan, S. Kazmi, S. & Latif, Z. (2003) A Comparative Institutional Analysis of Government, NGO and Private Rural Primary Schooling in Pakistan. Department of Economics Working Paper Series, Working Paper No. 2003-11, University of Utah.

La Roque, N. (2008) Public–Private Partnerships in Basic Education: an international review. CfBT. http://www.cfbt.com/evidenceforeducation/pdf/PPP.pdf

Muzaffar, I. (2010) Education in Pakistan: the nickel and dime route to ruin? Are Low Fee Private Schools (LFPS) the Route to Quality Education for All? CQE Working Paper Series. Lahore: Campaign for Quality Education. http://www.cqe.net.pk/pdf/The_Nickel_and_Dime_Route_to_Ruin_26.pdf

Naseer, M.F., Patnam, M. & Raza, R.R. (2010) Transforming Public Schools: impact of the CRI program on child learning in Pakistan, *Economics of Education Review*, 29(4), 669-683.

Patrinos, H. (2005) Education Contracting: scope of future research. http://www.ksg.harvard.edu/pepg/ PDF/events/MPSPE/PEPG-05-23patrinos.pdf

Smith, K.B. (1994) Policies, Markets and Bureaucracy: re-examining school choice, *Journal of Politics*, 56(2), 475-491.

van Zanten, A. (2005) New Modes of Reproducing Social Inequality in Education: the changing role of parents, teachers, schools and educational policies, *European Educational Research Journal*, 4(3), 155-169.

CHAPTER 4

The Relative Quality of Private and Public Schools for Low-income Families Living in Slums of Nairobi, Kenya

PAULINE DIXON,
JAMES TOOLEY & IAN SCHAGEN

An important part of any discussion on the impact of low-cost private schools on equity must concern the quality of provision in these schools, and in particular, their relative quality compared with available public schools. This chapter considers the quality of private and government schools that cater for children living in slum areas of Nairobi, Kenya by examining relative achievement in three key subjects. We consider whether parents in slum areas could be making choices taking into account quality factors. In particular, do factors such as class size and teacher commitment feed through to improved children's attainment?

There is a lacuna in the literature regarding pupil achievement in different school management types that cater for children from slum areas in developing countries. This chapter aims to address this issue by reporting a fresh analysis using multilevel modelling of data originally collected in 2004 in order to investigate whether, with regard to pupil achievement, these private schools offer a service that is of inferior quality. The chapter also reports general observations of the slum context on subsequent visits in 2007.

Background

The existence of low-cost private schools serving poor communities is becoming increasingly recognised, although it is not necessarily seen in a positive light. For example, the 2009 *Education For All Global Monitoring Report* has a section dedicated to low-fee private schools, and points to their ubiquity:

> Even a cursory observation of education provision in slums from Hyderabad to Nairobi demonstrates that private provision in some developing countries is no longer the sole preserve of the rich. Private primary schools charging modest fees and operating as small businesses, often with neither regulation nor support from government, are changing the education landscape... a growing marketplace in education provision is appearing by default. (UNESCO, 2008, p. 164)

However, this 'default' market is seen as a 'symptom of state failure' (UNESCO, 2008, p. 164) rather than as market success: 'Unplanned growth in private schooling for the poor in some parts of the world is symptomatic of an underlying malaise: underperformance, or outright failure, of public providers' (UNESCO, 2008, p. 164). So, for UNESCO, low-cost private schools are seen as less desirable than 'a publicly financed and operated education system that offers the option of good-quality, free education to all citizens' (UNESCO, 2008, p. 168). Other organisations taking a particular interest in low-cost private education include the University of Sussex Consortium for Educational Access, Transitions and Equity (CREATE) (see e.g. Cameron, 2010; Härmä, 2010).

An interesting aspect of the phenomenon reported in the literature has been the presence or emergence of low-cost private schools serving informal or 'slum' communities *even after* the introduction of free primary education (FPE) purportedly to benefit those same communities. Our earlier article examines this aspect with regard to Kibera, Nairobi, one of the largest slums in East Africa (Tooley et al, 2008). That article gave a 'snapshot' of what was happening some 10 months after FPE was introduced in Kenya in January 2003. It showed 76 low-cost private schools in the slum, serving 12,132 students, but reported a decline in enrolment in the majority of these schools, together with the outright closure of 33 private schools as a result of the introduction of FPE. Moreover, the article reported a dramatic increase (57%) in enrolment in the five government schools bordering Kibera. Private school proprietors had reported enrolment haemorrhaging to the free government schools, and feared for their future (Tooley, 2009). Taken together, these findings suggested that the impact of FPE was leading to a reduced role for low-cost private schools, with a likely further reduction in enrolment as the system of FPE became more established, particularly as some agencies pointed to early 'teething' problems with the introduction of FPE that were likely to be corrected over time (Save the Children, 2002, p. 34; Action Aid, 2003, p. 5).

We returned to Kibera in 2007 to assess how the situation on the ground had changed since 2003. The longitudinal evidence gathered in 2007, four years after our original data were collected, pointed to a dramatic increase in the number of private schools serving the slum. In total, 116 private schools were found to be operating in the slum, with private school enrolment showing an increase of 130%. So, why were parents still choosing to send their children to private schools in the slums when there was a free government alternative?

Oketch et al (2010), also focusing on Nairobi, Kenya, explore this question. Using data collected by the African Population and Health Resource Centre in two 'slum' (Korogocho and Viwandani) and two 'non-slum' (Jericho and Harambee) settlements, the authors seek to show that the reasons the poor use (low-cost) private schools are very different from the reasons that richer families use (high-cost) private schools. The authors try to explain why so many poor families send their children to low-cost private schools using the concepts of 'excess demand' versus 'differentiated demand'.

According to the authors, it is '*excess demand* which drives poorer parents to *low quality* private schools, but it is *differentiated demand* which is driving non-slum parents to choose private schooling for their children over free public schools' (Oketch et al, 2010, p. 24, emphases added). That is to say that poor parents only choose low-cost private schools because their 'preferred route of free state schooling is unavailable to them' (Oketch et al, 2010, p. 24); poor families 'would have preferred to enter the free public school system', but are 'crowded out' (Oketch et al, 2010, p. 24). Wealthier parents 'in the non-slum settlements' are 'sending their children to private schools ... for *quality* reasons, whereas in the slum settlements, those sending their children to informal/private schools are doing so because of low *quantity* of schools in these settlements' (Oketch et al, 2010, p. 25, emphases added). Poor parents' choices, in other words, are forced choices, made because of the inadequacy of state provision, and are nothing to do with quality considerations.

Importantly, according to Oketch et al, private schools in the slums are of poor quality – such poor quality that the poor could not possibly choose them above public provision unless forced to do so (although in other works - i.e. Ngware et al, 2009; Ngware et al, 2010 - the same authors do draw slightly different conclusions). Whenever low-cost private education is mentioned by Oketch et al, the epithet 'poor quality' also appears. For instance, they ask: 'why are poor parents paying for *poor quality* education when they could be getting fee-free schooling in the state sector?' (Oketch et al, 2010, p. 24, emphasis added). They further note that in the slums, nearly half of the pupils 'attend *poor quality* fee-charging private schools, in spite of the existing policy of FPE in Kenya' (Oketch et al, 2010, p. 24, emphasis added). However, there is no evidence adduced to support these claims regarding low quality. Others agree that private schools in the slums are of low quality. Mugisha (2006) claims that the 'schools that serve the slum communities are mainly non-formal. These schools are characterized by shortage of staff, congested classrooms and lack of scholastic materials' (pp. 472-473). However, as only a newspaper article is given as a reference, it appears that empirical evidence to make such an assertion is missing.

Nonetheless, in a previous article, the same group of researchers as those involved in the study by Oketch et al indicate that poor parents in slums may be guided by quality considerations in choosing low-cost private schools, rather than being crowded out by excess demand for public schools (Ngware et al, 2009). In this previous work, they state that the 'introduction of FPE ... resulted in overcrowding of classrooms, high teacher-pupil ratios (42 for Nairobi), reduced contact time with pupils, and an overall decline in quality in public schools' (Ngware et al, 2009, pp. 593-594, citing UNESCO, 2005 and Ruteere, 2007). Moreover, parents in slum areas 'perceived public schooling under FPE as inadequate and consequently sought alternative schools for their children' (Ngware et al, 2009, p. 594).

In Ngware et al (2010), the authors explicitly discuss comparative quality in terms of school inputs in government and private schools in Nairobi (p. 2). There, it is not entirely clear how many of the private schools researched were in the informal settlements. However, the following considerations suggest that the majority were: the analysis was based on 83 primary schools, of which 41 (49%) were government schools. Moreover, 36 (44%) schools were in informal settlements. As it is unlikely that government schools will be found in informal settlements in Nairobi (they are generally on the outskirts of these settlements), it is assumed that 36 of the private schools researched were in the slums, leaving six in formal settlements. In the discussion that follows, therefore, it must be assumed that the majority (86%) of private schools discussed are in informal settlements, and are therefore likely to be in our 'low-cost' private school category.

On a range of inputs, in some cases government schools fared better, and in others the private schools did, while for some indicators, there was no clear advantage for either management type. Regarding school size, government schools were larger, which may be beneficial in terms of curriculum scope, but may be disadvantageous for already disadvantaged students, who would do better, the authors suggest, in smaller schools (Ngware et al, 2010, p. 5). In terms of teacher qualifications, government schools fared better, with more than 40% of teachers in non-government schools untrained, compared with only 1% in government schools (Ngware et al, 2010, p. 8). Similarly, on pupil-textbook ratios and the quality of buildings, government schools performed better than private schools, although many private schools were within government norms regarding pupil-textbook ratios (Ngware et al, 2010, pp. 16-18).

Private schools, on the other hand, performed better than government schools according to the following indicators:

- On school facilities, the average pupil-toilet ratio in private schools 'was below 30 and within the recommended ratios'. In government schools, standards were not acceptable (Ngware et al, 2010, p. 12).
- Average physical space per child was also within government norms in private schools, while 'government-owned schools had the least student average physical space' (Ngware et al, 2010, p. 14).

- The average pupil-teacher ratio (PTR) was considerably smaller in private schools than government schools: 19:1 compared with 50:1 (Ngware et al, 2010, p. 10).
- In terms of teaching load, 'teachers in government schools not only taught larg[er] class sizes but also taught for many more hours than their peers in non-government-owned schools' (Ngware et al, 2010, p. 19), possibly leading to a less motivated government workforce (Ngware et al., 2010, p. 19).

In other words, Ngware et al (2010) suggest that there may be reasons based on the quality of provision that would lead poor parents in the slums to choose low-cost private schools. This is further reinforced by our earlier findings from focus groups that for poor parents who spoke to us, the great advantages of low-cost private schools were smaller class sizes and more motivated teachers (Tooley et al, 2008). Ngware et al (2010) confirm that these advantages were indeed the case for the private schools in their study, the majority of which, as we assume above, were likely to be low-cost private schools in the slums. Indeed, they conclude with a paragraph that appears to agree that poor parents are engaged in the same kind of 'differentiated demand' as exercised by richer parents:

> those moving from public to private perceive public schools to be of low quality, whereas those who move from one private to another may be searching for a private school which they perceive to be of better quality. One would have expected free primary education to reduce the use of private schools, *especially among the slum residents* ... but the results reveal that in spite of free primary education, parents still are searching for a 'good' school for their child. It appears this search is in favour of private schools rather than public schools. (Ngware et al, 2010, p. 19, emphasis added)

The research reported here was funded by the John Templeton Foundation and was part of a larger project conducted between April 2003 and June 2005 in multiple countries, including Kenya. This chapter reports new, recently conducted analyses on findings from Nairobi, Kenya. The main research question was: What is the relative achievement of public and private school children in low-income areas, controlling for background variables? A subsidiary question was: If there is an achievement advantage to any management type, is this because of greater levels of resourcing? Parallel research was undertaken in selected low-income areas in India, Ghana, Nigeria, China and Kenya, though only the results from Kenya are reported here.

Method

The research questions to be explored included:

- What are the relationships between pupil, school and teacher characteristics and pupil outcomes?
- Are there apparent differences in pupil attainment between school structures when other factors are taken into account?
- Do these differences vary according to pupil characteristics such as IQ, family income, sex or age?

The slums of Kibera, Mukuru and Kawangware, all in Nairobi, were chosen for the research. The research aimed, first, to discover whether or not low-cost private schools existed, and, if so, to catalogue their nature and extent. The first part of the research was conducted from October to November 2003, about 10 months after the introduction of FPE. A team of researchers, graduate students from Nairobi universities, were trained on finding and gaining access to schools, and on the use of an interview schedule for school managers. Maps were obtained of the areas to be covered and a systematic sweep conducted, with researchers instructed to go down every street and alley, as well as enquire of parents, children, market traders, etc., about the existence of schools. Only primary and secondary schools (both of which sometimes included nursery sections) were to be examined. Excluded from the research was 'non-formal education' (NFE) - that is, education taking place 'outside of standard educational institutions' (see e.g. Tight, 1996), such as after-school clubs, tuition centres, adult training centres, guided learning for those not in schools, and so on.

Data were gathered on background variables (including family possessions, family size, education levels of mother and father, material used for construction of home, distance of home from school, etc.) that earlier research on school effectiveness had shown to be significant for achievement (e.g. Jimenez et al, 1991; Kingdon, 1996; Bashir, 1997; Lassibille & Tan, 2001) through questionnaires sent to the pupils' parents, translated into Kiswahili. Since no measure of prior attainment at an earlier point was available, the main proxy was a measure of children's IQ, tested at the same time as the other achievement data. The Raven's Standard Progressive Matrices IQ test was used (Raven et al, 2003). Scores were normed using local published norms (see Deshpande & Ojha, 2002).

Owing to the unreliability of state examination results (e.g. mass cheating, copied examination papers, result tampering, etc.; see Kingdon, 1996 for India), standardised tests were given to the children in three subjects: Kiswahili, English and mathematics. The mathematics and English tests were adapted from those developed for USAID by the Educational Assessment and Research Centre, Accra, Ghana, adapted to suit local conditions by focus groups of teachers and educational experts. The Kiswahili test was developed by academics at Kenyatta University.

As in all such complex data analysis endeavours, a number of decisions had to be made about how the data should be modelled effectively in order to gain robust insights into the research issues. One challenge with this dataset was the relatively large number of variables in comparison with the amount of data. Many of these background variables are likely to be highly correlated with each other. Including all variables in a model would give very poor and generally uninterpretable results. The following strategy was therefore adopted in this case:

1. Background variables were divided into four categories: those relating to the pupil, the household, the school and the teacher. Certain important background variables (e.g. IQ, income, age, sex) were left as separate factors.
2. Exploratory factor analysis methods were applied to each group of variables to define a smaller set of combined factors, which explained most of the variance in the data.
3. Through inspection of the factor loading, it was possible to describe each of these combined factors in more general terms, and values for each pupil were estimated and rescaled to a mean of 50 and standard deviation of 10.
4. Multilevel modelling was used to explore the relationship between outcomes (scores in mathematics, English and Kiswahili) and background measures, including the combined scales and the separate initial variables, and taking into account management type.

Before discussing the method of factor analysis, it is important to note that the analysis discussed here does not permit any causal inference. Unless pupils are randomly allocated to private or government schools, there are always likely to be underlying unmeasured factors that may influence the school attended and be associated with outcomes. Parental motivation may be one example. All co-factor associations given below are correlations. We do not claim to have located any instrument that predicts pupil selection into school management type that would be unambiguously uncorrelated with pupil learning outcomes. Thus, the results need to be interpreted with appropriate caution, in common with other studies of this nature (e.g., Jimenez et al, 1991; Kingdon, 1996; Bashir, 1997, Lassibille & Tan, 2001). We present a brief profile of the sample before turning to the specifics of the factor analysis and multilevel modelling results.

Sample and Household Profiles

Using the lists of private schools generated in the survey and census part of the project for the three slums and the list of government schools on the outskirts of these slum areas, we created a stratified random sample of 3330 children at Standard 6 in primary school. Of these children, 1474 (44%) attended private schools and 1856 (56%) were enrolled at government schools. Importantly, the children attending low-cost private schools were from slum areas only, whereas those at public schools were from both slum and neighbouring 'non-slum' communities.

The low-cost private schools charged monthly fees ranging from KSh 50 (£0.42/$0.60) to KSh 500 (£4.17/$6.51), with the mean ranging from KSh 149 (£1.24/$1.94) for nursery classes to KSh 256 (£2.13/$3.33) per month for stream 8. It is suggested that the 'absolute poverty' line for Kenya was set at an income of KSh 3174 (£25.53/$41.33), excluding rent (Lauglo, 2004) at the time. The mean fees per child would thus range from 4.7% to 8.1% of this 'absolute poverty' income level.

On a range of indicators, the children in our sample at private schools were much less privileged than those attending government schools. Each of the following is statistically significant. The average monthly household income of the families in our sample was KSh 8852 (£74/$115 at contemporary exchange rates) [1] for government schools, but only KSh 5689 (£47/$74) for private schools. However, these were extended families. The average monthly income per earning adult member in the family was KSh 5779 (£48/$75) in government-school families, and KSh 3951 (£33/$52) in private school families. Looking at wealth indicators within the family, 18% of government pupils reported that their family owned a car or van, compared with 8% of private pupils; 21% of government families owned a fridge, compared with 10% of private families; 46% of government families had a separate kitchen at home, compared with 29% of private school families; 15% of government school families owned their home, compared with 9% of private school families; and 23% of government families had an inside toilet at home, compared with 16% of private families.

Regarding the families themselves, 19% of government pupils' fathers were unemployed, compared with 22% of private pupils' fathers; 29% of private school pupils had parents who spoke neither English nor Kiswahili at home, compared with 24% of government school pupils. In government schools, 37% of children's mothers were only educated up to primary school level or below, compared with 49% of private school children's mothers. For fathers, the corresponding figures were 25% (government), and 33% (private).

Factor Analysis

Factor analysis is a formal decision-making process to explicate subsets of co-varying variables (see Guertin & Bailey, 1970). It is developed to deal with the reduction of data where variables are difficult to define precisely. As a result, factor analysis is used to construct a number of relevant indicators/factors. For this study, factor analysis was carried out for data reduction and to show the variation and representation of the sample variables in terms of a rotated number of factors. With the results of the factor loadings, it was generally possible to explain each of the combined factors. Values of each pupil were estimated and rescaled to a mean of 50 and standard deviation of 10. With the imputation of missing values in order to have as complete a dataset as possible, the results of the factor analysis and combined loadings for each of the four datasets by using two and three factors are as follows.[2]

The factor analysis for the pupil dataset included 14 variables that were analysed using two rotated factors. The two main significant factors that contributed most to the variation of pupil dataset were those that explained parents' levels and years of education (PUP1 [Factor 1]) and parents' occupational level (PUP2 [Factor 2]). Figure 1 illustrates the pupil scree plot.

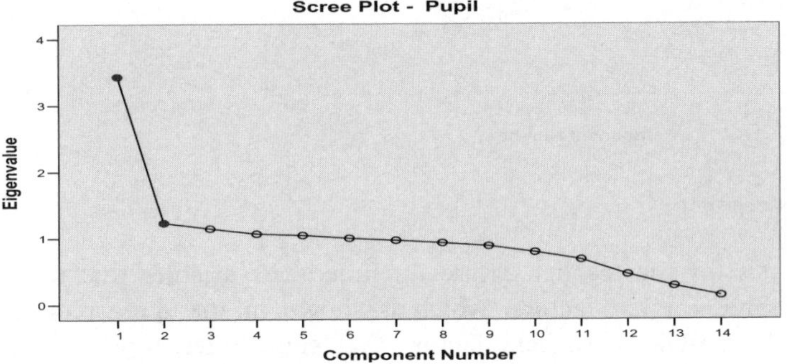

Figure 1. Pupil scree plot.

The factor analysis for the household dataset included 29 variables that were analysed using two rotated factors. The two main significant factors that contributed most to the variation of household dataset were HH1 (Factor 1), which explained mainly household possessions, and HH2 (Factor 2), which explained mainly family size (adults) (see Figure 2).

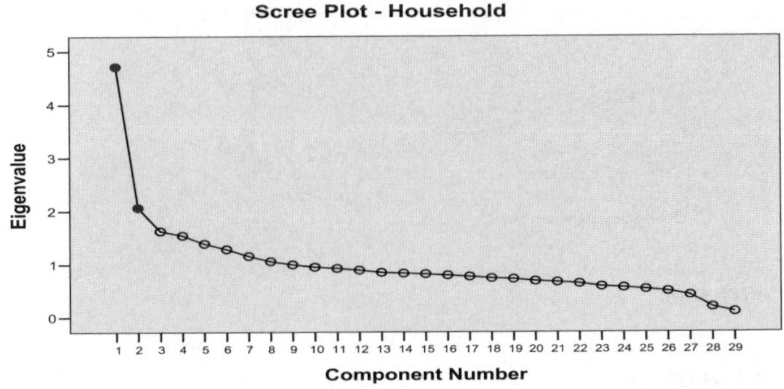

Figure 2. Household scree plot.

The factor analysis for the school dataset included seven variables that were analysed using three rotated factors. The three main significant factors that contributed most to the variation of school dataset were those that explained school size SCH1 (Factor1), school tools SCH2 (Factor 2) and school furniture SCH3 (Factor 3). The school scree plot is shown in Figure 3.

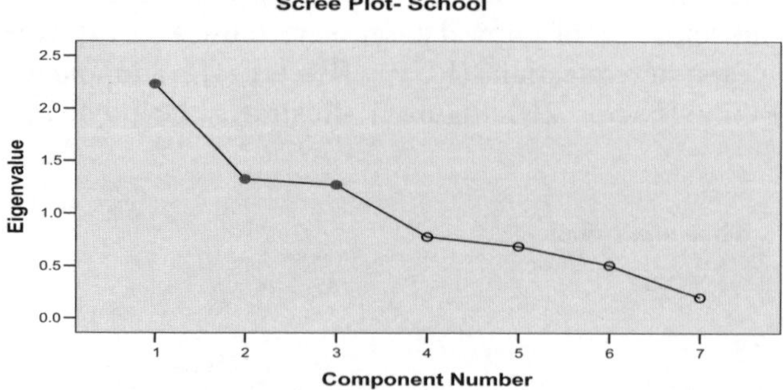

Figure 3. School scree plot.

The factor analysis for the teacher dataset included 16 variables that were analysed using three rotated factors, which is shown in the scree plot in Figure 4. The three main significant factors that contributed most to the variation of teacher dataset were those that explained mainly age and experience (TCH1 [Factor 1]), mainly access to teaching tools (TCH2 [Factor 2]) and mainly teacher qualifications (TCH3 [Factor 3]).

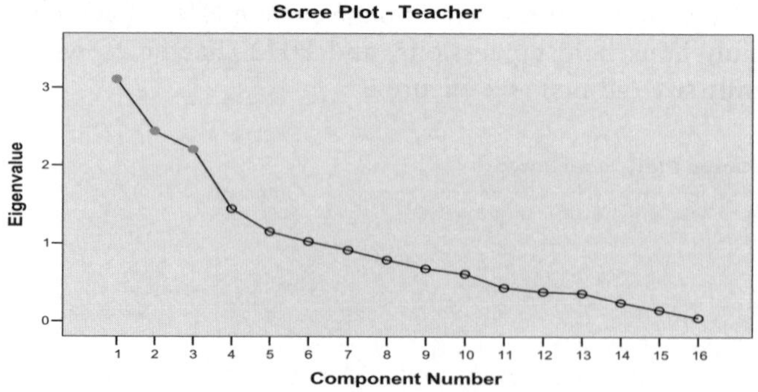

Figure 4. Teacher scree plot.

Multilevel Modelling

Multilevel modelling is a development of regression analysis which takes account of data that are grouped into similar clusters at different levels (see Goldstein, 2003). For example, individual pupils are grouped into classes, and those classes are grouped within schools. There may be more in common between pupils within the same class than with other classes, and there may be elements of similarity between different classes in the same school. Multilevel modelling allows us to take account of this hierarchical structure of the data and produce more accurate predictions, as well as estimates of the differences between pupils, between classes, and between schools.

In this dataset we were not able to identify classes within schools, so the model was set up with two levels: school and pupil. Three separate outcome measures were modelled - namely, mathematics, English and Kiswahili test scores, each standardised to have a mean of 50 and a standard deviation of 10. The background variables fitted in the model included all the composites defined above, plus certain variables which were kept separate (sex, age, IQ, average class IQ, household income). For some of these, squared terms were included in the models in order to allow for possible non-linear effects. The variables concerned were age, IQ and income.

In order to address some of the research issues, interaction terms were included in the models. These terms were created by multiplying together relevant variables in order to see if the coefficients of one variable were modified by the value of the other. For example, if we want to investigate whether the relationship between outcome and IQ is different in different management types, we create a new variable which is an indicator for the management type (e.g. private) and the IQ (subtracted from its mean value). A positive coefficient for this new variable would imply that the relationship with IQ was stronger in private schools than in government schools (the default type). In general, we created two sets of interactions – namely, with private and government schools (see Table I). We created the following variables for interactions: IQ; parental occupational level (PUP2); income; age; and sex (males versus females).

No.	Variable label	Variable details
1.	Priq	Private by IQ
2.	Goiq	Government by IQ
3.	Priqp2	Private by PUP2
4.	Goiqp2	Government by PUP2
5.	Incomesq	Income (k) squared term
6.	Pinc	Private by income
7.	Goinc	Government by income
8.	Pagesq	Age squared term
9.	Prage	Private by age
10.	Goage	Government by age
11.	Prsex	Private by sex
12.	Gosex	Government by sex

Table I. Multilevel modelling interaction terms.

The random variances in the model allow for differences between pupil performance in the same school, and differences between different schools overall, once other factors are taken into account. Variables that were clearly not significant in a particular model were deleted, but in some cases, borderline significant variables were retained. The final models for each outcome are presented in Table II, comprising random variances and fixed coefficients.

This table, however, may be quite difficult to interpret as it stands, and provides no indication of the relative strength of relationships between different factors and outcomes. A way around this is the use of 'quasi effect sizes' or 'adjusted coefficients' (see Schagen & Elliot, 2004). These enable us to present the results of complex models in a way that shows how much difference each factor makes to the expected pupil scores in each case. An adjusted coefficient shows the expected change in the outcome score which might be attributed to an 'average change' in the relevant background factor. Table III shows adjusted coefficients for all three outcomes, for background factors that are statistically significant at the 5% level.

(a) Mathematics

Parameter	Mathematics		
	Estimate	Standard Error	Sig.
Base case			
School variance	36.000	7.041	*
Pupil variance	163.000	4.043	*
Final model			
School variance	11.270	2.698	*
Pupil variance	129.000	3.197	*
Fixed coefficients			
Constant	84.440	3.590	*
The school is private	2.536	1.153	*
Pupil's age in years	-0.801	0.190	*
Pupil sex (males)	-1.918	0.414	*
Score on Raven's Test	0.685	0.029	*
Average IQ norm in the class	0.282	0.047	*
Total household income per month	0.040	0.027	
Pupil 1: Parents' level and years of education			
Pupil 2: Parents' occupation level	-0.050	0.021	*
HH 1: Household possessions	-0.051	0.024	*
HH 2: Household size			
School 1: Size			
School 3: Furniture			
Pupil IQ deviation sq	0.419	0.183	*
Private School by Income			
Private School by Pupil Sex			
Private School by Pupil IQ	-0.146	0.043	*
Private School by PUP2			

(b) English

Parameter	English		
	Estimate	Standard Error	Sig.
Base case			
School variance	52.180	9.699	*
Pupil variance	154.500	3.831	*
Final model			
School variance	20.180	4.187	*
Pupil variance	123.500	3.061	*
Fixed coefficients			
Constant	83.280	6.588	*
The school is private	3.232	2.048	
Pupil's age in years	-1.902	0.187	*
Pupil sex (males)	-2.601	0.529	*
Score on Raven's Test	0.530	0.023	*
Average IQ norm in the class	0.254	0.055	*
Total household income per month	0.093	0.030	*
Pupil 1: Parents' level and years of education	0.096	0.022	*
Pupil 2: Parents' occupation level			
HH 1: Household possessions			
HH 2: Household size	-0.038	0.023	
School 1: Size	0.252	0.104	*
School 3: Furniture			
Pupil IQ deviation sq	0.334	0.179	
Private School by Income	-0.208	0.066	*
Private School by Pupil Sex	1.584	0.789	*
Private School by Pupil IQ			
Private School by PUP2			

(c) Kiswahili

Parameter	Kiswahili		
	Estimate	Standard Error	Sig.
Base case			
School variance	26.780	5.678	*
Pupil variance	182.300	4.520	*
Final model			
School variance	10.860	2.777	*
Pupil variance	155.600	3.854	*
Fixed coefficients			
Constant	91.860	4.695	*
The school is private	5.502	1.759	*

Pupil's age in years	-1.254	0.208	*
Pupil sex (males)	-3.569	0.593	*
Score on Raven's Test	0.527	0.025	*
Average IQ norm in the class	0.190	0.048	*
Total household income per month	-0.039	0.030	
Pupil 1: Parents' level and years of education			
Pupil 2: Parents' occupation level			
HH 1: Household possessions	-0.081	0.026	*
HH 2: Household size			
School 1: Size			
School 3: Furniture	0.110	0.064	
Pupil IQ deviation sq	0.430	0.200	*
Private School by Income			
Private School by Pupil Sex	1.870	0.882	*
Private School by Pupil IQ			
Private School by PUP2	-0.088	0.043	*

Note: *Estimate is significantly different from zero at the 5% level.
Confidence intervals not shown in table, but can be obtained by multiplying 1.96 times the standard error, then adding this value to the estimated parameter to obtain the upper bound of the confidence interval. Subtract this value from the estimated parameter to obtain the lower bound of the confidence interval.

Table II. Detailed multilevel model results for mathematics, English and Kiswahili.

Variable	Mathematics score	English score	Kiswahili score
The school is private	2.5		5.5
Pupil's age in years	-1.3	-3.0	-2.0
Pupil sex (males)	-1.9	-2.6	-3.6
Score on Raven's Test	9.6	7.4	7.4
Average IQ norm in the class	3.6	3.2	2.4
Total household income per month		1.0	
Pupil 1: Parents' level and years of education		1.3	
Pupil 2: Parents' occupation level	-0.7		
HH 1: Household possessions	-0.7		-1.1
HH 2: Household size			
School 1: Size		3.6	
School 2: Tools			
School 3: Furniture			
Teacher 1: age & experience			
Teacher 2: access to equipment			
Teacher 3: qualification			
Pupil IQ deviation sq	0.7		0.7
Private School by Pupil IQ	-1.4		

Private School by PUP2			-1.9
Income (k) sqd term			
Private School by Income		-1.0	
Pupil Age sqd term			
Private School by Pupil Age			
Private School by Pupil Sex		1.6	1.9

Note: Adjusted coefficient = expected change in outcome score due to average change in variable.

Table III. Adjusted coefficients from multilevel modelling.

On the basis of Table III, we may draw the following main conclusions from the analysis:

- Taking all other factors into account, there is a significant positive relationship between attendance at a private school and test scores in mathematics and Kiswahili.
- Allowing for IQ (Raven's test), older pupils tend to have lower attainment on all three tests.
- Boys tend to have lower scores than girls on all three tests.
- Test scores are strongly related to IQ scores, and to average IQ in the class.
- Total household income per month and parental level of education are positively related to test scores in English only.
- Parental occupational level is slightly negatively related to attainment in mathematics.
- Household possessions are negatively related to test scores in mathematics and Kiswahili.
- Pupils in larger schools tend to have higher scores in English.

The above results relate to the overall relationships between background variables and outcomes, but do not include the significant interaction terms. We will now attempt to interpret these.

- There is a non-linear relationship with IQ for mathematics and Kiswahili.
- The relationship with IQ is less strong in private schools.
- There is a negative relationship with parental occupational level for Kiswahili in private schools only.
- The relationship between income and English scores is reduced, and even eliminated, in private schools.
- The attainment gap between boys and girls is reduced in private schools, for English and Kiswahili.

Another way of understanding the model results is to plot graphs showing expected outcomes for different groups of pupils, as a function of factors such as IQ or age. Some examples are given in Figures 5-9. Figures 5 and 6 show mathematics scores as a function of IQ and age respectively, for boys and girls in government and private schools. Figures 7 to 9 show expected English scores as a function of IQ, age and income.

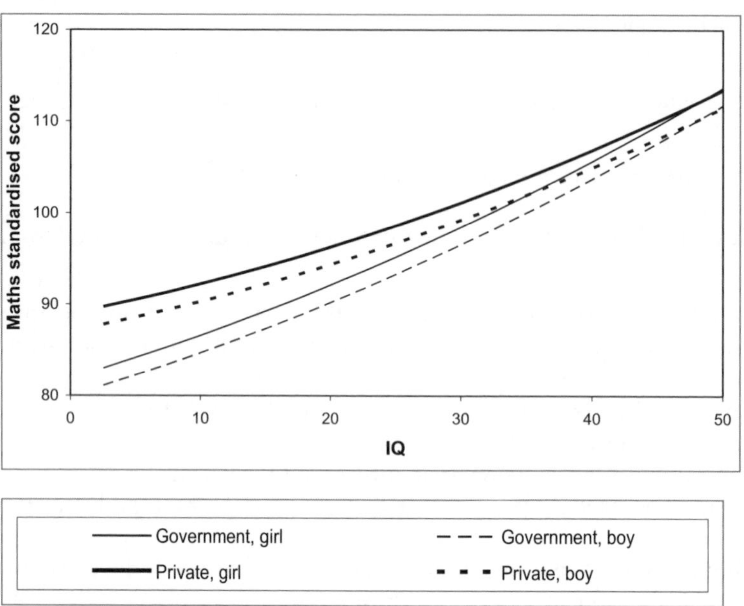

Figure 5. Expected mathematics score as a function of IQ.

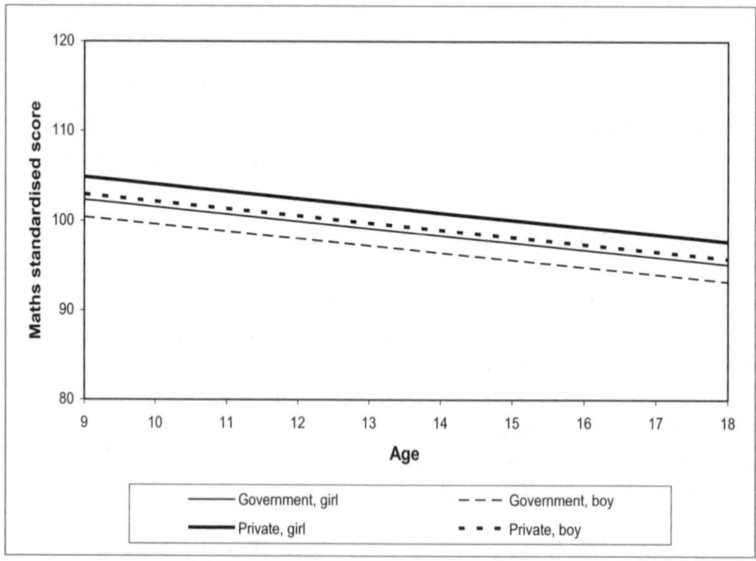

Figure 6. Expected mathematics score as a function of age.

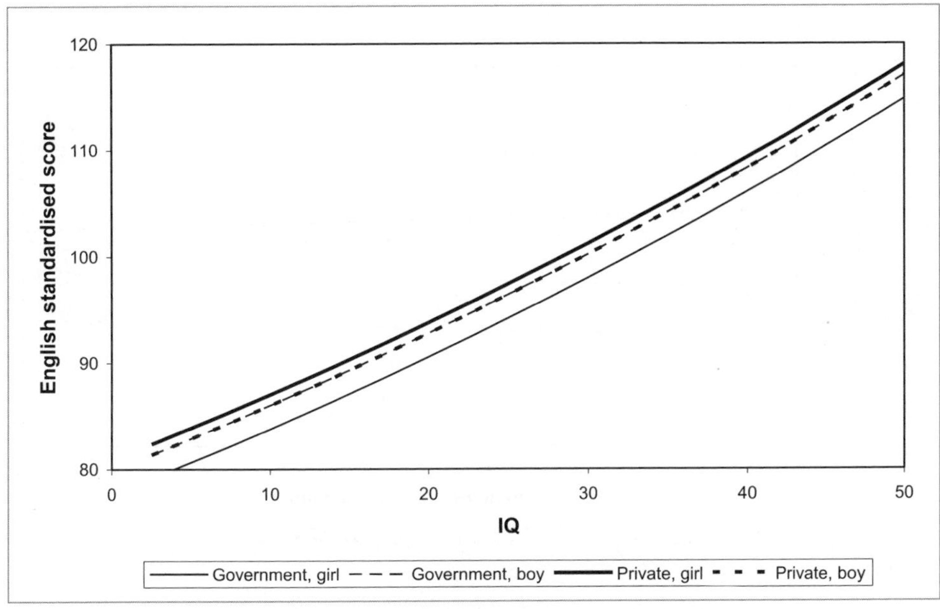

Figure 7. Expected English score as a function of IQ.

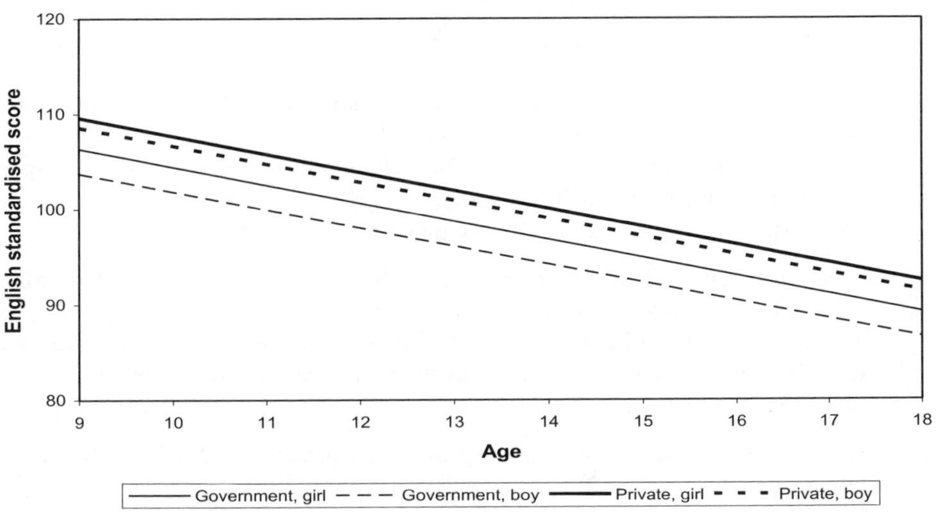

Figure 8. Expected English score as a function of age.

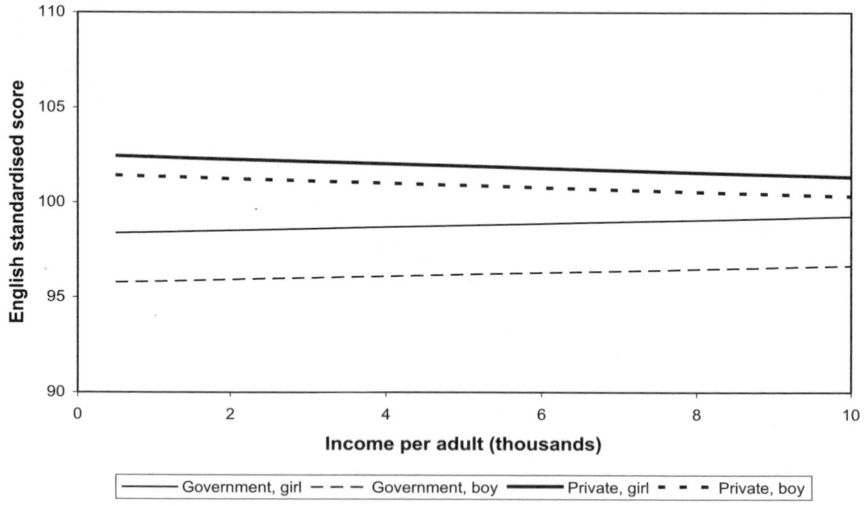

Figure 9. Expected English score as a function of income

Summary of Findings

It is worth revisiting the original research questions and considering to what extent the analysis described above has addressed them.

1. What are the relationships between pupil, school and teacher characteristics and pupil outcomes?
The strongest relationships are with IQ, sex and age, with other background characteristics appearing to some extent. There may be some interest in the variables which do *not* appear to be related to outcomes. For example, income is only related to English scores, and most of the derived scales are not related, once age, sex and IQ are taken into account.

2. Are there apparent differences in pupil attainment between school structures when other factors are taken into account?
There is a clear difference between outcomes for government and private schools, controlling for IQ and age in the two of the outcomes, but this is not significant for English.

3. Do these differences vary according to pupil characteristics such as IQ, family income, sex or age?
There are some apparent variations in the 'private school effect'. It is reduced, at least in English and Kiswahili, for boys, such that the attainment gap with girls is reduced. The small effect of income for government school pupils seems to mostly vanish for private schools.

Discussion and Conclusion

Concerns have been expressed in the literature regarding the quality of private schools that cater for children living in slum areas. One suggestion in the literature, as discussed above, is that parents send their children to low-cost private schools because they are unable to access free government education, owing to excess demand. Therefore, poor parents in these areas have no 'choice' but to send their children to private schools. Moreover, some of the research makes the assumption that private schools in slums are of low quality and, presumably, of lower quality than available government schools. The analysis reported here suggests that such concerns may be unwarranted, at least in comparison to what is available in the government alternative.

Using data from a preliminary survey that had located private schools in three slum communities of Nairobi (Kibera, Mukuru and Kawangware), the research elicited data on achievement and background variables from a stratified sample of 3300 pupils from government and private schools serving children from slum and non-slum areas. The results show that private schools outperformed government schools in Kiswahili and mathematics. For English, there was no significant difference between management types.

We consider the following reasons for this. As mentioned above, *all* of the children in the private schools were from the slums, whereas the children in the government schools were from both the slums and middle-class areas surrounding them. Descriptive statistics from the sample above indicate that children in the private schools were from poorer, less educated families than their government counterparts. Hence, it is possible that the advantage in government schools in English could arise because English is picked up outside of school - for example, through discussion with parents, watching television, and so on. The private school advantage in mathematics and Kiswahili, however, is likely to indicate advantages to children that have come only from school. The results, therefore, provide data concerning the relative quality of private and government schools regarding pupil achievement in Kenya, and they suggest that government policy, aid agencies and academics might benefit from being more sympathetic to the achievements of private schools.

The literature reviewed at the beginning of this chapter suggested that poor parents are denied opportunities to send their children to public schools due to a lack of space, and send them to low-cost private schools out of necessity, not choice. These arguments were framed around the assumption that low-cost private schools are of lower quality than available government schools, but this assumption was not supported by evidence in this study. This chapter has presented evidence on relative achievement in public and private schools showing that, after controlling for background variables, children in low-cost private schools do better than their counterparts in public schools in mathematics and Kiswahili, and that there is no significant difference between student achievement in English. Coupled with other findings showing smaller class size in private than public schools and more committed teachers, this suggests that the choices favouring low-cost private schools made by parents in the slums are based on quality considerations, like those made by wealthier parents.

Notes

[1] Exchange rate at £1 = KSh 119.62 and $1 = KSh 76.80.

[2] Imputed missing values are carried out as the mean.

References

Action Aid (2003) Response to World Development Report 2004. The World Development Report 2004: making services work for poor people. Washington, DC: World Bank.

Bashir, S. (1997) The Cost Effectiveness of Public and Private Schools: knowledge gaps, new research methodologies and an application in India, in C. Colclough (Ed.) *Marketizing Education and Health in Developing Countries: miracle or mirage?*, pp. 124-164. Oxford: Clarendon Press.

Cameron, S. (2010) Access to and Exclusion from Primary Education in Slums of Dhaka, Bangladesh. CREATE Pathways to Access Research Monograph No. 45. Brighton: Centre for International Education, University of Sussex. http://www.create-rpc.org/pdf_documents/PTA45.pdf

Deshpande, C. & Ohja, J. (2002) *Indian Norms for Raven's Standard Progressive Matrices: a normative study in Delhi and Maharashtra*. Delhi: Manasaya.

Goldstein, H. (2003) *Multilevel Statistical Models*, 3rd edn. London: Arnold.

Guertin, W.H. & Bailey, J.P., Jr. (1970) *Introduction to Modern Factor Analysis*. Ann Arbor, MI: Edwards Brothers.

Härmä, J. (2010) School Choice for the Poor? The Limits of Marketisation of Primary Education in Rural India. CREATE Pathways to Access Research Monograph no. 23.

Jimenez, E., Lockheed, M.E. & Paqueo, V. (1991) The Relative Efficiency of Private and Public Schools in Developing Countries, *World Bank Research Observer*, 6(2), 205-218.

Kingdon, G. (1996) The Quality and Efficiency of Private and Public Education: a case study in urban India, *Oxford Bulletin of Economics and Statistics*, 58(1), 57-81.

Lassibille, G. & Tan, J. (2001) Are Private Schools More Efficient than Public Schools? Evidence from Tanzania, *Education Economics*, 9(2), 145-172.

Lauglo, J. (2004) Basic Education in Areas Targeted for EFA: ASAL districts and urban informal settlements in Kenya. Washington, DC: World Bank.

Mugisha, F. (2006) School Enrollment among Urban Non-slum, Slum and Rural Children in Kenya: is the urban advantage eroding?, *International Journal of Educational Development*, 26(5), 471-482.

Ngware, M.W., Oketch, M. & Ezeh, A.C. (2010) Quality of Primary Education Inputs in Urban Schools: evidence from Nairobi, *Education and Urban Society*, 43(1), 91-116.

Ngware, M.W., Oketch, M., Ezeh, A.C. & Mudege, N.N. (2009) Do Household Characteristics Matter in Schooling Decisions in Urban Kenya? *Equal Opportunities International*, 28(7), 591-608.

Oketch, M., Mutisya, M., Ngware, M. & Ezeh, A.C. (2010) Why are There Proportionately More Poor Pupils Enrolled in Non-state Schools in Urban Kenya in Spite of FPE Policy? *International Journal of Educational Development*, 30(1), 23-32.

Raven, J., Raven, J.C. & Court, J.H. (2003) *Manual for Raven's Progressive Matrices and Vocabulary Scales. Section 1: general overview.* San Antonio, TX: Harcourt Assessment.

Ruteere, M. (Ed.) (2007) Falling Short: the right to free primary education. Discussion paper. Urban Primary Education Advocacy Initiative, DARAJA. Kenya.

Save the Children (2002) Private Sector Involvement in Education: a perspective from Nepal and Pakistan. Submission to *The Private Sector as Service Provider and its Role in Implementing Child Rights*, Office of the High Commissioner for Human Rights, Geneva, 20 September.

Schagen, I. & Elliot, K. (Eds.) (2004) *But What Does it Mean? The Use of Effect Sizes in Educational Research.* Slough: National Foundation for Educational Research (NFER)/Institute of Education. http://www.nfer.ac.uk/nfer/publications/SEF01/SEF01.pdf

Tight, M. (1996) *Key Concepts in Adult Education and Training*. London: Routledge.

Tooley, J. (2009) *The Beautiful Tree: a personal journey into how the world's poorest people are educating themselves*. Washington, DC: CATO Institute.

Tooley, J., Dixon, P. & Stanfield, J. (2008) The Impact of Free Education in Kenya: a case study in private schools in Kibera, *Educational Management, Administration and Leadership*, 36(4), 449-469.

UNESCO (2005) *Challenges of Implementing Free Primary Education in Kenya: experiences from the districts*. Nairobi: UNESCO Nairobi Office.

UNESCO (2008) *2009 Education for All Global Monitoring Report. Overcoming Inequality: why governance matters*. Paris/Oxford: UNESCO-IIEP & Oxford University Press.

CHAPTER 5

Low-fee Private Schooling: the case of Kenya

JONATHAN M.B. STERN &
STEPHEN P. HEYNEMAN

This investigation, part of a larger study commissioned by the United States Agency for International Development (USAID) with case studies on six countries (i.e. Ghana, Indonesia, Jamaica, Kenya, Pakistan and Tanzania), was undertaken in order to gain a more complete understanding of the low-fee private education sector in Kenya, as well as the impetuses for increased low-fee private schooling in relation to Education For All (EFA). We present data from the commissioned case study on Kenya, and provide a description of 23 low-fee private schools in four districts (i.e. Nairobi, Nakuru, Eldoret West and Kisumu), the challenges and issues they face, and the regulatory context within which they operate.

In this chapter we begin with a discussion of the education policy context in Kenya, briefly highlight the arguments surrounding non-government schooling, and contextualize the non-government and low-fee private sectors in Kenya. We then explain our method of inquiry before presenting our results, which include a description of the case study school contexts and characteristics, pedagogical quality issues, and the regulatory environment. We also examine the impact of external actor activities on low-fee private primary schools in Kenya before concluding with observations and recommendations for the sector. As a final note on terminology, the terms 'non-government', 'private' and 'independent' are used interchangeably throughout this chapter, owing to their common use in the Kenyan context.

Education For All, the Kenyan Policy Context, and Free Primary Education

Although it is well documented that some countries are lagging behind in their progress toward universal basic education and gender parity, it is important to understand why this is occurring. We posit four main reasons: (1) lack of government capacity and, on occasion, commitment; (2) decreases in donor support/funding; (3) the recent global economic crisis; and (4) the prevalence of failed states and post-conflict circumstances. Additionally, concerns have been raised about the unrealistic nature of EFA goals. By setting such high standards without taking into account the magnitude of the problem in some countries, it is not unreasonable to assume that certain among these countries may be unable to meet the goals despite a concerted effort. In fact, far-reaching goals may increase problems in the public sector, if the focus is placed on access without sufficient attention to quality. For example, while net primary enrolment rates in Kenya increased from 61% in 2002 to 82% in 2009, pupil-teacher ratios increased by nearly 40% during the same time (World Bank, 2010). This is likely due to capacity and funding issues.

While national spending on education increased in a majority of countries after the EFA declaration in Dakar, 40 of 105 countries with available data actually experienced *a decrease in the share of national spending* between 1999 and 2006 (UNESCO, 2008). Some of this was in failed states and post-conflict contexts. In Kenya, public spending on education decreased from 26% of total government expenditure in 2000 to 18% in 2005 (World Bank, 2010). Combined with the fact that aid commitments have been decreasing, this lack of government support (i.e. funding) for basic education has caused some researchers, donors and education experts to call into question the ability of poor nations to provide free high quality basic education to all children, youth and adults even with international assistance. It is in this context that the low-fee private education sector in a number of developing countries, such as Kenya, has been filling the gap.

Before examining the private sector, it is necessary to gain an understanding of the more recent history of the Kenyan education system and its focus on free primary education (FPE). There have been several attempts at providing FPE in Kenya. The first FPE initiative came in 1974 with the abolition of formal school fees. In 1979, a second initiative was passed, prohibiting building levies and non-fee charges on parents. These first two FPE initiatives saw significant increases in enrolments in primary education. However, the 1980s saw the implementation of a cost-sharing programme, along with increased private costs, which led to enrolment stagnation throughout the primary sector (Somerset, 2008).

In 1986, core subjects were added to the curriculum, though the public system suffered due to a lack of additional resources. Throughout the 1990s, decreases in economic growth and per capita incomes, rising poverty rates, deterioration of public infrastructure, and increases in corruption exacerbated the problem. With a growing budget deficit, many families were forced into the sprawling Kenyan slums; however, the provision of government education did not follow suit (Bauer et al, 2002).

In 2003, a third and final FPE initiative was passed and was heralded by development experts and world leaders alike. However, it has been argued that this final initiative did not provide the expansion in primary enrolment that is often attributed to it, and that despite admirable government efforts, the public system is still far from 'free' (Tooley, 2005, 2009; Tooley & Dixon, 2006b; Musani, 2008; Tooley et al, 2008; Verspoor, 2008a). Musani (2008) sums up the consensus by noting that the Ministry of Education had trouble providing education for all, and that high costs (e.g. textbooks, materials and uniforms), high student–teacher ratios (up to 100 students per class), insufficient schools, and limited facilities and activities remain problems for public education in Kenya. Additionally, Verspoor (2008a) notes that out-of-pocket costs are on the rise in public schools and that, as of 2008, more than half the funding of public schools came from fees and parental contributions.

With regard to enrolments, Tooley (2005) found that approximately 6500 students in the slums of Kibera left private schools during the introduction of FPE in 2003. An additional 4500 students dropped out because they were enrolled in private schools that closed, but only 3300 students enrolled in Kibera's public schools during that same period. This led to an estimated reduction of 8000 students enrolled from one slum alone (Tooley, 2005). However, these numbers are based on estimations by private school managers, and therefore they may be exaggerated. Additionally, Tooley did not necessarily account for all possible schools to which students may have transferred, and these numbers do not take into account transfers from one private school to another.

Arguments Surrounding Non-government School Expansion and Low-fee Private Schools

Private schooling across the globe is on the rise. According to UNESCO's *Education for All Global Monitoring Report*, approximately 16% of the world's primary school students were enrolled in private schools in 2000, and by 2009, the figure rose to more than 20% (UNESCO, 2010). It has been noted in many countries that much of this increase is due to the rise of the low-fee private school sector. Although the specific reasons for this growth are unique to each country, there is an underlying theme. Simply put, the demand for private education derives from the public sector's inability to meet the needs of parents at all income levels.

While the relative size, support and impact of low-fee private schools vary by country, there are two seemingly ubiquitous reasons for the rise of the sector. The first is that inadequate or uneven distribution of government financing leads to demand for schooling that non-government schools can fill (Colclough, 1997). The second is low quality and/or inefficient public education. In other words, non-government schools have proliferated in developing countries in order to meet excess demand resulting from an insufficient supply of public school spaces, and/or to provide alternatives to a failing public education system. While, in many countries, private schools were traditionally used by wealthy families as alternatives to the public system, in the past few decades, this same trend has been seen for low-income families.

Phillipson (2008) provides additional reasons for the expansion of this sector. He suggests that low-fee private education has increased in developing countries in recent years due in part to an oversupply of teachers, hidden costs in government schools, high private tuition fees (in high-fee schools), a preferable language of instruction being used, poor public school performance (i.e. poor academic achievement), and religious preference. In addition, Tooley (2009) claims that low-fee private schools are likely to experience lower teacher absenteeism (because of increased accountability to parents and school owners), more engaged teachers (because of more local recruitment), smaller class sizes and more individualised attention. Although there is evidence in the literature and from our fieldwork in Kenya to support both Phillipson's and Tooley's claims, low-fee non-government schools are not without their problems and controversies.

Debates and Controversies

Lewin (2007) outlines four arguments against the use of non-government schools to achieve universal basic education. The first concerns the concept that basic education is a human right that only states can deliver. According to this argument, for-profit institutions have no essential interest in delivering education services to the poor, and non-profit charities cannot deliver services on a national scale without relying on a public subsidy, essentially making them a public responsibility even if the state outsources service delivery. This argument holds that states have the moral and legal responsibility to protect minorities, promote equity and diminish exclusion (Lewin, 2007, p. 42).

Second, if non-subsidised providers in low-income communities depend on community revenue, including tuition, they are essentially drawing down the community's wealth. The availability of income to support non-government schools is much more limited in low- rather than in high-income countries, among other things because of differences in age-dependency ratios. Relative to gross domestic product (GDP) per capita, teacher salaries in low-income countries may be six times those in high-income countries. Additionally, available domestic revenue is only 15% of GDP, compared with 40% in wealthy countries (Lewin, 2007). This suggests that the relative social cost of basic education is significantly higher in low-income countries; hence, arguments for non-government schools in high-income countries cannot easily be applied in low-income countries (Lewin, 2007, p. 43). Ultimately, as Watkins (2004) puts it, '[s]hould the world's poorest people really be expected to choose between the health and the education of their children? And what is the market rationale to suggest that such choices make sense for the rest of society?'(p. 9).

Third, the claims of greater efficiency, lower cost, higher quality and higher relevance in the non-government sector can only be true under certain conditions. According to Lewin (2007), these include 'informed choice, transparent accountability, adequate regulation and an effective legal framework' (p. 44), and they rarely, if ever, pertain to the reality of the poorest households in developing countries. The lack of informed choice, in particular, is especially troubling. Opponents of non-government schooling claim that, without sufficient information, low-fee private schools will simply take advantage of poor parents (Probe Team, 1999; Watkins, 2004). Fourth, Lewin alleges that there is no OECD or rapidly developing country that has depended on non-government provision to achieve universal attendance in basic education. This is because basic education has a wide range of externalities, which are naturally provided through state involvement (Lewin, 2007, p. 44).

Two additional arguments against the use of non-government schools are raised in the literature. One is that relying on non-government schools can undermine the public education system. While enrolling children in non-government schools because of public system shortcomings may prove to be an appropriate short-term fix for some, 'failure to address the challenge through increased public investment and improvements in service delivery will inevitably undermine public education' (Watkins, 2004, p. 10). Second, much of the literature raises the point that private schools charging low fees will be unable to accommodate the poorest households (Probe Team, 1999; Watkins, 2004; Rose & Adelabu, 2007; Srivastava & Walford, 2007). We kept these important arguments in mind throughout our work in Kenya, and feel that, for the most part, they are compelling. However, our fieldwork found evidence that both supports and belies these concerns.

Non-government Schools in Kenya: history and context

Less than a decade ago, researchers had a difficult time convincing certain governments that private schooling catering to poorer groups existed in their respective countries. In fact, we encountered this issue in our recent research in Jamaica in the broader USAID study. The Kenyan government, on the other hand, has been aware of the low-fee or community private school sector since the early 1960s. Shortly after independence in 1963, grassroots organisations in Kenya took it upon themselves to expand the secondary education sector to places beyond the reach of the government system (Verspoor, 2008a).

These *Harambee* (translated from Kiswahili as 'Let's all pull together') schools were established without approval from the Ministry of Education and were therefore not only unrecognised, but technically illegal. Despite initial funding shortages and regular conflicts with the government, by 1973 government provisions and recognition were offered to *Harambee* schools, which ultimately afforded some of the best students the opportunity to transfer to government schools (Kitaev, 1999). Although course offerings and resources were limited and there was a high proportion of unqualified teachers, the provision of schooling opportunities for low-income students who could not afford to travel to government schools significantly increased secondary school enrolments throughout rural Kenya as a result of increases in numbers of schools (from 19 government-assisted and 244 unassisted schools in 1969 to 1142 assisted and 741 unassisted schools in 1987). Bray (1997) notes that the expansion was not due to increases in quality but was because these schools were the only ones available to certain populations. In the early 1990s, *Harambee* schools were subsumed by the government system, and are no longer distinguished from public, government schools (Verspoor, 2008a).

In the current context, a new brand of private school has emerged. In one of the earliest pieces on private education in Kenya, Karmokolias and van Lutsenburg Maas (1997) offer a useful starting point for understanding the main impetuses for private education expansion, which may also help to explain its growth over the last 15 years or so. The authors assert that the reasons for increased demand in private education in Kenya are as follows: (1) population growth; (2) fiscal constraints in the public sector; (3) better image of private schools; (4) increased expenses for parents (i.e. government cutbacks); (5) opportunity costs (i.e. lack of public school efficiency leads to wasted time, and thus less time for children to contribute to labour); (6) long waiting lists at private schools; and (7) significant increases in private enrolments (leading to even further demand).

While it may appear on the surface that some of these reasons are somewhat outdated, especially in light of post-2003 FPE, the majority of the more recent literature still draws upon a very similar set of causes for the expansion of the sector. More specifically, the low quality of public schools, inadequate supply of public school spaces (and schools in remote areas) and high school fees (i.e. hidden costs of schooling) have become the most prevalent responses to the question of why the private sector has expanded so rapidly in Kenya in recent years (Lewin & Caillods, 2001; Lewin & Sayed, 2005; Tooley, 2005; Tooley & Dixon, 2005, 2006a; Musani, 2008; Somerset, 2008; Tooley et al, 2008; Verspoor, 2008a; World Bank, 2008).

The prevalence of low-fee private primary schools is greatest in slum areas but is not limited to them. Similar to Tooley's work, our team found that low-fee primary schools can be found throughout the country in urban slums, small cities and rural areas. However, due to the high population density in urban slums and the low supply of government schools serving them, low-fee schools are often viewed as more necessary and prevalent there. Low-fee private primary schools in Kenya are almost universally run by local community members or local organisations, such as churches and/or small non-governmental organisations (NGOs). In both slums and rural areas, they are generally housed in small rented buildings or semi-permanent structures, electricity being an uncommon luxury, and facilities are typically not up to the standards of public primary schools.

A previous analysis by Tooley and Dixon (2005) of relative achievement of students in Nairobi slums found that, on average, students in low-fee schools scored about the same as their public school counterparts in all subjects, with slightly better scores in mathematics and Kiswahili, but slightly worse in English. It is important to note, however, that although the researchers controlled for family/background characteristics in that analyses, it is not entirely clear that they sufficiently accounted for selection bias (i.e. controlling for unobserved characteristics, such as motivation) that may cause students to enrol in private over public schools, and influence their achievement.

In a new analysis presented in this volume of those data using multilevel modelling techniques (see Chapter 4, by Dixon et al), the researchers found a significant positive relationship between private school attendance and test scores in mathematics and Kiswahili, but not in English. Although both analyses were only on students in Nairobi slums, the results provide some evidence about relative achievement in low-fee schools. Differences in achievement between government and non-government schools are not consistent across subjects, suggesting that the demand for non-government schools cannot simply be reduced to higher test scores/achievement.

Due to insufficient official data, and because so many private schools (and therefore students) are unregistered with the government, it was difficult to obtain accurate or consistent private school enrolment figures in the literature. Thus, while the literature and our field research point to a relatively large low-fee private sector, the exact figures on how non-government schools accommodate low-income children are non-existent. Nonetheless, there are some relevant statistics that may be useful in developing a deeper understanding of non-government and low-fee private schools in Kenya.

As of 2001, Bauer et al (2002) noted that there were an estimated 700 primary and 300 secondary private schools registered in Kenya. Tooley (2009) offers that only a year later, there were 76 private primary schools serving 12,132 students in Kibera slum alone, a third of which were managed by women. By 2008, Musani (2008) claimed that more than 5000 independent schools were found to serve over 500,000 students throughout the country. Additionally, Musani (2008) noted that many of these schools served HIV/AIDS orphans and provided subsidies to those who could not afford tuition and fees.

Perhaps most illustrative are the table and figure, reproduced here as Table I and Figure 1, from recent work by Oketch et al (2010), showing that more than 40% of the poorest students in slums in their study attended private schools, and that this number steadily increased since the introduction of FPE in 2003 (see Table I). While these numbers are high, with so few public schools and so many unregistered low-fee private schools in many of Kenya's slums, they are not necessarily surprising. Table I also shows that while poorer populations in slums are more likely to enrol in private schools than their wealthier counterparts, the reverse is true for those living in non-slum areas. The most intriguing trend in Figure 1 is that since the introduction of FPE, the percentage of private school students in slums has remained above the percentage of public school students.

Variable	Private	Total	% Private
Site			
Korogocho	1712	3921	43.66
Viwandani	793	2235	31.45
Jericho	97	779	12.45
Harambee	112	348	32.18
Total	2624	7283	36.03
Wealth Index: All			
Poorest 20%	705	1559	45.22
2	542	1361	39.82
3	558	1450	38.48
4	514	1457	35.28
Least poor 20%	305	1456	20.95
Wealth Index: Slum			
Poorest 20%	529	1232	42.94
2	490	1231	39.81
3	504	1231	40.94
4	485	1233	39.33
Least poor 20%	407	1229	33.12
Wealth Index: Non-slum			
Poorest 20%	12	227	5.29
2	25	224	11.16
3	39	227	17.18
4	55	228	24.12
Least poor 20%	78	221	35.29
HHG			
Female	720	2196	32.79
Male	1904	5087	37.43

Table I. Private school enrolment by wealth and study site.
Source: Oketch et al, 2010.

From our field experience, it is clear that the number of registered schools grossly underestimates the actual number of operating private schools. Additionally, there is a distinct concentration of schools in Nairobi's slum areas and, as evident in World Bank (2010) statistics, private enrolments in Kenya have been on the rise, increasing from 4% in 2005 to 11% in 2008. However, our work leads us to believe that even Musani's (2008) numbers may be underestimated. This is due to the fact that those estimations are based on the assumption that low-fee private schools are primarily found in urban slums. While we found a concentration of low-fee schools in the slums around Nairobi, we were surprised to find large numbers of small low-fee primary schools throughout the rural areas of western Kenya as well. The great majority of these schools were off the beaten path, and very few of them were recognised by any government organisation. We now turn to the method of inquiry used for the broader study and for the Kenyan case study before discussing results.

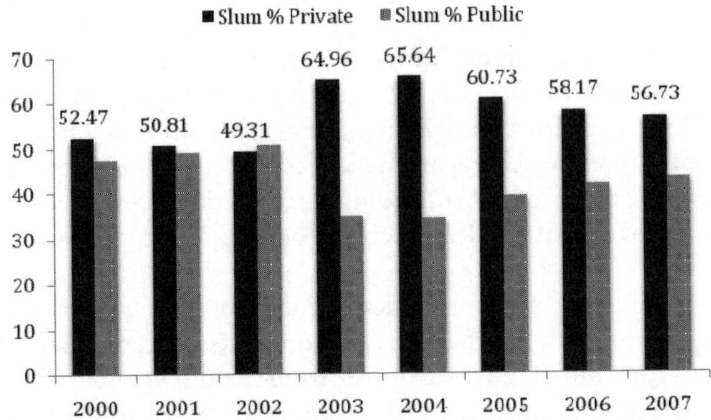

Figure 1. Public and private enrolments by year (in slum areas).
Source: Oketch et al, 2010.

Method of Inquiry

As noted in the introduction, this chapter stems from a larger study commissioned by USAID-Washington to assess the growth and impact of low-fee private schools. The full study included a global literature review, as well as case studies from six countries (i.e. Ghana, Indonesia, Jamaica, Kenya, Pakistan and Tanzania). All case studies included in-country interviews as well as school site visits. Interview protocols were created by the principal investigators (Stephen Heyneman, Jonathan Stern and Thomas Smith) prior to visiting the first country, and were adapted as necessary to suit the education context of each subsequent country. The overall study ran from January 2010 until May 2011. All interviews and site visits in Kenya were conducted by Heyneman and Stern during May-June 2010.

We began our investigation of the low-fee private primary education sector in Kenya with a review of the available literature and background information. We then obtained a list of contacts from the Director of the Education Development Office at USAID-Kenya. The list included representatives from donor organisations, NGOs and government officials relevant to the sector. All representatives were contacted prior to our arrival in Kenya in order to schedule in-country interviews.

Interviews with representatives from donor organisations (i.e. Department for International Development [DFID], International Development Association [IDA], International Finance Corporation [IFC] and USAID) were conducted in order to obtain information about current policies on low-fee private schools, opinions on the promise/obstacles of the sector, ideas for appropriate public policy, and intentions regarding future assistance. NGOs and service providers (e.g. Bridge International Academies, Dignitas and the Kenya Independent Schools Association [KISA]) were interviewed on sources of funding, regulatory environments, motivations (e.g. for-profit or non-profit), scholarships/subsidies, growth prospects and major challenges. Finally, Kenyan government officials (i.e. from the Ministry of Education [Basic Education, Adult and Continuing Education] and the Ministry of Gender, Sports, Culture and Social Services, as well as District Education Officers) were interviewed regarding government data collection, school registration, government support/funding, accreditation, regulatory frameworks, monitoring/oversight and perceived benefits/concerns about low-fee private schooling.

While ministry interviews were intended to obtain lists of private schools for site visits, we quickly learned that complicated and inefficient registration procedures precluded any such list from being created. The reality was that no government agency, local or national, knew how many non-government schools existed, where they were located or who (teachers or students) was involved. Unlike Tooley's previous work, we did not have the resources to do a catchment sample.[1] As an alternative, we chose several rural and urban districts, using convenience sampling techniques to locate schools. Since we knew we would not be able to generate a representative sample, our objective was different – namely, to find schools that illustrated each of the six official categories of non-government schools that exist in Kenya (discussed further below). Ultimately, we adopted a school selection method similar to snowball sampling. After learning about a particular school from one of our initial interviews, we would use those contacts in order to pinpoint other schools.

Although monetary restrictions and incomplete data prevented us from using an expansive random sampling procedure, we worked with Ministry of Education officials and local USAID offices to create a sampling frame that would allow for the most appropriate sample of schools possible (taking into account geography, religion and tuition), given time and monetary restraints. Our final sample included one public government and 23 non-government schools across four districts (Nairobi, Nakuru, Eldoret West and Kisumu). These included non-government schools registered with the Ministry of

Education Department of Basic Education, the Ministry of Education Directorate for Adult and Continuing Education and the Ministry of Gender, Sports, Culture and Social Services, and schools operating but not registered with any government organisation.

We conducted interviews with principals or directors and teachers. Whenever possible, school visits were announced. There were, however, occasions when we would simply 'come upon' a school and ask if they would be willing to provide us with an interview. The purpose of school interviews/visits was to obtain information about the number of students enrolled, tuition and fees, scholarships, class size, hours and days of operation, religious affiliation, sources of funding, management structure, parental involvement, teacher salaries and qualifications, facilities and materials, student background (including ability to pay full tuition) and performance on the Kenya Certificate of Primary Education (KCPE) exam. Although several school owners and/or principals were initially hesitant to provide information on tuition, teacher salaries and funding, none refused to participate entirely.

As a consequence of segmentation across the six categories, all organisations, including departments within ministries, had differing views on the scope of the sector. This stems in no small part from inconsistencies about the language surrounding non-government schools in Kenya. In the Ministry of Gender, Sports, Culture and Social Services, non-government schools are referred to as 'self-help groups' or 'community projects'. In the Ministry of Education Department of Basic Education, they are referred to as 'private schools', whereas, in the Ministry of Education Directorate for Adult and Non-Formal Education, they are referred to as 'non-formal schools'. They are additionally referred to as 'independent schools'.

Additionally, since there is no universally accepted definition of low-fee private schools in the literature (which has an impact on the generalisability of studies), a definition was created for the purpose of the larger commissioned study. Low-fee private schools were defined as those with tuition rates that were less than 50% of the minimum wage, which we took as a conservative figure. For Kenya, however, the mean school fee at case study schools was much less, at KSh 968, representing 14.4% of the minimum monthly wage rate in 2010 for a general labourer in Nairobi and Kisumu, 15.6% in all other municipalities, and 17.5% of the overall mean monthly wage for a general labourer (Ministry of Labour, 2010).[2] All study schools in Nairobi slums had a tuition fee at or below KSh 600, representing a maximum of 9% of the minimum monthly wage rate.

Characteristics of Low-fee Private Schools

Table II presents the range and mean for a variety of characteristics for the 23 private schools in our study. Although the table provides a good overview of our case-study schools, it is important to examine these numbers with some context and scrutiny. For example, while the lowest performing school had a pass rate of 71% on the eighth grade exit exam, it is important to contextualise what this means relative to nearby primary schools. As it happens, this mark ranked the school first in its zone and fourteenth in the district on KCPE exam rates in 2009, among all public and private schools. In general, case study schools regularly placed at or above the level of nearby public schools in terms of district-wide Grade 8 exam rankings. Perhaps even more interesting is the fact that the top-scoring public school in the district ranked twenty-second overall, out of 81 schools. In other words, the top 21 schools in the district were all private schools, many of which were low-fee schools like the ones in our study.

	Range	Average
Years in operation	1-23	9
Monthly tuition (KSh)	200-2100	968
Monthly teacher salary (KSh)	1500-12000	6186
Number of students	35-856	220
Scholarship or subsidized tuition (%)	5-100	61
KCPE pass rate (%)	71-100	89

Table II. Description of the 23 private primary sample schools in Kenya.
Source: Researcher fieldwork.

Several other characteristics require further explanation. Opponents of low-fee private schools have raised concerns about the 'fly by night' nature of the sector, but we found that, on average, case study schools had been in operation for nine years. Half were run by women. While interviewees informed us that some low-fee schools had shut down in recent years, this was purported to be the result of decreased enrolments and families' inability to pay after the post-election violence in 2007-2008. For example, two schools in our sample finished the 2007 school year with more than 300 students, but re-opened after the post-election violence with less than a tenth of their previous year's cohort. Conversely, one public primary school in Nakuru increased its enrolment by nearly 40% between 2007 and 2010. This led to serious concerns about capacity in the public sector, especially since the school had a student-teacher ratio of approximately 90 to 1 as a result.

As for funding and resources, Table II tells an interesting but incomplete story. Although the average monthly tuition across these schools was KSh 968 (under $13), 40% of sample schools had tuition fees below KSh 675, including all the schools we visited in Nairobi slums (which had a mean tuition fee of KSh 450). With regard to teacher salaries, the average is skewed upward due to the disproportionate increases for head teachers. The majority of teachers averaged closer to KSh 4300 per month, while head teachers averaged approximately KSh 8100. Finally, it is important to note that while the percentage of students receiving scholarships or subsidised tuition ranged from 5% to 100%, only four schools provided such concessions to under a quarter of their students.

More generally, in addition to accounting for the public system overflow in demand for schooling, low-fee private schools in Kenya have been found to fill a particular niche regarding religious preference. Many non-government schools are associated with local religious groups and local community churches. In our interviews, school owners claimed that they adhered to a moral philosophy that parents believed is necessary for the proper educational experience of their children in addition to the national curriculum. In terms of religious affiliation, the schools in our study were found to be non-selective. Church-run schools, for instance, regularly enrolled Muslim students.

Furthermore, while all sample schools enrolled poor students and charged relatively low fees, many catered specifically to orphans and street children who could not afford to attend public schools. As mentioned above, 'free' public education in Kenya is not necessarily free of private cost. To be admitted, a child needs to have shoes, uniform shirt, socks, tunic and shorts, and donate a desk and chair, all of which costs an estimated KSh 4500. Verspoor (2008a) claims that the cost is actually higher, with public school fees ranging from KSh 10,000 to KSh 26,000 per year.

Of the schools in our sample, the majority fell below the KSh 10,000/year mark, and none charged more than the upper end of the public school range noted by Verspoor (2008a). The majority of schools provided some sort of scholarship or subsidy to students who could not afford tuition fees. Ultimately, while Kenya has many high-fee private primary schools, it seems that the majority of independent and/or unregistered schools target poorer students and provide access to education that is unavailable in the public system due to a severe under-supply of public school spaces and relatively high fees.

Finally, the financial stability of the low-fee private sector relies almost entirely on the business acumen of school proprietors and their ability to attract a sufficient number of students to pay their teachers, and this did not appear to be promising. Nearly all school owners we interviewed were local community members who wanted to provide a much-needed service to the community, but who had no business experience and little understanding of the regulatory framework. Many school owners were unaware of how or with whom to register their school, and some even feared that the registration and/or monitoring process would only result in having to pay bribes to officials. Complicated tax structures and issues regarding property rights, especially in slum areas, are likely to play a further role in frustrating the long-term financial sustainability of the sector. While the sector is continuing to grow in the aggregate, without financial assistance from the government or aid organisations, individual schools are unlikely to provide assurance of long-term sustainability to their students.

Pedagogical Considerations

We found that the pupil-teacher ratio reached 80:1 in a government school, but was about 15:1 in a non-government school in Nairobi slums, Kisumu, Eldoret West and Nakuru.[3] In earlier analyses, Tooley and Dixon (2005) found the student-teacher ratio in government schools to be 60:1, as opposed to 21:1 in low-fee private schools in Kibera. Musani (2008) also claimed that independent schools had lower student-teacher ratios and better facilities than public schools. Regarding teacher pay, we found that, in general, public schools can pay teachers as much as twice the salary of top earners in non-government schools and offer pensions and health insurance. Despite the fact that we found teacher salaries to be as low as KSh 1500 per month in private schools (and as high as KSh 35,000 in public schools), teacher absenteeism in private schools was reported to be lower or non-existent.

We also found that class periods in public schools are meant to be 35 minutes regardless of subject, whereas, class length in non-government schools may be altered according to the demands of the curriculum. Furthermore, while public schools are obligated to maintain national schedules (7.30 am to 12.30 pm for grades 1-4, and 7 am to 4 pm for older students), non-government schools can open as demanded by the parents. Some schools in our study opened as early as 6 am, catering to parents in peri-urban areas with long commutes, and closed at 6 pm. Public schools are normally open five days per week, with three months of holiday (one month after each of three terms), while many non-government schools remain open on Saturdays and year-round.

As a result of our interviews and site visits, we also found many differences with regard to teacher hiring/firing practices, as well as differences in financial support and funding streams. For example, public schools use teachers of standard quality but find it difficult to transfer or sanction a teacher for absenteeism or non-performance. Non-government schools, conversely, have flexibility in hiring and dismissal procedures. Public schools may appoint teachers without regard to their education philosophy; non-government schools often appoint teachers as a result of their education philosophy.

Public schools may appoint teachers from widely dispersed areas; non-government schools often appoint teachers from the same village community, and frequently those who have graduated from the same school in which they teach. Although knowledge of the local community is seen as a benefit, this can have adverse effects, since local recruitment may result in a limited supply of teachers (especially those with strong educational backgrounds). Public schools depend on the government for financial support; non-government schools depend less on the government for financial support. Often the school management committees, church committees and parent groups in non-government schools may take a more active role because they may feel they 'own' the school to a greater extent.

In several instances, we opportunistically spoke with family members at the schools we visited. In these cases we asked why they accessed that particular non-government school for their children. Most of these informal interviewees mentioned the school's 'control' or discipline, and often talked about the ability of parents to speak to teachers/principal if there were concerns. Finally, due to concerns about sexual harassment, parents of female students often noted that they felt that the non-government school could provide greater 'protection' than the overcrowded public system.

Regulatory Environment

The complex structure of the Kenyan administration system with regard to education presents a barrier towards effective policy implementation and monitoring (Verspoor, 2008b). The Ministry of Education, Science, and Technology (comprised of 10 divisions), Kenya Teachers Service Commission, Kenya Institute of Education, and Ministry of Labour and Human Resource Development are all involved in education provision (World Bank, 2008). Furthermore, the management of public schools is the responsibility of the Boards of Governors (BOGs) who report to District Education Offices. However, BOG members are political appointees who are not necessarily qualified for their roles, and may not accurately represent their constituents (World Bank, 2008). Additionally, school-level parent-teacher associations rely on BOGs to pass their messages on to District Education Offices, but there are often breakdowns in the lines of communication. Finally, transitions from primary to secondary schools are poorly aligned in the system. There have been reports of student files being lost, which is not helped by the fact that there is little local accountability in schools (World Bank, 2008). The following highlights some of the issues that were most apparent during our analysis.

Registration Procedures

In addition to the complex administrative system, private school owners are faced with a complex set of procedures for opening and registering a school (see Box 1). Glassman and Sullivan (2006) contend that the main problems with this overly complex procedure have to do with inadequate manpower. Whether it is a result of delayed inspections, lost forms, postponed committee meetings, or cumbersome paperwork, this process can take a significant amount of time, potentially delaying school openings. Thus, many private school owners with whom we spoke pre-emptively opened their doors prior to being registered, knowing that there was insufficient monitoring to face immediate consequences. This issue of private schools opening without even attempting to register with the Ministry of Education is exacerbated by the fact that many schools do not meet the criterion of owning the land on which their school resides (Musani, 2008).

Application for registration of a school is made in a prescribed form and is submitted to the Registrar through the district, municipal, or city education officer.

Application form is accompanied by the following documents:
- Inspection report from the public health officer indicating whether the institution complies with the set of health standards
- Inspection report from the inspector of schools
- Minutes of the district education board in which the application was discussed
- Certification of registration of business name from the registrar general
- An application for the approval of the district manager
- Names of school managers and copies of their education certificates
- School size in terms of land (rules differ depending on locality)
- Proof of ownership of the land on which the proposed school is now or is to be built

Once the registrar receives the application, it is presented to the Ministerial Committee on Registration of Schools for evaluation in accordance with the relevant provisions.

If the application is approved, it is forwarded to the Ministry of Education for authorization.

The Minister issue [*sic*] two letters to the manager of the school approving and authorizing the operation of the school.

The Registrar of the school will then issue a certificate to the institution after the final inspection.

Box 1. Official procedure for opening a private school in Kenya.
Source: Glassman & Sullivan, 2006.

However, it is possible for schools to be registered even if they are not under the Ministry of Education. Schools that do not own land can register as self-help groups or community organisations through the Ministry of Gender, Sports, Culture and Social Services, but they are then registered as businesses for taxation purposes. It does not seem appropriate that basic education institutions (particularly those that are non-profit) following the national curriculum, and established because of excess demand due to insufficient public school supply, should be taxed differently from other formal (government) schools. While we do not claim that all schools registered with the Ministry of Gender, Sports, Culture and Social Services are non-profit, the majority of schools we visited claimed to reinvest their income into materials and facilities. Many school owners and directors claimed to pay themselves a lower salary than their teachers.

Land Ownership: related issues

As indicated above, the condition of land ownership poses significant issues for low-fee private school owners, but also for the wider education sector. Because many low-fee private schools do not own the land on which they reside and are unable to register with the Ministry of Education, available data on their numbers and enrolments are limited. Additionally, the dual registration process with the Ministry of Gender, Sports, Culture and Social Services makes data collection at the national level significantly more complicated, as the two ministries do not appear to cross-reference school databases in their statistical analyses.

More pointedly, however, while the land requirement precludes private school owners from registering with the Ministry of Education, land issues have also contributed to limiting the number of public schools established in slum areas. Due to the fact that slums are technically illegal settlements, public schools are generally built outside them. This has led to the under-provision of public schooling, as noted in the literature above and in our own fieldwork. Musani (2008) estimated that there was one public school for each 10,000 students in a five-kilometre radius in some urban slums. Thus, people living in the middle of Mathare Valley, for example, would have to send their children through the expansive slum in order to reach the nearest public school. This is one of the main reasons for the expansion of low-fee private schools in Nairobi.

Donor and Other Actor Activities in Private Education in Kenya

Although there are a number of international aid organisations and NGOs in Kenya, the programmes/activities of these organisations in private education are limited. The major bilateral aid organisations in the country (i.e. the Canadian International Development Agency [CIDA], DFID, the Japan International Cooperation Agency [JICA] and USAID) are aware of the burgeoning sector, but have yet to develop projects focusing on low-fee private schools. The World Bank has also been limited in its private education work in Kenya. However, the recently designed Kenya Education Sector Support Programme II (KESSP), although public sector focused, is intended to provide some assistance to private schools by way of textbooks, although the exact nature of support is unclear.

On the other hand, the IFC has recently commissioned Gray Matters Capital, a private operating foundation, to map the country's private schools in order to gain an understanding of the size and needs of the sector. While the mapping initiative was expected to have been completed by the time of writing, no information was available about the results. Nonetheless, the work of the IFC and Gray Matters Capital indicates the likelihood of other organisations entering the sector, particularly if that study shows that the number of low-fee private schools is far greater than currently estimated by the government.

There are other organisations focusing on the private sector in Kenya. For example, the Aga Khan Foundation (AKF) is one of the larger organisations recently making claims about entering the private sector. Our research found that the AKF may incorporate 50 private schools into its Education for Marginalized Children in Kenya programme, intended to mainly serve 800 public schools with a 'whole-school' approach (from education access to teacher training and education management) once the programme is under way. Among smaller organisations working with private schools in Kenya, two were interviewed in our study. The first, the Dignitas Project, sought to address key barriers in education, such as access, retention, completion and performance, in Mathare (Cheng & Kariithi, 2008). After conducting a needs assessment, Dignitas found that while the people of Mathare valued education highly, access was extremely restricted to the public system. Therefore, it decided to focus on assisting low-fee private schools in the professional development of teachers and schools and the provision of supplies, and on increased community involvement in the schools.

The second organisation, Bridge International Academies, is a private equity-owned company seeking to provide 'high quality' low-fee private primary education. Its stated goal is educating 'at scale', with a focus on sustainability and accountability to parents and communities. The company employs a franchise approach to the development of what it calls a 'school-in-a-box', costing under $4 per month per student. The package includes a scripted curriculum, teacher/management training materials, and other essential materials and supplies. Bridge International recruits and trains a local school manager and local teachers, all of whom must have completed secondary education at minimum. Managers have a 'performance contract' linked to their salary (i.e. they may begin with an annual salary of $1000, and with 'good' performance, may end up with a salary of six times the original over a number of years). Much of the support and financial measures are centralised, with payments to schools and teachers done mainly via mobile phone. All transfers between school managers and Bridge International are conducted via specially encoded SMS texts.

The process of starting a franchise school owned by Bridge International begins with the lease of land from traditional authorities (generally untitled land in slums), followed by constructing a school, costing approximately $2000 per classroom, fully equipped. Again, due to complications with land tenure, in many cases it is not possible to obtain a clear title to the land. Permission from local community leaders and municipal authorities is obtained, through which the school is operated without clear title. The risk of expropriation is reduced by diversifying school locations, maintaining good relations with political leaders, and registering with the World Bank Group's Multilateral Investment Guarantee Agency and the United States' Overseas Private Investment Corporation to insure against political risk. After training, schools open for operation. The entire process can take as little as five months from procuring land to the school opening.

Finally, given the complications of registration, many private schools belong to the Kenya Independent Schools Association (KISA), in order to increase their legitimacy. According to its director, KISA aims to support these schools from its own budgetary resources coming from membership subscriptions and donor support. Support was mentioned in the form of advocacy to lower government restrictions, networking, capacity building, micro-finance and scholarships for needy students. While KISA's plans for achieving its goals and the extent of the work accomplished were unclear, it seemed that simply becoming a member provided a sense of legitimacy for member schools. Ultimately, while international aid agencies have taken a relatively minor role in assisting private primary education up to this point, providing technical and other assistance to organisations representing private schools may be an effective means of assisting the low-fee private school sector as a whole.

Conclusions and Recommendations

By presenting data from our commissioned case study on Kenya, this chapter provided a description of 23 low-fee schools in four districts (i.e. Nairobi, Nakuru, Eldoret West and Kisumu), the challenges and issues they face, and the regulatory context within which they operate. Due in large part to land rights issues, we found public schooling options to be woefully inadequate for the number of school-aged children in the country's largest slums. With a strong desire for education, many individual proprietors and small community organisations have established low-fee schools that are accessible to children whose parents are unwilling to allow them to travel the distances necessary to reach the nearest public school. Even those old enough to make the trip are often greeted by educational institutions that are severely overcrowded. Therefore, we contend that low-fee private schools are meeting a demand for accessible schooling in some of the country's poorest neighbourhoods. Based on our case study, we make the following recommendations for the public and private education sectors in Kenya.

All schools, whether operated by the government or any other organisation, should be listed under one ministry. This centralised listing procedure would allow all schools to be recognised under one registry, providing significant benefits for assessing the size of the public and private education sectors. It would also help determine the overall proportion of out-of-school youth in the country. The central listing should contain schools in the following categories.

- Category A: operated by the Ministry of Education or Municipal Councils
- Category B: operated by churches or mosques
- Category C: operated by private proprietors

- Category D: operated by NGOs (including informal organisations)
- Category E: operated by the Ministry of Education Directorate for Non-formal Education
- Category F: temporary or provisional licence

Currently, schools in Categories A-E can be found across several ministries, while Category F does not yet exist (although some schools are being run with no registration/licensing). For schools in Category F, there should be no fee to register for a temporary or provisional licence. However, it is our view that these schools should be assigned permanent registration before being eligible for textbook and pedagogical material assistance, in order to militate against non-regulated schools using scarce government resources.

Relevant public policy initiatives should apply to all schools in all categories. This does not imply that the government should assist all categories of schools equally. However, national objectives should be applied to all Kenyan children regardless of where they are being schooled, since non-government schools, like government schools, enrol future Kenyan citizens. For example, cash transfers to the most vulnerable children (MVC) are available only to children in state-run schools, but should be extended to students in non-government schools. Currently, vulnerable children are targeted through public school registration, effectively neglecting those children in private schools who may also meet the criteria many of whom enrol in the private sector due to a lack of public school places.

The taxation system for non-government schools causes confusion. Non-government schools within municipal councils are taxed as businesses on the grounds that they charge for services. While some non-government schools may charge for reasons of profit, most schools in our study claimed to reinvest income in the school. As such, they should be considered non-profit private enterprises. However, legal distinctions between for-profit and non-profit institutions in Kenya need to be more clearly defined, taking into account school operations. There should be a legal distinction between schools established for reasons of personal profit, and those in which owners may not, other than stated salary, profit from the income. These latter schools should be categorised as non-profit organisations and should not be taxed.

Another serious impediment is corruption, which directly affects low-fee private schools in the form of bribery. Several school directors explained that yearly monitoring visits were nothing more than opportunities for officials to collect bribes in exchange for allowing schools to remain open. At the national level, corruption has affected the education sector as a whole, with the public school system not receiving the full amount of development aid earmarked for educational services. A scandal was recently exposed in which nearly $100 million of funding from the World Bank, CIDA, DFID and UNICEF could not be accounted for during a financial audit of the Ministry of Education (Agence France-Presse, 2010). This may have serious implications for the type and amount of aid for education in Kenya in the future, affecting the public and private sectors.

Finally, while the demand for low-fee private schools in Kenya is unlikely to diminish soon, there are two significant barriers to the growth and sustainability of the sector. Arguably, as highlighted above, the largest obstacle is the issue of (official) land rights. This stems largely from the fact that slums are technically illegal settlements, and therefore land cannot be purchased or owned. While land outside of slums can be owned and registered by official government agencies or owned and managed by tribal authorities, only schools on land in the former category are considered primary schools under the authority of the Ministry of Education. Since land ownership is a registration requirement, this matter will continue to hinder many low-fee private schools' attempts at becoming recognised as legitimate education institutions. Unfortunately, the land issue has deep historical roots, and is far beyond the purview of the Ministry of Education.

Ultimately, insufficient supply (in quantity and quality) of public schools seems to be the overriding reason for the rise in low-fee private schooling in Kenya. While this issue is most prevalent in urban slums, there is additional evidence of this phenomenon in rural areas where infrastructure, roads and public services are limited. These independently owned low-fee schools therefore address a very important need in the lives of many poorer Kenyans. While this sector faces some significant obstacles, it seems inevitable that low-fee private schools will play an important role in assisting Kenya to reach its goal of universal access to basic education.

Acknowledgements

The authors acknowledge support from USAID. The opinions and views represent those of the authors alone, and do not necessarily represent the views of any institution or agency.

Notes

[1] A catchment sample is analogous to how a biologist might survey for a particular species. A boundary is drawn around a particular area and all species within it are counted. Since no government agency had adequate data on non-government schools, this technique would have been the only way to answer the question of how many non-government schools there were in a particular area where all schools had been identified and counted.

[2] Exchange rate at time of fieldwork was 75.78 Kenyan shillings to the US dollar on 1 June 2010.

[3] The public school figure is an estimated average, although the pupil-teacher ratio was as high as 90:1 in lower-primary public schools.

References

Agence France-Presse (AFP) (2010) Kenya Must Prosecute Education Graft Culprits: donors. *Education-News.us*. http://education-news.us/2010/12/15/kenya-must-prosecute-education-graft-culprits-donors/

Bauer, A., Brust, F. & Hubbert, J. (2002) Entrepreneurship: a case study in African enterprise growth. Expanding Private Education in Kenya: Mary Okelo and Makini schools, *Chazen Web Journal of International Business* (Columbia Business School), Fall, 1-19.

Bray, M. (1997) Community Financing of Education: rationales, mechanisms, and policy implications in less developed countries, in C. Colclough (Ed.) *Marketizing Education and Health in Developing Countries: miracle or mirage?*, pp. 185-204. New York: Oxford University Press.

Cheng, T.K. & Kariithi, S. (2008) *More Than One Struggle: ensuring quality education for the next generation in Mathare Valley*. Dignitas Project Report. Mathare: Kenya.

Colclough, C. (Ed.) (1997) *Marketizing Education and Health in Developing Countries: miracle or mirage?* New York: Oxford University Press.

Glassman, D. & Sullivan, P. (2006) Governance, Management, and Accountability in Secondary Education in Sub-Saharan Africa. Working Paper Series., SEIA Thematic Study No. 3. Washington, DC: World Bank.

Karmokolias, Y. & van Lutsenburg Maas, J. (1997) The Business of Education: a look at Kenya's private education sector. Discussion Paper, No. 32. Washington, DC: World Bank.

Kitaev, I. (1999) *Private Education in Sub-Saharan Africa: a re-examination of theories and concepts related to its development and finance*. Paris: International Institute for Educational Planning, UNESCO. http://unesdoc.unesco.org/images/0011/001176/117631e.pdf

Lewin, K. (2007) The Limits to Growth of Non-government Private Schooling in Sub-Saharan Africa, in P. Srivastava & G. Walford (Eds) *Private Schooling in Less Economically Developed Countries: Asian and African perspectives*, pp. 41-67. Oxford: Symposium Books.

Lewin, K. & Caillods, F. (2001) *Financing Secondary Education in Developing Countries: strategies for sustainable growth*. Paris: International Institute for Educational Planning, UNESCO.

Lewin, K.M. & Sayed, Y. (2005) Non-government Secondary Schooling in Sub-Saharan Africa: exploring the evidence in South Africa and Malawi. Researching the Issues, No. 59. London: Department for International Development.

Ministry of Labour (2010) Regulation Of Wages (General) (Amendment) Order, 2010. Nairobi: Kenya. Legal Notice No. 98, The Institutions Act (No. 12 of 2007). http://www.kenyalaw.org/LegalNotices/pop_ln.php?file=435

Musani, Y. (2008) Understanding the Kenya Independent Schools Sector: study of the Kenya Independent Schools Association (KISA). Gray Matters Capital Foundation Working Paper. Atlanta, GA: Gray Matters Capital Foundation.

Oketch, M., Mutisya, M., Ngware, M. & Ezeh, A.C. (2010) Why are there Proportionately More Poor Pupils Enrolled in Non-state Schools in Urban

Kenya in Spite of FPE Policy? *International Journal of Educational Development*, 30(1), 23-32.

Phillipson, B. (Ed.) (2008) *Low-cost Private Education: impacts on achieving universal primary education*. London: Commonwealth Secretariat.

Probe Team (1999) *Public Report on Basic Education in India*. New Delhi: Oxford University Press.

Rose, P. & Adelabu, M. (2007) Private Sector Contributions to Education for All in Nigeria, in P. Srivastava & G. Walford (Eds) *Private Schooling in Less Economically Developed Countries: Asian and African perspectives*, pp. 67-87. Oxford: Symposium Books.

Somerset, A. (2008) Access to Primary Education in Kenya: a case study of the impact of the 2003 FPE initiative at nine schools in Nairobi City and Nyeri District. CREATE Work in Progress. Brighton: Centre for International Education, University of Sussex. http://www.dfid.gov.uk/r4d/PDF/Outputs/ImpAccess_RPC/TS_Report_Phase1_Kenya_WiP.pdf

Srivastava, P. & Walford, G. (Eds) (2007) *Private Schooling in Less Economically Developed Countries: Asian and African perspectives*. Oxford: Symposium Books.

Tooley, J. (2005) Private Schools for the Poor: education where no one expects it, *Education Next*, 5(4), 22-32.

Tooley, J. (2009) *The Beautiful Tree: a personal journey into how the world's poorest people are educating themselves*. Washington, DC: CATO Institute.

Tooley, J. & Dixon, P. (2005) *Private Education is Good for the Poor: a study of private schools serving the poor in low-income countries*. Washington DC: Cato Institute.

Tooley, J. & Dixon, P. (2006a) 'De Facto' Privatisation of Education and the Poor: implications of a study from sub-Saharan Africa and India, *Compare*, 36(4), 443-462.

Tooley, J. & Dixon, P. (2006b) The Failures of State Schooling in Developing Countries and the People's Response, in M. Miles, K.R. Homes & M.A. O'Grady (Eds) *2006 Index of Economic Freedom*, pp. 27-37. Washington, DC: Heritage Foundation and Wall Street Journal.

Tooley, J., Dixon, P. & Stanfield, J. (2008) Impact of Free Primary Education in Kenya: a case study of private schools in Kibera, *Educational Management Administration & Leadership*, 36(4), 449.

UNESCO (2008) *2009 Education for All Global Monitoring Report. Overcoming Inequality: why governance matters*. Oxford: University of Oxford Press-UNESCO.

UNESCO (2010) *2010 Education for All Global Monitoring Report. Reaching the Marginalized: summary*. Paris: UNESCO. http://unesdoc.unesco.org/images/0018/001865/186525E.pdf

Verspoor, A. (2008a) The Power of Public-Private Partnership: coming together for secondary education in Africa. Working Document Draft. Paris: Association for the Development of Education in Africa.

Verspoor, A. (2008b) *At the Crossroads: choices for secondary education in sub-Saharan Africa*. Africa Human Development Series. Washington, DC: World Bank.

Watkins, K. (2004) Private Education and 'Education For All' or How Not to Construct an Evidence-based Argument: a reply to Tooley, *Economic Affairs*, 24(4), 8-11.

World Bank (2008) Governance, Management, and Accountability in Secondary Education in Sub-Saharan Africa. World Bank Working Paper, No. 127. Washington, DC: World Bank.

World Bank (2010) Education Statistics [data file]. http://Ddp-ext.worldbank.org/ext/DDPQQ/report.do?method=showReport

CHAPTER 6

Scaling Up: challenges facing low-fee private schools in the slums of Lagos, Nigeria[1]

JOANNA HÄRMÄ & FOLASADE ADEFISAYO

Introduction

Lagos is the thriving economic heart of Nigeria that exists (to some extent) outside of the oil industry, and it is characterised by great wealth, entrepreneurialism and innovation on the one hand, while in certain areas there is still great inertia and apathy, with many living in poverty. Some public services have gone from non-existence to strength in recent years, a highly visible example being the clean-up of Lagos's streets, with the ubiquitous piles of rubbish having been banished. For many, though, the quest for essential services of acceptable quality and in sufficient quantity has led them to the private sector, education being a prime example. Alongside a modest public education system there is a rapidly expanding private education sector, with 12,098 private schools in Lagos State in the 2010-2011school year compared with the government's 1606 schools (Lagos State Government, 2011a).

The education landscape in Lagos is dominated to such an extent by private schools that they account for 70% of pre-primary- and primary-level pupils (Härmä, 2011b). The most common is the low-fee private school, operating on tight margins, and catering to poorer communities and the less well-off in middle-class neighbourhoods. These schools can be found across the city and in outlying peri-urban areas, sometimes in great concentration. They are often hard to find, and want to remain so, as many do not meet government norms and run the risk of being closed down. They may be housed in apartment buildings, behind unassuming metal gates, and in shoddy makeshift structures. Often the only clue to their existence is the sound of children's voices in the air, or the sight of uniformed pupils emerging unexpectedly from anonymous gates and doorways.

There is scope for much more evidence to be published on this type of school. There is a small but growing literature on low-fee private schooling in India and Pakistan (e.g. Alderman et al, 1996; Srivastava, 2006, 2008; Andrabi et al, 2008; Härmä, 2011a; Fennell, Chapter 2, this volume; Ohara, Chapter 7, this volume; Humayun et al, Chapter 8, this volume), whereas African contexts experiencing similar developments have received less attention. The body of evidence is even more limited with regard to the Nigerian context (e.g. Tooley & Dixon, 2006; Rose & Adelabu, 2007; Umar, 2008). This chapter explores the nature of private schools, taking into account the divide between those recognised by the government and those operating illegally (in Nigerian terminology, 'approved' and 'unapproved' schools), with a focus on schools serving families in the lower part of the socio-economic spectrum.

This chapter seeks to answer the following questions: what are these schools like in Lagos? What are their defining characteristics? Do these schools serve the needs of poor children, especially girls? If schools have major development needs, as the limited existing evidence suggests (e.g. Rose & Adelabu, 2007), what are the barriers they face in terms of improving their quality and generally scaling up? Do these schools truly reach out to the poor, and how significant is competition between neighbouring schools?

We chose to explore these issues in Makoko, a poor slum area, and neighbouring Iwaya, which, while still a slum area, appears to be slightly less poor, and a lagoon community. Both slum areas are immediately adjacent to each other and front onto the Lagos Lagoon, visible to the west from the Third Mainland Bridge which carries road traffic to the affluent islands. The basis of the local economy is predominantly fishing, sawmill work, and petty market trading or vending. Inhabitants are greatly deprived in terms of basic facilities and amenities, and they suffer from endemic flooding. Unexpectedly, we also found a community of fishermen and their families both working and living literally on the Lagos Lagoon. This community was found to face the greatest challenges with accessing education for their children. These combined areas are referred to in the rest of the chapter as 'the study area'.

The UK's Department for International Development Education Sector Support Programme in Nigeria (DFID-ESSPIN), which funded this study, has a working definition of a 'low-cost school' as one that charges N30,000 or less per year, not counting all other direct education costs. This was adopted for the fieldwork for our study. In our relatively small study area, we found 35 private schools, one of which was a charity school and charged no fees, and thus was excluded. This chapter reports findings from the remaining 34 low-fee private schools. We found a mean fee level of N19,500 per annum at study schools, much less than the working definition.[2]

In summary, our research found the following: 'low-fee' was still quite expensive as a proportion of the minimum wage; there did not seem to be a gender divide in terms of where parents sent their children in schools on land; schools tended to have sub-standard facilities and infrastructure; and teachers were often unqualified. On the other hand, we also found: small class sizes; teachers present and usually active (to varying degrees); and that schools were close enough to people's homes for them to feel confident in sending even the smallest children.

The structure of the chapter is as follows. We begin by defining private schooling and exploring the existing literature on Nigeria, before turning to the context and study methods. Next, we present the characteristics of study schools, detail the challenges faced by the proprietors, and finally, make some concluding remarks.

Review of the Literature

Definition of Private Schooling

Private schooling can take many forms, and private schools may be run by a wide variety of actors, including 'NGOs, faith-based organisations, communities and commercially-oriented private entrepreneurs, each with different motives for their involvement in education' (Rose, 2007, p. 2). The type of private school that is growing in the Lagos context (and in other parts of Nigeria) is the small school, owned and run by a private individual, and funded through school fees. Sometimes these schools are run by a church. In our study, church schools did not receive any funding that was additional to the fees paid by parents, and classes would be held either in the church hall or in a small structure on church grounds.

Our research experience has shown that the private unaided sector in Nigeria is now highly heterogeneous and varies significantly in scope and quality, encompassing the elite to the poor and shoddy (see also Adelabu & Rose, 2004; for India, see De et al, 2002). As in India, lower-cost private schools in Nigeria are often run at the lowest possible fee level in order to appeal to as wide a market as possible - hence the term 'low-fee private' (Srivastava, 2006). These fully private unaided schools are distinct from some private schools in Nigeria which have benefited historically from grants-in-aid (mostly mission schools) (see Adelabu & Rose, 2004). Proportionally, however, there are few private-aided schools, and none were found in the study area. Private unaided schools include elite schools for the wealthy and expatriate communities, schools for the upper- and lower- middle classes, and lastly, the low-fee schools that target poorer segments of society. Private schools in Nigeria have complete autonomy in terms of management, hiring and pedagogy, including the low-fee schools studied here. This is similar to the situation of low-fee private unaided schools described in India (De et al, 2002; Srivastava, 2007).

For households in the study area, the only other alternative was government schools on the outskirts of the community, owned, funded, run and managed by the government, with little autonomy at the school level.

Government schools in Nigeria are necessarily recognised by the government irrespective of the quality of their infrastructure and facilities; indeed, the quality of teaching and infrastructure in these schools varies widely.

Private schools, on the other hand, can be disaggregated by approval status (Adelabu & Rose, 2004; for India, see Härmä, 2011a), with only 26% of schools in Lagos being government approved (Härmä, 2011b, p. 9). It is technically illegal to operate a private school without government approval (Lagos State Government, 2011b), and it is also against government regulations to operate a private school for profit (Adelabu & Rose, 2004). However, as other researchers have noted in the Indian context (e.g. Kingdon, 2007; Srivastava, 2008; Ohara, Chapter 7, this volume), our combined research experience between 2008 and 2011 in Lagos State found that, similar to Kingdon's (2007) following assertion about the Indian context, in Nigeria too, 'government "recognition" is an official stamp of approval... though hardly any private schools that get "recognition" actually fulfil all the conditions of recognition' (p. 183).

Government schools are nominally free, though some costs still remain (e.g. parent-teacher association levies, uniforms), while monthly fees and a range of other direct costs are payable at private schools. As data from our study showed, these are, on average, lower in unapproved schools than they are in approved schools. Schools in the study charged low fees relative to middle-class and elite schools, and on average, the fees were much lower than DFID-ESSPIN's working definition. Nonetheless, fees were still quite high in relation to the minimum wage at the time, ranging from 11% to 48% of the annual minimum wage at the time of data collection. Study schools tended to be run by individuals, often as small family businesses, and of the 34 sample schools from the study area, 12% were approved and 88% unapproved.[3]

Estimating the Size of the Private Sector

In a rare study of private provision in Lagos and Enugu, Adelabu and Rose (2004) point out that 'there is extremely limited existing literature on private schooling in Nigeria' (p. 47). The literature that exists corroborates the emerging story that 'parts of central and southern Nigeria ... [have] seen a notable growth in the enrolments and relative importance of private nursery-primary schools in the period since 1980' (Urwick, 2002, p. 134). Furthermore, there is evidence of 'flight from the public sector' reportedly due to 'the inadequate funding of government schools, and the related problem of teacher strikes' (Urwick, 2002, p. 142) in the 1980s and 1990s. This trend, echoed by Umar (2008) and Rose and Adelabu (2007), has continued into the 2000s (Härmä, 2011b).

Administrative data in Nigeria have historically been extremely weak (Umar, 2008), as demonstrated through many blank entries for Nigeria in successive UNESCO Education for All Global Monitoring Reports. Nigeria's education management information system (EMIS) has been especially lacking data on the private sector as a whole, with many approved schools not participating in the Annual School Census, and no real effort being made to gather data on the myriad unapproved schools.[4]

In order to collect data on such schools, it is necessary to send trained enumerators to elicit information, record them properly, and return completed questionnaires to the government. For the 2010-2011 school year, DFID-ESSPIN conducted a full and comprehensive census of private schools in Lagos State using such methods. Since no school list covering even half the schools existed, the census was designed as an exploratory exercise for which enumerators combed every street and back alley to find all schools as thoroughly as possible.[5]

According to the census, Lagos's 12,098 private schools of all types and sizes were serving 1,408,420 pupils from kindergarten through senior secondary levels.[6] To put these figures in context, 1606 public schools were serving 1,034,072 pupils in the same school year (Lagos State Government, 2011a). The recent 2010 Nigeria Demographic and Health Survey Education Data Survey (DHS EdData) (covering the 2009-2010 year) found that only 3% of children in the primary school age range (ages 6 to 11) were out of school. These figures point to a situation in Lagos State where parents value education highly, with most children enrolled in school, and the majority (57%) in private schools. At the nursery and primary levels even more enrolments were private (70%) (Härmä, 2011b). There is clear evidence of growth in the private sector, as reported and explained by Härmä elsewhere:

> In 1998 only 24 percent of today's schools were in existence, and until the 1990s the numbers of schools opening per year remained below 90. In 1991 the number of new schools reached 100, and through the course of the decade there was year on year growth in the sector. The upwards curve continued into the 2000s and accelerated in 2005, with 961 schools established in 2010. (Härmä, 2011b, p. 11)

What Are Low-fee Private Schools in Lagos Like, and What Are Their Challenges?

Adelabu and Rose (2004) have described the low-fee private sector in Nigeria as serving low-income families in mostly urban and peri-urban areas, but remaining unaffordable to the poorest. Fee levels are determined by: the socio-economic status of the local area's client base; what other schools in the area are charging; and the relative level of quality of the service provided or perceived to be provided (i.e. largely based on infrastructure and whether teachers are present).

These schools tend to have difficulty with their revenue streams, charging what are nominally termly fees, but which are difficult for poor parents to budget. This often leads to piecemeal payment of whatever parents can afford (Adelabu & Rose, 2004; Tooley et al, 2005). Indeed, in practice, these schools might find it more effective to charge monthly, weekly or even daily fees (Tooley, personal communication, January 2011), but our study found that only the very poorest schools chose to have such a payment system. Nonetheless, children are sometimes allowed to remain enrolled in school when parents experience difficulty in paying fees, mostly for the combined reasons of philanthropy and care for their pupils (Adelabu & Rose, 2004; Tooley et al, 2005) and also, as our study found (in line with Adelabu & Rose, 2004), in order to keep enrolments up, project a positive image, and in the hope that parents will eventually pay.

The limited literature yields general agreement on the appeal of these schools for poor parents. They tend to be close to home and have small class sizes. Additionally, they have longer opening hours (often operating afternoon 'lessons') and serve the child-minding needs of working parents. It appears that teachers spend more time on task and have fewer pupils to attend to. The fact that teachers may be teaching more at low-fee private schools appears to spring from the direct 'short-route' accountability of the school to the fee-paying parent, which is absent in government schools. Short-route accountability refers to direct power of fee-paying clients over service providers through the ability to 'vote with their feet' and exit, while traditional or political accountability requires an effective political process to affect real change. Short-route accountability may lead to more teaching activity in the absence of motivation (in some cases) for the work, as private school teachers are paid extremely low wages (Adelabu & Rose, 2004).

Interestingly, and consistent with the Indian context (see Härmä, 2008), many teachers at low-fee private schools are not qualified, and yet appear to impart more learning to pupils than government school teachers (Tooley & Dixon, 2006), nearly all of whom in Lagos State have the requisite Nigerian Certificate in Education (Lagos State Government, 2011a). School buildings in private schools are often worse in some respects than those at government schools (Adelabu & Rose, 2004), suggesting that this factor is less important to parents than others.

An area of disagreement in the literature surrounds the quality of provision in these schools. Government schools tend to have more qualified teachers, although in practice, this may mean little. For example, teachers may be qualified but not teaching, or they may be qualified on paper, but may not have the necessary subject knowledge, let alone the skill to deliver it.[7] While private school teachers are often more present and on-task than government school teachers, they do not employ child-centred techniques (neither do government teachers), largely, as we have seen, because they are self-taught or briefly trained by the head teacher or school proprietor. Adelabu and Rose (2004) are highly sceptical about the quality of provision at these schools, although their evidence is admittedly impressionistic.

Tooley et al (2005) have been more positive about the quality of these schools, backing their view with results of achievement tests that they administered in government and approved and unapproved private schools. In one study, they found that 'the mean math score advantage over government schools was about 14 and 19 percentage points respectively in private registered and unregistered schools, while in English it was 22 and 29 percentage points' (Tooley & Dixon, 2006, p. 454). When a range of background variables, including peer-group effects and school choice process, was taken into account, the differences in scores were 'reduced but still large in favour of both types of private school' (Tooley & Dixon, 2006, p. 454). Specifically, scores for mathematics at unapproved and approved private schools were 9 and 13 percentage points higher respectively, while English scores were 19 percentage points higher in private schools (with no significant difference according to approval status) (Tooley & Dixon, 2006, p. 454). DFID-ESSPIN has recently conducted a study monitoring learning achievement in three Nigerian states, the results of which indicate a raw private school advantage. The final results of that study, when available, will shed further light on the quality debate.

In terms of the challenges facing private schools, the limited evidence throws up various areas of difficulty for private school proprietors, whose views need to be taken into greater account (Adelabu & Rose, 2004). As corroborated in our study, low-fee private schools face financial constraints, first because of parents' non-payment of fees (Adelabu & Rose, 2004; Tooley et al, 2005). Under these circumstances, banks are unwilling to lend to these schools (Adelabu & Rose, 2004), leaving little to no capital for school improvement or expansion. Financial issues also have an impact on the challenge of meeting overly stringent government approval requirements, most of which entail considerable expense. For example, private schools have been required to have an owned (not rented) site, a purpose-built building of considerable size, and qualified teachers (amongst other things).

The inability of most schools to meet these requirements has led to conflict with the government, resulting in the Ministry of Education closing or threatening to close small private schools. Such threats led to the creation of private school associations, particularly, the Association for Formidable Educational Development, which was formed to defend member schools against government enforced closure (Adelabu & Rose, 2004). These problems are further exacerbated by the fact that the vast majority of government schools do not meet approval criteria to which private schools are subject. The relationship between government and private school proprietors has been extremely strained, with the government generally viewing private schools as operating solely for profit and cutting corners to maximise returns, while private school proprietors view the government as interested only in taxing schools and penalising them (or possibly shutting them down) when they fail to meet required standards.

Study Context and Methods

We embarked on this study having worked in private education provision and private education research, with previous experience in Nigeria. The study was shaped out of the currently growing international interest in low-fee private schooling, and in particular, out of a growing interest on the part of DFID-ESSPIN.

Study Area

The selection of the study area was based on an earlier situational analysis undertaken for DFID-ESSPIN, conducted in 2008-2009 (Adefisayo, 2009). School-level fieldwork for the present study was conducted between November 2010 and February 2011. The study area is considered to be generally poor, and a household element, while not part of this study, has since been conducted and is under review for publication elsewhere. All households served by the study schools were housed in slum dwellings, and most of the sample schools were found to be of the poorest type of private school (i.e. in terms of infrastructure, school organisation and teaching arrangements) prevailing in the state, indicated by Härmä's simultaneous other work with the DFID-ESSPIN private school census.[8]

The physical environment of the neighbouring Makoko and Iwaya slums lying along the coast of the Lagos Lagoon provides easy access to livelihoods such as fishing and fish processing, but proximity to the water also brings hardships to these communities. There is severe flooding during the rainy season, which tends to be worse approximately every three years. The ground is generally swampy and unstable, making it difficult to build on. In parts, it is necessary to walk via flimsy wooden planks in order to avoid wading through water which is filled with raw sewage and refuse. Rubbish collection takes place, but the area does not benefit from the same level of street cleaning and waste disposal as other parts of the new Lagos, and in parts, the springy ground is made of a significant proportion of rubbish. Habitations are mostly fairly solid slum houses, not generally rising above the ground floor.

News of private schools on the lagoon itself, the existence of which were unknown to many in the Lagos education sector, led to some expansion of the study area to cover these 'houses-on-water' – that is, the sprawling communities of houses and businesses on stilts, with waterways for roads and canoes of all sizes for necessary transportation. The community was served by a *Médecins Sans Frontières* clinic and private schools, rather than by any government services. The lagoon community, like its parallel community on land, was an informal settlement. Considerable parts of the habitation have been threatened with demolition, averted only through civil society organisation efforts.[9]

Several different groups lived on the lagoon, including Egun- and Yoruba-speaking people originating from the Badagry area of south-west

Nigeria; Egun- and French-speaking fishing families that migrated from Benin; and some Yoruba families that have lived in the area for four generations. The lagoon community was demonstrably poorer than parallel communities on land, with far fewer girls than boys enrolled in school, and many children visibly seen to be out of school. Those who were in school paid tiny daily sums rather than monthly or termly fees.

Description of Schooling Options in Makoko and Iwaya

The only government primary school provision for land and lagoon communities in the study area existed on the physical fringe of the area at Makoko Anglican Primary School, Adekunle Anglican Primary School and Aiyetoro African Primary School. These were all housed in the same building, on the same site, catering to 1823 children, with very limited outside space. Children from the inner Makoko and Iwaya slums would have to walk some distance. These schools were essentially inaccessible to children living on the water who would first need to pay for canoe transport to land and then proceed by foot. The schools were overcrowded and lacked resources to effectively teach existing pupils, with no spare capacity to comfortably accommodate any more.

Approved and unapproved private schools were found in the study area. As our data indicate, the former were 2.2 times more expensive on average. Public schools in Lagos generally have better buildings, although they are not well equipped in terms of furniture and other basic items. Low-fee private schools in Lagos tend to have poor quality, often makeshift structures. Effectively, the choice available to parents is to send a child to a somewhat distant but (technically) fee-free public school which is visibly overcrowded, or to a neighbourhood private school which is close to home and has smaller class sizes, and which may be observed to have had more teaching activity, but is inevitably relatively expensive (echoed in Tooley & Dixon, 2006; Umar, 2008).

Sampling and Survey Methodology

This study is a small-scale school-based survey (conducted as a structured interview). Schools were drawn from the selected study area. All low-fee private schools that were found were asked to participate in the study. Our interest was also piqued by information about French-speaking schools on the water which had not been documented in any previous study of private schooling in Nigeria. This news was fascinating and improbable in the context of English-speaking Lagos and the very difficult physical conditions on the lagoon. The sample was expanded to cover some of these 'lagoon' schools in order to see how schools could operate under such challenging conditions.

Thirty-seven schools were identified in all. One declined to be interviewed, while one lagoon school was not interviewed at the end of the study as it had become clear that similar and consistent messages were emerging from the research (see the discussion of result below); no substantially different responses were emerging from successive respondents. Another lagoon school's data were not included as it turned out to be a charity school, did not charge fees, and thus did not fit with the low-fee model. The final analysis included 34 schools (5 lagoon and 29 schools on land), of which only four schools, all on land, were government-approved.

The authors and one additional researcher worked independently to conduct interviews mostly in English.[10] Translators were only required from Egun and French to English, sometimes via Yoruba in lagoon communities. The interviewer would arrive at the school unannounced during school hours and ask to speak to the proprietor. All data for each school were collected in a single interview. The proprietor was interviewed in 20 of 34 schools; the head teacher in 13; and the manager in one. All participants were told the purpose of the study. Verbal consent was granted in all cases. Some schools participated but declined to provide information about teacher qualifications and/or salary levels and school running costs. In one instance, the language barrier was too great to ask certain questions on the interview schedule. Interviews lasted anywhere between 45 minutes and two hours, depending on the respondent's openness.

The instrument was piloted in several schools, with alterations and additions made as a result. The following topics were covered: basic school characteristics (enrolment, facilities and infrastructure); teachers' details (e.g. titles, experience, qualifications, age and whether or not they were present on the day of the visit); issues and problems in running a private school and challenges faced; respondents' perceptions of the poverty of client families; ease or difficulty of dealing with government; and whether competition affected how their schools functioned. All three interviewers also recorded qualitative perceptions on any aspects of the school visit and interview that were of particular interest. Data recorded in the structured interview schedule were entered and analysed in SPSS, a statistical package for data analysis in the social sciences, and simple descriptive statistics were used.

General Overview of Sample Low-fee Private Schools

What Were the Sample Schools Like?

Some basic characteristics of the schools are detailed in Table I. Most were owned and run by individual owners; one was owned by a faith-based organisation and one by the community, but since these fell in the designated fee range, they were included. Only 29% of proprietors owned their school premises. The mean enrolment at approved and unapproved schools did not differ greatly (165 and 150, respectively). Of the four approved schools, the range of enrolments was 90 to 348 pupils, while the range was 15 to 361 for unapproved schools. Approved schools were substantially older than unapproved schools, and tended to have more secure tenure in their premises.

	Approved schools	Unapproved schools	All schools
Number of sample schools	4	30	34
% owned by an individual	75	97	94
Mean year of establishment	1990	1999	1998
Mean enrolment	165	150	152
Median enrolment	111	158	153
% premises owned	25	30	29
% premises up to 1 year lease	25	47	44

Table I. Basic characteristics of sample schools.

Low-fee Private School Teachers

Selected characteristics of private school teachers in the sample are presented in Table II. Approved schools had around one and a half times as many teachers as unapproved schools, while a third of unapproved schools had five or fewer teachers. Approved schools paid almost one and a half times as much as unapproved schools. The lowest approved school salary was N10,000 per month, compared with N6000 per month in unapproved schools. Approved school teachers were found to be present more often – on the day of the visit, all were present, while at unapproved schools only 83% of teachers were. However, absenteeism without permission was not reported as a major problem in any sample school (similar to Umar, 2008).

	Approved schools	Unapproved schools	All schools
Number of teachers - mean	12	8	9
Number of teachers - range	9-17	1-17	1-17
% Female	70	57	61
Mean age in years	30	28	28
% Present on day of visit	100	83	89
Mean monthly salary in Naira	16958	10750	11495
Median monthly salary in Naira	17500	9500	10000

Table II. Selected characteristics of private school teachers.

Schools serving the primary level almost always had pre-primary sections. Schools could have one nursery class feeding into primary 1, or two (the most common) or even three nursery classes, preceded by one or two kindergarten classes (pre-nursery). This means that with six primary classes, schools could have between seven and ten classes in total. A total of 50% of all schools used multi-grade teaching, the proportion being the same for approved and unapproved schools. This was despite low pupil-teacher ratios of 13:1 for approved schools and 23:1 for unapproved schools.

All low-fee private schools in the sample had a large proportion of unqualified teachers, larger in unapproved schools (see Table III). Nearly half of unapproved school teachers were secondary school certificate holders or lower. Salaries were largely below the minimum wage of N18,780 per month, with the lowest salary at unapproved schools being N6000 per month, and N10,000 per month at approved schools. Most schools stated that they offered their teachers some form of in-service training, although the description of what 'training' consisted of was vague and less than satisfactory. Most proprietors or head teachers said that they instructed new recruits in how to teach, subsequently telling them from time to time how to improve their teaching, as opposed to an organised and systematic training regime. While half of all schools from both groups used multi-grade teaching, no training in these methods was provided at any school.

Respondents were not able to respond accurately in terms of teachers' level of experience in the profession, simply because they were not aware of how long teachers had been teaching before working at their school. Thus, the data in Table III report minimum years of experience (i.e. the number of years the teacher taught at the current school). Some would have had prior experience unaccounted for here, while many would be new to the profession when joining sample schools.

	Approved schools	Unapproved schools	All schools
% teachers qualified	54	38	43
% up to secondary school certificate	18	49	43
% received in-service training	60	65	66
Mean minimum years of experience	4.8	3.8	4.0
Mean pupils per teacher	13	23	22
% of schools using multi-grade teaching	50	50	50

Table III. Teachers' qualifications, in-service training, and experience at private schools.

Low-fee Private School Facilities

Study schools tended to have one of two types of building in varying states of repair (see Table IV). The first consisted of solid block construction with rendered and sometimes painted walls. Roofs were constructed using corrugated sheeting on a timber frame, and windows often had wooden shutters and doors. These would sometimes have raised concrete floors to avoid seasonal flooding. The second was a makeshift structure consisting of a timber frame with plywood sheets for walls. Sometimes the walls were made of old packing crates, complete with 'This Side Up' printed on the outside. Roofs were also of corrugated sheeting on timber frames, and sometimes had plastic sheeting affixed to the outside to keep out the damp. These buildings sometimes had raised floors, but more often did not, and suffered flooding as a result. The exceptions were two approved schools accommodated in proper, purpose-built buildings that met or came close to meeting government regulations.

	Approved schools	Unapproved schools	All schools
% proper, purpose-built building	50	0	6
% unfit, makeshift plywood structure	0	47	41
% with separate classrooms	50	5	12
% with toilets for students	100	52	58
% with water source	50	14	18
% with electricity connection	100	67	70
% with playground	100	47	53

Table IV. School buildings and facilities.

School Fee, Total Costs and the Minimum Wage

Table V compares the yearly fee (calculated by multiplying the termly fee by three), and this fee plus all other direct costs (textbooks, stationery, uniforms and possibly transport) as reported by schools. The difference between the two figures is remarkably similar across the three school groups, with fees at approved and unapproved schools representing 82% and 81% of total costs, respectively. However, the total reported schooling costs must be treated with a degree of caution. While there were no directly comparable school and household data, it has been found elsewhere that proprietors tend to under-report schooling costs compared with expenditure reported by households where children are attending these schools (see Härmä, 2008 for India). Prior research experience indicates that the fees and schooling costs quoted here are likely to represent the lower bound.

The mean costs at unapproved schools on land were more than twice those of schools serving people on the lagoon, ostensibly the poorer community. Unapproved schools on land had a mean total cost per year of N20,513, while it was N9670 per year for lagoon schools. When these costs are compared with the minimum wage (in the absence of household asset and income information), a picture of parental sacrifice to access private schools emerges.[11]

The data collection period for this study straddled a significant upward revision of the national minimum wage, from N7500 per month to N18,000 per month. In Lagos State this was further increased to N18,780 per month. Table V indicates the proportions of the minimum wage before and after the increase required to access a sample school based on the mean fee (and all other costs) charged by each school type in the study for one child for one year. These figures must be considered in context. As Lewin (2007) notes, 'most household surveys of expenditure in SSA show that educational expenditures are below 10% of total household income, and often below 5% amongst the poorest' (p. 10). Arguably, new minimum wage laws take time to be enforced, and therefore the old figure may be more appropriate for the 2010-2011 school year regarding costs in our study. Based on Lewin's observations and the old minimum wage, the unapproved and approved schools on land were substantially more costly, while unapproved lagoon schools fell just outside the upper bound of this limit. Approved schools remain very expensive even with the introduction of the new minimum wage.

	Approved schools	Unapproved schools on land	Unapproved schools on lagoon	All schools
Yearly fee in Naira – mean	33750	16977	6280	17377
Yearly fee in Naira – median	31500	15000	6000	15000
Total cost in Naira – mean	41116*	20513**	9670***	21342
Total cost in Naira – median	39233*	19340**	8900***	18571
Total costs as % old minimum wage N7500/ month	47.7	22.8	10.7	4.3
Total costs as % revised minimum wage N18,780/ month	18.3	9.1	4.3	9.5

Note: *Standard deviation 25,195; **standard deviation 7405; ***standard deviation 1,792.

Table V. School costs and the minimum wage.

Equity

There are equity implications to relying on private schools in poor areas. Where fees must be paid, there will inevitably be many families that cannot afford to access schooling. Most schools in our study, of their own volition, provided free and concessionary places for the poor (see Table VI).

	Approved schools	Unapproved schools	All schools
Mean enrolment	165	155	156
Mean number concessionary places	27	13	15
Concessionary places as % of total enrolment	16	8	10
% schools not offering these	0	8	7

Table VI. Concessionary places offered at schools.

Only 7% of schools did not. The proportion of total enrolments that these free seats represents appears to be high, with 16% of places in approved schools and 8% of places in unapproved schools in our sample, compared with Tooley et al's (2005) findings from a larger sample of schools of 4.9% and 4.8% of places, respectively (p. 136). However, reports by schools must be treated with caution. Elsewhere (see Härmä, 2008), proprietors have been found to over-report their philanthropy and under-report fees and other schooling costs. Our current study did not have a household element, whereas Tooley et al (2005) used household data to triangulate the level of school philanthropy, arriving at the lower figures reported above.

Schools in our study purportedly offered concessions and free places out of compassion for children whose parents could not afford to pay (also reported in Tooley et al, 2005). However, our findings also indicate that concessions were given in the hope that parents would eventually pay the full fee or close to it (see Srivastava, 2007 for India). A further motivation may be to boost the reputation of the school (Adelabu & Rose, 2004).

While conducting their own outreach is a positive aspect of these schools, the total number of free or concessionary places at study schools amounted to just 10% (516 places) of total enrolments of all 33 reporting schools (one school refused to report enrolments) in a densely populated area. When asked, schools readily insisted that many children in the study area were unable to pay private school fees and were, consequently, out of school. Indeed, the one charity school we found on the lagoon stated that it had a waiting list of some 1000 or more students who were out of school because the school charged no fees and parents were too poor to send their children to fee-paying schools. We asked schools how they would feel about more of the poorest children accessing their schools if they were supported in so doing. None expressed objection to access being widened, indicating that social position or school status was not a major consideration; however, they may have been concerned about appearing discriminatory.

Apart from economic equity issues, it is often assumed that parents may prioritise boys over girls when they have to pay fees. In the case of the sample schools, Table VII illustrates that there was near gender parity in enrolments at schools situated on land. However, this was not the case with schools on the water. Enrolments in lagoon schools were skewed towards boys, with girls representing only 41.9% of children enrolled at these schools.

	Schools on land	Schools on the lagoon	Approved schools	Unapproved schools	All schools
% girls	49.0	41.9	49.1	47.2	47.4

Table VII. Percentage of girls in relation to total school enrolment by school type and approval status.

Lagoon schools were questioned extensively on why girls from lagoon communities tended to be under-represented. They reported that these families were extremely poor. Indeed, as our data show, fees at lagoon schools were less than half of those charged by schools on land. Since private schools were the only option, it seemed that many families chose not to educate their daughters or to prematurely end their education, causing drop-out.

Challenges Facing Low-fee Private Schools

One intention of this study was to examine the challenges facing low-fee private school proprietors, particularly regarding day-to-day operations, in becoming approved schools, and also in scaling up and improving operations. Interviewees raised issues largely consistent with previously published evidence (Adelabu & Rose, 2004; Umar, 2008). Existing literature highlights the deficiencies of low-fee private school facilities. We wondered whether schools were content with their current operations, or whether they had aspirations to hire what they would perceive as better teachers (possibly better qualified, or simply more experienced) and have better facilities and more students.

This study found perhaps a much worse situation than described by Tooley et al (2005). As a consequence of the terrible conditions that some of these schools operated under (i.e. flooding; flimsy, makeshift shacks, some of which were built on rubbish piles), it was supposed that there must be obstacles to investment, since few regarded their circumstances as optimal. Below we examine schools' concerns relating to a number of operational challenges they faced.

Challenges to School Improvement

We asked schools whether they could access the funds necessary to carry out school improvement, and 70% reported that finance was their single biggest obstacle (75% of approved schools and 69% of unapproved schools). Indeed, a lack of funds hindered efforts to making lasting improvements to school buildings which could permanently solve problems such as flooding. In the absence of a suitable credit market for low-fee private schools, they were forced to rely on temporary fixes, which tended to cost more in the end. Some desired school grants, but most just wished for reasonable loans (i.e. longer loan periods with lower interest rates) in order to make capital investments in their schools.

Only 29% of owners had been able to access funds for school development. In these cases, the repayment terms were invariably short (typically three to six months), and the interest rates extremely high (15-50% over the term). Difficulties in the credit market were confirmed during an interview with an international investment banker now working in Lagos to encourage innovation and expansion in the Nigerian banking sector.[12] The Nigerian banking sector has focused in recent decades on the oil and gas sectors, ignoring to a large extent banking needs of the individual and the micro-entrepreneur. Part of this narrow focus is a result of high levels of identity and financial fraud in Nigeria, and also because, even where collateral is connected to a loan, systems for debt recovery are extremely weak. This leads banks to be overly cautious and punitive in their lending practices. As the interviewee above claimed, these practices seem to result from the practical need to protect the bank's investment. In this context, microfinance banks and informal sector private money lenders are the only option available to low-fee private school owners.

Challenges Related to Teachers and Teaching Quality

When asked about school improvement plans, we noted the lack of mention of improvements to teaching staff (i.e. hiring better qualified teachers; providing more rigorous in-service training). Most schools described training as in-house instruction by proprietors or head teachers, while outside training was mostly provided by the main textbook publishing company, Macmillan Nigeria Publishers Limited. As our previous experience indicates, the latter mostly consisted of guiding teachers on the use of the company's books rather than on child-centred pedagogies, for example, or other direct teaching methods.

Most interviewees expressed little concern for the quality of teaching at their schools, which may partly have been due to lack of awareness of other methods. Most schools reported no major challenges regarding teaching quality, even in schools where minimal active teaching was observed during school visits. Indeed, where teachers appeared particularly demotivated (in approximately a quarter of sample schools), there was no inclination to put up even a pretence of active teaching during our visit. Alternatively, some proprietors may have been all too aware that when teachers are better trained they often find better-paying jobs elsewhere, making staff development seem a futile exercise.

When specifically asked about challenges related to teachers, 49% of interviewees reported no problems; only 6% complained that teachers did not write their lesson notes on time; 6% complained of lack of specialisms; while another 12% complained that teachers lacked commitment and were unwilling to learn. No complaints were made about the quality of instruction. Other complaints focused on important issues such as excessive corporal punishment (3%) and tardiness (6%), as well as other minor discipline issues.

Other Challenges

Most other challenges facing the low-fee private schools in our study could be traced to a lack of funding, even in cases where the original source of the problem was the physical environment. Many schools face seasonal flooding for two to three months of the year in the autumn. This problem is essentially impossible to overcome, since communities straddle the land/water divide, extending to the lagoon. Families living in the study area are mostly involved in fishing, meaning that their homes are convenient for their livelihoods, but less than convenient in other aspects, such as getting children to school. Despite these environmental issues, the slums are extremely overcrowded.

The landscape presents particular challenges to school owners: 20% of respondents reported that finding sufficient space is extremely difficult, and 14% reported the cost of running 'school boats' to ferry pupils from home and back as a challenge. Such issues could be ameliorated with sufficient funding. For example, school floors could be raised permanently rather than temporarily by sand-filling, boat operators could be hired, and more land could be bought or leased.

Schools also reported interference by government officials. Some school proprietors reported that staff from the 57 Local Council Development Areas (LCDAs) tended to visit private schools to extort money. Although it is generally known to government officials that most proviate schools are unapproved, this problem is mitigated through cash payments. Some schools reported the charging of an 'illegal school tax' – essentially a bribe referred to as a 'tax' – by concerned government employees that, when paid, would simply get them to go away, leaving the school in peace. Such relationships with government units mean a continuing distrust of the state by private school proprietors.

However, official requirements for approval status were reported as the major government-related challenge. Requirements were so stringent that most schools could not even think of applying.[13] Indeed, 40% of the unapproved schools reported their inability to meet requirements as the reason that they would not consider applying. There was a persistent fear that the government would embark on another round of school closures. However, this was reportedly not a significant daily challenge to schools, and by extension, neither was unapproved school status because the government was less than zealous in enforcing regulations on private schools and effectively accepted that many such schools existed.

The main issues seemed to be related to lack of access to credit markets. It is reportedly more difficult for schools to access loans when they are unapproved, resulting in a vicious cycle, since it is difficult to meet approval requirements without credit. Without access to credit to invest in their schools, proprietors have developed coping mechanisms, such as association membership, where private schools band together to fight the government at times of threat, as well as adopting the strategy of flying under the radar as far as possible.

Our interview data indicate that the current business model results in difficulties. Schools are generally small and charge low fees because their client base consists of low-income families. Cash flow is unpredictable because of families' financial constraints, and schools have little leverage because parents can withdraw their child and enrol elsewhere. Difficulties with cash flow lead to difficulties paying teachers' salaries (reported by 75% of approved schools and 59% of unapproved schools) and could, by extension, lead to difficulties repaying a standard loan. Our data show that many school proprietors do not have the necessary skills to draw up business plans and keep proper school records and accounts. In our sample, all approved schools and only 39% of unapproved schools claimed to keep accounts ledgers, but these were not inspected.

Conclusions

Private schools are the majority provider in Lagos State, accounting for 57% of all enrolments and 70% at the pre-primary and primary levels in the 2010-2011 school year (Härmä, 2011b). Yet, until the comprehensive 2010-2011 school census, there was only patchy information on the sector. What was already clear was that in Nigeria 'unapproved [private] schools are providing schooling opportunities to a significant number of children, particularly in urban and peri-urban areas' (Adelabu & Rose, 2004, p. 64; see also Tooley et al, 2005; Tooley & Dixon, 2006). In particular, existing literature has mainly discussed private schools as a homogeneous group, without differentiating between approved and unapproved schools, and it is noted that the views of proprietors are deserving of further attention (Adelabu & Rose, 2004, p. 48). This chapter has presented, from an admittedly small sample of schools, data disaggregated by approval status, giving voice to some of the challenges and concerns of proprietors.

In terms of outreach to the poor, schools seemed already to be doing what they could, with mixed motivations. They charged the lowest possible fees in order to attract the largest number of clients, and tended to allow some children who were unable to pay to stay in school tuition-fee-free, although other non-discretionary direct costs such as exam fees and charges for books and uniforms still applied.

Irregular cash flow emerged as one of the most pressing challenges. The business model dictates that costs must be kept down for profitability through being accessible to the widest possible client base. For the schools in our study, this client base was made up of unskilled workers operating in the informal sector, with unpredictable incomes, resulting in irregular and sometimes incomplete fee payments to schools. Therefore, schools often had trouble meeting their financial commitments, the largest of which comprised teachers' salaries. By extension, these schools may well have difficulty paying a traditional bank loan with fixed monthly repayments.

Proprietors reported that access to credit for school improvement was their single biggest obstacle. Very poor facilities often dictate the fee that a school can charge in the absence of readily available information or criteria on teaching quality for parents. This, in turn, dictates the level of wages a school can pay, creating a vicious cycle. The Nigerian banking and law enforcement context, in which it is difficult, if not impossible, to recover debts even where collateral is involved, means that there is little legal back-up to mitigate the current situation of unaffordable borrowing for small low-fee private schools.

It is unclear, because it has not been tried in this context, whether schools would be able and willing to meet repayments of a relatively long-term loan (e.g. five years) at a low interest rate. Such loans would only be possible through a non-profit organisation set up by the government or international donor agencies, since extremely low interest rates are not possible in the private market. Schools require capacity building in terms of business planning, record and account keeping, and general school management, and even more so where potential borrowing and expansion are concerned. Conditions could be attached to loans or grants to schools, such as a commitment to teacher development and a minimum percentage of free places for the poor.

Nonetheless, improvements to fee-paying schools are insufficient to serve equity considerations. Many children are unable to access private schools, and the majority enrol in public schools, or are out of school (3% of children in the state). In our study area, such large and densely populated slums are highly likely to have more than the 7208 children reportedly enrolled at the public, private and charity schools found in the area, which was also the contention of the schools in our study. In order to reach these children, either the government must step in to purchase land and build more schools, or private school costs must be subsidised.

However, evidence from India suggests that private schools whose teachers' salaries are paid by the state do not perform as well as independent private schools (Kingdon, 2007). Arguably, where private schools are to be subsidised, funding must follow the student to sustain competitive pressure. Short-route, direct accountability to the fee-paying parent and proximity to the families served are arguably the source of advantage of this form of provision. Indeed, 79% of sample schools felt they had to compete with other schools, mostly by providing a 'good' service and keeping fees low.

Nonetheless, funding pupils to attend private schools would only add to the existing state education budget, as the public system will continue to require the same and, arguably, increased funding. In addition, there are considerable administrative costs associated with running such schemes. Lastly, active support for private schools will prove difficult politically because teachers are often paid far below what is now the minimum wage, meaning a clear-cut breach of state employment policy.

While not the basis for wider generalisations, our findings indicate that the low-fee private sector serves the needs of poor families, who are otherwise not served or under-served by government provision. In that sense, they make a serious contribution. However, our repeated visits and continued work in the study area indicate that the poorest and most marginalised, which may be very many in slum areas such as these, are likely left behind.

Their access to education of acceptable quality must be facilitated, whether through improved government schools or through private schools.

Acknowledgements

The authors would like to thank DFID-ESSPIN for supporting this research, and the participating schools, who were so welcoming. Sincere thanks go to researchers Abiola Modupeoluwa Lawal and Olufunke Tawa Kehinde for their enthusiasm, insights and hard work. Their company has been a joy during this research.

Notes

[1] Joanna Härmä's views expressed in this chapter and the study conducted with Folasade Adefisayo do not represent the views of UNESCO or any other organisation, and are unconnected to her current work with the *Education for All Global Monitoring Report*.

[2] At the time of the fieldwork, UK£1 = N260; US$1=N155.

[3] The proportion of unapproved schools was higher in the study area than in the state overall (88% as opposed to 74% for the state), most likely because these schools are cheaper, and therefore more likely to exist in such a context.

[4] Efforts to capture private schools in the Annual School Census have been piecemeal at best, relying on schools to voluntarily come forward to supply data. School proprietors do not want to do this because they fear taxation (and multiple taxation) and forced closure if they do not meet government guidelines (i.e. their reluctance is due to their illegal status).

[5] It is accepted that some small number of schools may still have been missed out.

[6] The confidence in these numbers is high. A verification team monitored the quality of coverage and individually confirmed the existence of a large sample of the overall total (i.e. 46% of all schools reported by enumerators).

[7] This was evidenced by the Teacher Development Needs Assessment carried out in Kwara State, Nigeria, with the support of DFID-ESSPIN. Virtually no teachers could pass a Class 4 test.

[8] Joanna Härmä was simultaneously conducting the first comprehensive private school census in Lagos (school year 2010-2011) with the support of DFID-ESSPIN. Her experience with the verification team and through visiting all types of schools in all Local Government Areas (LGAs) in the state confirmed that while such schools also existed in many other locations across Lagos, the typical Makoko school was amongst the poorest type in the state.

[9] Despite civil society efforts, Lagos State Government finally carried out the long-threatened demolition of the Makoko community on the water in mid-July 2012, giving residents only 72 hours' notice. It is likely that many of the study schools on the lagoon no longer exist as a result.

[10] One of the authors was accompanied by a research assistant who had worked on the 2009 study, in the capacity of guide, aide and translator, where needed.

[11] The minimum wage was also used by Tooley et al, 2005 and Tooley & Dixon, 2006.

[12] An initiative through the DFID-funded project EFINA, working with banks to expand credit and general banking opportunities to a range of potential customers hitherto not served by the sector.

[13] At the time of writing, schools only had the old guidelines (Lagos State Ministry of Education, n.d.). These have since been slightly relaxed. For example, it is now accepted that schools can operate in rented premises rather than owning their own substantial plots (Lagos State Ministry of Education, 2011a). The updated guidelines still contain onerous requirements, however.

References

Adefisayo, F. (2009) Lagos State Private Primary School Survey. A study commissioned by ESSPIN. Unpublished.

Adelabu, M. & Rose, P. (2004) Non-state Provision of Basic Education in Nigeria, in G. Larbi, M. Adelabu, P. Rose, et al (Eds) *Nigeria: study of non-state providers of basic services*. Country Studies. Commissioned by Policy Division, Department of International Development, UK. Birmingham: International Development Department, School of Public Policy, University of Birmingham. http://www.birmingham.ac.uk/Documents/college-social-sciences/government-society/idd/research/non-state-providers/nigeria-report-23march05.pdf

Alderman, H., Orazem, P.F. & Paterno, E.M. (1996) School Quality, School Cost, and the Public/Private School Choices of Low-income Households in Pakistan. World Bank Working Paper Series on Impact Evaluation of Education Reforms, No. 2. Washington, DC: World Bank.

Andrabi, T., Das, J. & Khwaja, A. (2008) A Dime a Day: the possibilities and limits of private schooling in Pakistan, *Comparative Education Review*, 52(3), 329-355.

De, A., Majumdar, M., Samson, M. & Noronha, C. (2002) Private Schools and Universal Elementary Education, in R. Govinda (Ed.) *India Education Report*. New Delhi: Oxford University Press.

Härmä, J. (2008) Are Low-fee Private Primary Schools in Rural Uttar Pradesh, India, Serving the Needs of the Poor? Unpublished doctoral thesis, University of Sussex, Brighton.

Härmä, J. (2011a) Low Cost Private Schooling in India: is it pro poor and equitable? *International Journal of Educational Development*, 31(4), 350-356.

Härmä, J. (2011b) *Lagos Private School Census 2010/2011 Report*. Report No. LG 501. Education Sector Support in Nigeria. ESSPIN-UKAID DFID. http://www.esspin.org/index.php/resources/abs/lagos/296/LG%20501%20Lagos%20Private%20School%20Census%202010/2011%20Report

Kingdon, G. (2007) The Progress of School Education in India, *Oxford Review of Economic Policy*, 23(2), 168-195.

Lagos State Government (n.d.) *Guidelines for the Establishment of Private Schools.* Alausa, Lagos: Ministry of Education.

Lagos State Government (2011a) *Annual School Census Report.* Alausa, Lagos: Ministry of Education.

Lagos State Government (2011b) *Guidelines for the Establishment of Private Schools.* Alausa, Lagos: Ministry of Education.

Lewin, K. (2007).*The Limits to Growth of Non-government Private Schooling in Sub-Saharan Africa.* CREATE Pathways to Access Research Monograph, No. 5. Brighton: Centre for International Education, University of Sussex. http://www.Create-rpc.org/pdf_documents/PTA5.pdf

Rose, P. (2007) *Supporting Non-state Providers in Basic Education Service Delivery.* CREATE Pathways to Access Research Monograph, No. 4. http://www.Create-rpc.org/pdf_documents/PTA4.pdf

Rose, P. & Adelabu, M. (2007) Private Sector Contributions to Education for All in Nigeria, in P. Srivastava & G. Walford (Eds) *Private Schooling in Less Economically Developed Countries: Asian and African perspectives.* Oxford: Symposium Books.

Srivastava, P. (2006) Private Schooling and Mental Models about Girls' Schooling in India, *Compare*, 36(4), 497-514.

Srivastava, P. (2007) For Philanthropy or Profit? The Management and Operation of Low-fee Private Schools in India, in P. Srivastava & G. Walford (Eds) *Private Schooling in Less Economically Developed Countries: Asian and African perspectives.* Oxford: Symposium Books.

Srivastava, P. (2008) The Shadow Institutional Framework: towards a new institutional understanding of an emerging private school sector in India, *Research Papers in Education*, 23(4), 451-475.

Tooley, J. & Dixon, P. (2006) 'De Facto' Privatisation of Education and the Poor: implications of a study from sub-Saharan Africa and India, *Compare*, 36(4), 443-462.

Tooley, J., Dixon, P. & Olaniyan, O. (2005) Private and Public Schooling in Low-income Areas of Lagos State, Nigeria: a census and comparative survey, *International Journal of Educational Research*, 43(3), 125-146.

Umar, A. (2008) Nigeria, in B. Phillipson (Ed.) *Low-cost Private Education.* London: Commonwealth Secretariat.

Urwick, J. (2002) Determinants of the Private Costs of Primary and Early Childhood Education: findings from Plateau State, Nigeria, *International Journal of Educational Development*, 22(2), 131-144.

CHAPTER 7

The Regulation of Unrecognised Low-fee Private Schools in Delhi: potential implications for India's Right to Education Act[1]

YUKI OHARA

Studies have shown that a lack of quality government provision has resulted in the emergence of low-fee private schools catering to lower-income groups in India (De et al, 2002; Tooley & Dixon, 2003; Srivastava, 2007; Härmä, 2009). It is important to note, however, that a number of low-fee private schools are unrecognised and, until recently, were not the immediate focus of government education departments. Effective as of April 2010, the Right of Children to Free and Compulsory Education Act, 2009 (RTE Act) has changed the scenario for unrecognised schools, compelling them to apply for recognition and formalise their status.[2]

In particular, Section 18(1) of the act prescribes: 'No school, other than a school established, owned or controlled by the appropriate Government of the local authority, shall after the commencement of this Act, be established or function without obtaining a certificate of recognition' (Government of India, 2009), and gives schools a period of three years from the commencement of the act to fulfil specified norms and standards (Section 19(2), Government of India, 2009). The act carries with it a harsh fine of Rs. 100,000, or Rs. 10,000 per day of contravention, for any owner who runs a school without obtaining a certificate of recognition, or continues to operate a school once recognition is withdrawn (Section 18(5), Government of India, 2009). However, obtaining recognition is a costly and lengthy process, and despite the vigour of the act, many unrecognised schools are unlikely to meet recognition standards due to financial restrictions, thus facing an uncertain future and potential closure.

While the existence of unrecognised schools in India had not been widely challenged by the legislative body until the RTE Act came into effect, in Delhi the dispute concerning the regulation of unrecognised schools occurred earlier. In 2005, Social Jurist, a Delhi-based non-governmental organisation (NGO) opposed to unrecognised schools, filed a public interest litigation (PIL) in the Delhi High Court requesting their closure. The PIL was filed on the basis that unrecognised schools did not conform to requirements regarding equipment, teacher qualifications or salary, as stated in the Delhi School Education Act, 1973 and the Delhi School Education Rules, 1973 (DSEAR), the guiding act and rules stipulating the establishment, recognition, management, and terms and conditions of service for Delhi schools.

Within this context, this chapter presents analysis from a larger field study on low-fee private schools in Delhi that aimed to address the following question: Do state regulations imposing standardised recognition criteria on unrecognised schools achieve the main aim of the RTE Act, which is to ensure children's right to education? Results show that unrecognised schools in Delhi, feeling threatened by the state's legislative body, and to fend off a High Court ruling ordering their closure, made an effort to affiliate with recognised schools and other organisations considered to carry more legitimacy and power in order to increase their credibility and ability to function as low-fee private schools. They also suggest that recognised schools in Delhi, particularly larger more profitable ones, were opposed to the ruling because many among them ran unrecognised schools, later seeking to expand their operations by 'chaining' or 'branching'. We thus examine the potential contribution that recognised schools made to the existence and expansion of unrecognised schools at the level of policy and practice.

The chapter presents two distinct areas of analysis stemming from the results of the larger study that was conducted on low-fee private schools in Delhi.[3] The first demonstrates the way that low-fee private schools in Delhi operated, and their interactions with other private schools and the state. The second presents an analysis of the Delhi High Court dispute on the regulation of unrecognised schools which took place during the fieldwork period. As a result of the analysis, we explore the possible implications of three potential options to regulate unrecognised schools in Delhi under the RTE Act: (1) standardised regulation; (2) non-state- or self-regulation; and (3) classified regulation.

The chapter begins by outlining the Delhi school system and context, followed by a discussion of the conceptual framework, and a presentation of methods and case-study school profiles. The bulk of the chapter discusses results in three sections. First, we examine the institutional arrangements and operations of a set of unrecognised low-fee private schools in Delhi. Second, we consider the Delhi High Court case – particularly Social Jurist's arguments maintaining the necessity of standardised regulation, and counter-arguments by the Co-ordination Committee of Public Schools in Delhi, an association of more than 250 recognised and unrecognised private schools and a proponent of unrecognised schools. Finally, we discuss potential options for regulation given the emerging compulsions of the newly instituted RTE Act.

On the basis of responses by education experts at the Centre for Civil Society (CCS) – a Delhi-based NGO active in advocacy and research-based projects in education – and the Co-ordination Committee, this study estimates the monthly fees to be around Rs. 300 for low-fee private schools, between Rs. 800 and Rs. 2000 for medium-fee schools, and above Rs. 2000 for high-fee schools. A monthly tuition fee of Rs. 300 represented approximately 7.8% of the mean monthly minimum wage for unskilled workers in Delhi between 2008 and 2010 (the fieldwork period).[4] The mean fee charged at case study schools in this study was lower, representing 6.5% of the minimum wage for unskilled workers in Delhi during this time.

Delhi School System

In Delhi, pre-primary (lower and upper kindergarten) and primary schools (Class I to V) are under the purview of local authorities such as the Municipal Corporation of Delhi, the New Delhi Municipal Corporation and the Delhi Cantonment Board, while the Directorate of Education generally runs upper primary (Class VI to VIII), secondary (Class IX to X) and senior secondary schools (Class XI to XII). Table I presents the number and proportion of different school types in elementary education in Delhi.

Total number 4946	Government schools 2733 (55%)				Private schools 2213 (45%)	
Type	Department of Education	Local body	Tribal/Social Welfare Department	Other departments	Aided	Unaided
Number (%)	922 (18)	1811 (36)	0 (0)	0 (0)	258 (5)	1955 (39)

Table I. Total number and proportion of elementary schools in Delhi.
Source: NUEPA, 2011a, *Education in India under Government Managements 2009-10* (selected tables based on the District Information System for Education [DISE] data).

According to the latest DISE data available at the time of writing, 2733 schools (55%) were run by government authorities and 2213 (45%) were run by private organisations registered under the Societies Registration Act (NUEPA, 2011a).[5] As indicated above, the proportion of private (recognised) unaided schools (39%) (i.e. schools independently managed and financed) surpassed local body/authority schools (36%) (Mehta, 2008; NUEPA, 2011b). The proportion of private unaided schools in Delhi is higher than in any other state and union territory in India, suggesting the rapid growth of fee-charging schools in Delhi at elementary level.

It is important to bear in mind that official DISE data do not capture unrecognised schools. Therefore, it is likely that the actual number of private unaided schools in Delhi is greater than reported in official sources. Furthermore, for obvious reasons, there is no indication of the number of 'falsely' recognised schools (i.e. schools granted recognition without meeting norms) that are included in official estimates of recognised schools, given the surreptitious manner in which recognition is acquired by this sub-set of schools. During the dispute over unrecognised schools in Delhi, the High Court ordered government authorities, including the Directorate of Education and the Municipal Corporation of Delhi, to survey unrecognised schools, resulting in a list of 1593 such schools. A quarter of these (398 of 1593) were located in Shahdara, the location in which the fieldwork for this study was carried out. Given their self-financing status, private unaided schools typically have higher fees than their private aided or government counterparts.

Private aided schools – that is, privately managed schools whose operational expenses are aided to a large extent by the government (up to 95% of a school's budget) – represent merely 5% of schools in Delhi. Although aided, these schools are officially categorised as a type of 'private' school. They are in fact considered by the bureaucracy to be closer to government schools due to the strong level of state control that accompanies handsome financial aid. Their tuition fees are meant to be nominal (Rs. 10-15 per month), but De et al (2002) found schooling costs in aided schools to be considerably higher than in government schools despite substantial government subsidy (p. 142), and that they cater to the relatively better-off among lower middle-class clientele compared with government schools.

Three types of government schools are operated by the Directorate of Education: *sarvodaya vidyalaya* (Class I to XII) (*sarvodaya* means 'universal uplift' or 'awakening of all' and *vidyalaya* means 'school'); non-*sarvodaya vidyalaya*; and *pratibha vikas vidyalaya* (Class VI to XII) (*pratibha* means 'talent' and *vikas* means 'development'). As of 2008, there were 367 *sarvodaya* schools, 447 non-*sarvodaya* schools and 19 *pratibha vikas vidyalayas* in Delhi (Government of the NCT of Delhi, 2008, p. 17).

The establishment of *sarvodaya* and *pratibha vidyalaya* schools is an important development to note. As 'composite schools' (i.e. housing multiple levels within the same school), they can be viewed as an attempt by the Directorate to reform the organisational structure of its schools by mimicking the model of how 'good' (typically, higher fee) private schools operate. In fact, this is explicitly stated by the Government of NCT of Delhi regarding the aim of *sarvodaya vidyalaya* schools: 'to provide quality education to the children from Class I to XII under one roof as is being provided in the private public schools' (Government of NCT of Delhi, n.d.).[6] *Pratibha vikas vidyalaya* schools were initiated to provide quality education from class VI to XII for talented students from disadvantaged sections of society. The majority of existing schools that do not follow this model began to be called non-*sarvodaya* schools.

Pratibha vikas vidyalaya schools are typically better equipped than *sarovodaya* schools, which in turn, are generally better equipped than non-*sarvodaya* schools. Whereas non-*sarvodaya* schools, in principle, accommodate all students from their locality, *sarvodaya* and *pratibha vikas vidyalaya* schools have limited seats. The former select students by lottery and the latter hold admission tests (Juneja, 2010, p. 20). The issue of testing in *pratibha vikas* schools is interesting, since Section 13 of the RTE Act prohibits schools from screening for admission in elementary schools, but does permit random selection by lottery (National Commission for Protection of Child Rights, 2010, p. 6).

Owing to their higher numbers and more open admission policies, non-*sarvodaya* or local body schools remain the most accessible to children from poorer backgrounds compared with the other two state-run types. However, these schools are also reported as being the most malfunctioning in the school system. It is in this context that unrecognised schools in Delhi emerged to cater to poorer groups dissatisfied with the schools otherwise available to them.

Conceptual Framework: inter-organisational relations and the 'Shadow Institutional Framework'

Several studies on inter-organisational relations provide insightful perspectives on the mechanism of organisational affiliation. Higgins and Gulati (2003) argue that 'because organizations are not able to generate internally all of the resources required to maintain themselves, they often face situations of dependence which necessitate matching up with powerful groups in their environment' (p. 245). Similarly, Pfeffer and Salancik (1978) claim that 'organisations act to achieve social legitimacy and occasionally achieve this legitimacy through a process involving identification with other legitimate social actors' (p. 222). Furthermore, Galaskiewicz (1985) suggests three aims/motives of an organisation in affiliating with other organisations: resource procurement and allocation; political advocacy; and organisational legitimation.[7]

With this in mind, the following studies examining regulatory processes in the Indian context draw our attention to the potential risks associated with the implementation of the RTE Act on unrecognised schools. First, studies have revealed that state regulation of the private sector may often serve as a rent-seeking opportunity (Lambsdorff, 2002; Harriss-White, 2003; Sharma & Ramachandran, 2009). Studies of low-fee private schooling in India have found that some unrecognised schools failing to meet recognition criteria succeeded in obtaining it through informal procedures and unofficial payments to education officials (Tooley & Dixon, 2003, 2005a; Srivastava, 2007, 2008). I use the term 'falsely recognised schools' to refer to schools that obtained recognition through corrupt practices (including bribery) or political connections.

In this regard, conceptually, Harriss-White (2003) outlines two types of informal economy: (a) an informal economy 'that is not registered for the purpose of taxation and/or regulation by the State' (p. 4); and (b) an informal economy functioning 'in the formal economy' but 'not covered by state regulation or record-keeping' (p. 6). We can conceive of falsely recognised schools as occupying a place in the part of the informal economy that falls within the formal institutions (Type B), while unrecognised schools occupy a place in the informal economy outside the framework of formal institutions (Type A).

Similarly, according to Srivastava (2008), the 'shadow institutional framework', a concept empirically constructed from her study on low-fee private schooling in Uttar Pradesh, is 'a codified yet informal set of norms and procedures' (p. 452). According to Srivastava (2008), '[d]espite the fact that LFP [low-fee private] case study schools were independently owned, managed and financed, they used the shadow framework to manipulate and mediate the formal policy and regulatory framework for their benefit and formed part of the *de facto* LFP sector, a sub-sector of the greater private unaided sector' (p. 452). Srivastava (2008) explains that the shadow institutional framework gained practical legitimacy for low-fee private schools because it reduced 'uncertainty by employing organisational structures and institutional mechanisms that were proven successful in the experience of other LFP schools' (p. 452), allowing unrecognised low-fee private schools to function since they did not meet required norms to operate officially.

Srivastava identifies two elements of the shadow framework – namely, common internal institutions and external institutions. The former enables 'schools to be identified as LFP school organisations and reduce information asymmetries on properties of the formal institutional framework and on the informal arrangements of the shadow framework' (Srivastava, 2008, p. 462). The latter is 'established to minimise transaction costs of interacting with the state in key areas of organisational performance, identified by case study school owners as obtaining recognition and qualifying students for examinations' (Srivastava, 2008, p. 466). She identified four elements of common internal institutions: fee practices and fee collection structures; admission procedures; internal management and processes; and hiring of and employment terms for staff. She also identified four elements of external institutions: affiliation procedures between unrecognised low-fee private and recognised schools; procedures for delivering formal secondary schooling; state board examination provision; and norms and practices for obtaining recognition. These were identified as key areas of performance because they were quality signifiers and helped in gaining legitimacy.

In the context of the RTE Act, obtaining recognition for unrecognised low-fee private schools in Delhi is even more politically charged. Given the actual practices of granting recognition, it is possible that if the RTE Act is forced on unrecognised schools, unofficial regulation by government authorities and the numbers of falsely recognised schools may increase, rather than the desired outcome of increased compliance by unrecognised schools to the formal rules and policy framework. Consequently, the right to quality education would be hindered. Furthermore, while unrecognised schools have emerged because of the perceived and actual poor quality of state schools, there is little evidence to suggest that the quality of private schools (in particular, low-fee private schools) is much better. They have, nonetheless, added to the total supply of schools available to some lower-income groups. If, in this context, unrecognised schools are closed under the RTE Act, increasing access may be harmed, hindering the right to access education.

Methods

This chapter stems from a doctoral study on low-fee private schools in Delhi. Data were collected during a 10-month period over nearly two years, from September 2008 to February 2009, from September 2009 to February 2010, and during August 2010. Results presented in this chapter are from primary data collected from interviews and observations at nine case study schools, a sub-set of interviews with relevant policy and school officials, and analysis of relevant Delhi High Court documents. The wider study also included questionnaires for teachers and parents at three focus schools (from among the nine case study schools) and follow-up interviews with selected respondents. In the interest of space, those results are presented only as contextualising comments in this chapter as necessary.

Upon consultation with the Directorate of Education, private school managers (recognised and unrecognised) and several NGOs, the author selected nine unrecognised schools in Shahdara, most from the official unrecognised school list, as case study schools for this study. Shahdara is known as the most disadvantaged area in Delhi and, as mentioned above, contains the largest number of unrecognised schools identified by the Directorate of Education and the Municipal Corporation of Delhi. Of the nine schools that were selected for this study, six were randomly chosen from the list of unrecognised schools. The other three were included during fieldwork to incorporate unrecognised schools that were not included on the initial list.

To investigate school managers' backgrounds and build rapport, multiple visits to case study schools were made, with the exception of two schools (Schools H and I), which refused to provide information on certain aspects.[8] In each visit, an interview lasting approximately 90 minutes was conducted with the manager to collect background data on each school, including: manager's background; year of school's establishment; recognition status; level of instruction; number of students; fee structure; and curriculum content. For School G, an unrecognised school operating as part of a chain, the manager of a recognised school in the chain was also interviewed to clarify the institutional arrangements between it and School G. Three schools (Schools A, D and G) were chosen as focus schools to further investigate the status of teachers and parents at unrecognised schools. Each focus school was visited a maximum of 10 times to obtain detailed observations of operational procedures and mechanisms, and to administer questionnaires to teachers and parents.

Data on socio-economic backgrounds of households, together with parents' and teachers' general understandings and perceptions of focus schools, were collected from 30 teachers and 129 parents. Three teachers and 10 parents with different socio-economic backgrounds from each focus school were selected for follow-up interviews. Teachers were selected on the basis of their qualifications, salary level, marital status and teaching experience at schools other than unrecognised schools. Parents were selected on the basis of their educational qualifications, salary levels, job types and children's experience at schools other than unrecognised schools. Interviews with teachers lasted 30 to 60 minutes, and 60 to 90 minutes with parents.

Finally, interviews were conducted with representatives from Social Jurist, the Co-ordination Committee of Public Schools, the Directorate of Education, the Municipal Corporation of Delhi and an unrecognised school manager affiliated with the Co-ordination Committee to gain insight on past litigation. The following Delhi High Court documents were obtained and analysed for this chapter: the final High Court judgment Delhi dated 8 February 2008 (see High Court of Delhi, 2008a); Special Leave Petition (Civil) No. 21952 of 2008 (see High Court of Delhi, 2008b); list of dates and synopses; relevant affidavits and action reports submitted to the court by concerned authorities; and the list of unrecognised schools.

Case-study School Profiles

Table II presents case-study school profiles. Most schools in the study were established after 2000, with the exception of School G, which was much older (1960), and H, established somewhat earlier (1993). Five of the nine schools operated up to Class V (primary), and the rest up to Class VIII (upper primary/junior). All schools except School D, which was recognised at the primary level but operated until upper primary, were fully unrecognised. School G had been running on an unrecognised basis for nearly 50 years. With the exception of School D's primary section, at the beginning of the fieldwork for this study, all case study schools were unrecognised, and six schools were in the process of applying for recognition. However, during the course of fieldwork, School A's primary section, School C, and School D's junior section obtained recognition.

Parents' questionnaires (n=129) at focus schools revealed that most fathers were engaged in daily labour jobs, such as shop-keeping, factory labour, or driving a cycle-*riksha*. Nearly all the mothers were homemakers. The average monthly family income was approximately Rs. 3000-5000, significantly lower than the official cut-off for groups defined as 'economically weaker sections' of society, earning less than Rs. 100,000 per year (Government of NCT of Delhi, 2011). The range of monthly incomes of the parents at each focus school was as follows: School A: Rs. 2500-3000; School D: Rs. 2500-4000; and School G: Rs. 3000-10,000. The educational background of parents at School A was the lowest among the three focus schools. Most parents at School D had Class X certificates (high school), whereas many of the parents at school G had Class XII certificates (higher secondary).

School	Year established	Applied for recognition?	Level of education	Number of students	Tuition fee	Concession?
A	2007	✓	Nursery-8th	198	Rs.200	✓
B	2002	✓	Nursery-8th	276	Rs.50-100	✓
C	2006	✓	1st-8th	300	Rs.500	✓
D	2000	✓	Nursery-8th (1st-5th recognised)	750*	Rs.300	✓
E	2006	✓	Nursery-5th	120	Rs.120-240	✓
F	2000	✓	Nursery-5th	216	Rs.100-200	✓
G	1960	×	Nursery-5th	360	Rs.300	✓
H**	1993	×	Nursery-5th	N/A	Rs.225-400	✓
I**	2000	×	Nursery-5th	N/A	N/A	✓

School	Manager's background (gender)	Textbooks	Medium of instruction
A	Ex-government school teacher (M)	Government & Private	Hindi and English (Separate)
B	Entrepreneur (M)	Private (Class 1-5); Government (Class 6-8)	Hindi and English (Combined)
C	Entrepreneur (M)	Government	Hindi and English (Separate)
D	Ex-government school principal (M)	Private	Hindi and English (Separate)
E	Ex-tailor (M)	Private	Hindi and English (Combined)
F	Housewife (F)	Government & Private	Hindi and English (Combined)
G	Principal of private recognised school (F)	Private	English Only
H**	Housewife (F)	Private	Hindi and English (Combined)
I**	Housewife (F)	N/A	N/A

*The number of students at School D includes 180 from Class I to V which are recognised; **School H and School I refused to provide data on certain aspects. These cases are marked as not available (N/A).

Table II. Case study school profiles.
Source: Researcher field data. Data supplied by case study school managers.

Institutional Arrangements of Unrecognised Low-fee Private Schools

Similar to Srivastava's (2008) analysis, results of the study revealed common internal and external institutions across case study schools. However, just two of the four external institutional elements (i.e. affiliation procedures and norms and practices for recognition) were investigated here since the other two were not applicable because schools did not offer secondary education. Also similar to Srivastava's (2008) findings, this study found that although unrecognised low-fee private schools were not formally recognised by the government, they nonetheless managed to provide transfer certificates (official school records) for students who attended them through informal procedures, such as enrolling their students on the books of recognised schools for a fee and/or purchasing transfer certificates from recognised private schools and charging parents an extra fee. As a result, many unrecognised low-fee private school students eventually managed to transfer to recognised schools and/or sit for official exams. Results about the institutional arrangements are presented in more depth below.

Common Internal Institutions

Fee practices and collection structures. Since the parents of students at case study schools overwhelmingly belonged to lower-income groups, they could not afford to pay high tuition fees. The highest fee charged was Rs. 500/month (School C), and the mean fee was Rs. 252/month, which represented approximately 6.5% of the mean monthly minimum wage for unskilled workers in Delhi between 2008 and 2010 (the fieldwork period). All case study schools claimed to offer fee concessions for the neediest families. Examples of concessions included full fee exemption in cases where family income fell below the poverty line or fee exemption for one child if three or more children from the same family attended. However, despite fee concessions and relatively lower fees, it was difficult for some families to pay. Most schools were flexible on payment, as described by School D's manager, who termed his fee collection approach as 'lenient', claiming:

> Most parents do not pay on the due date. It happens quite often that we wait for two to three months. Some parents don't pay the fee for half a year. Last year, we had difficult time collecting fees and we had a negative balance because of this. (Manager, School D interview, translated from the original in Hindi)

Admission procedures. Admission procedures at case study schools were flexible compared with those at government and recognised private schools, and particularly compared with those at schools targeting elite and middle-class groups. For example, case study schools did not observe the official enrolment period, allowing students to enrol at any time of the year, and official documents usually required for admission at recognised schools (e.g.

parents' affidavit or students' transfer certificates) were not necessarily requested. According to school managers, almost all children who sought admission to their schools were accepted. It is important to note that the provisions of the RTE Act had not been implemented during the time of the fieldwork. The scenario has since changed for all schools operating in Delhi, and these practices are now required of schools in general (see Noronha & Srivastava, 2012).

Internal management structure and processes. Case-study school managers' or their families' inside knowledge of and experience of education networks with recognised or government schools helped unrecognised schools reduce information asymmetries with regards to the formal regulatory framework's requirements, minimising uncertainty of operating as unrecognised schools. This observation is similar to Oliver's (2001) notion of 'network learning', wherein organisations acquire knowledge from other organisations 'through alliances to facilitate the development of their internal capabilities' (p. 482). Consequently, case study schools appeared to enhance their credibility and succeeded in attracting parents.

Some case-study school managers had direct experience of working at recognised or government schools (Schools A, D and G). School A's manager was an ex-government school teacher and had obtained three different awards from the Directorate of Education for his teaching achievements. Parents at this school explained that it convinced them about the wisdom of accessing it. Although a former government school principal was officially registered as School D's manager, his son, an incumbent government school teacher, assumed his father's position in practice.

School G was an interesting case. It was managed by a family that also operated a recognised private aided and unaided school. Some parents at this school claimed that they had a strong attachment to it, believing it to be a 'good school' because it was managed by a family that operated a renowned private school group with a bigger recognised private school. Of the managers who did not have direct experience in these settings, most had close family members or contacts in recognised or government schools. For example, the fathers of the managers of Schools B and C were former government school teachers.

The analysis showed that unrecognised schools in Delhi could provide formal education regardless of whether or not they were recognised. Case study schools generally followed curriculum practices similar to those of recognised schools. While government schools use only textbooks published by the National Council of Educational Research and Training (NCERT), similar to recognised schools, many case study schools used privately published books in addition. As is the case in recognised schools, all case study schools held end-of-semester exams to evaluate students' learning. However, whether these exams actually measured learning levels was questionable, as, similar to Tooley and Dixon's (2005a) and Srivastava's (2007) findings, one teacher claimed:

> The examinations are prepared according to the students' ability so that they won't fail and will remain at school. This lenient examination system allows unrecognised schools to retain students and maintain popularity among the poor. (Interview with Teacher, School G)

Most case study schools offered instruction in English and Hindi. Some schools had separate English- and Hindi-medium classes (Schools A, C and D), while others had combined English and Hindi classes (Schools B, E, F and H) in which both languages were used by teachers. However, the study revealed low English competency among teachers at case study schools. Classroom observations and teacher interviews showed that although they were able to read out English textbooks, most teachers were unable to construct sentences necessary to instruct in English, and spoken fluency was low. Nonetheless, all case-study school managers were unanimous in explaining that English instruction was an important element in attracting parents from poorer backgrounds.

Hiring and employment terms for staff. Many teachers at focus schools revealed that they were hired by managers through family/friend connections. Many teachers at Schools A and G were family members, relatives or close friends of the managers. Some teachers (mainly at School D) explained that they had approached the manager directly for the job. While most teachers at Schools A and G were retained during the fieldwork period from 2008 to 2010, there was high turnover at School D because many of them, young women, got married (only three of 12 teachers were retained by the end).

School D's de facto manager explained that it was difficult to find and recruit teachers with appropriate qualifications from the local area, given its low socio-economic profile. The majority of teachers had an undergraduate degree or high school/higher secondary certificates, but did not have official qualifications required to teach at recognised schools. School G employed the highest number of teachers with university qualifications, but only four of the 17 teachers at that school had professional teaching qualifications.

Case-study school managers stated that since their schools relied on tuition payments from low-income parents, it was impossible to pay teachers government prescribed rates. According to the DSEAR, teachers' salaries at recognised private schools should not be lower than at government schools, and should be in line with levels set by the Central Pay Commission. The latest recommendation of the Sixth Central Pay Commission suggested a minimum monthly salary of Rs. 22,000 for a primary school teacher and Rs. 27,000 for an upper primary teacher (Puri, 2010). Many teachers in this study were paid as little as or less than one-tenth of the prescribed salary (between Rs. 1500 and Rs. 2500). However, it is likely that salaries at recognised private schools also did not meet government norms. According to one teacher who transferred to School A from a recognised private school:

> I decided to work here because the salary was better than other recognised and unrecognised schools where I searched for a post ... [and] because the quality of education there was not good. (Interview with teacher, School A, translated from the original in Hindi)

External Institutions

Affiliation procedures. This study found that unrecognised low-fee private schools managed to transfer students to recognised schools. According to official DSEAR rules, students from unrecognised schools at the elementary level could transfer to recognised schools on the basis of an affidavit by the parents stating the child's schooling history. However, when transferring to recognised schools at the secondary level, students had to have valid transfer certificates (official school record) issued by a recognised school, or else they had to pass a public examination set by the Directorate of Education.[9] Since unrecognised schools do not have the authority to issue transfer certificates, single-operation case-study elementary schools affiliated themselves with recognised schools in order to provide students with transfer certificates by negotiating with them or purchasing them from recognised schools (similar to Srivastava, 2008).

For example, School D's de facto manager explained that he purchased transfer certificates at a reasonable price from a nearby recognised low-fee private school. School A's manager stated that he received transfer certificates for free from a reputed recognised higher-fee school catering to middle-class families, because it was operated by a relative. By forming a bilateral contract, or leveraging family relations with recognised private schools, single-operation unrecognised schools in the study succeed in securing students' transition to recognised secondary schools without government involvement. This affiliation arrangement was mutually beneficial for unrecognised and recognised schools. It provided an extra revenue stream for recognised schools, while allowing unrecognised schools to secure student transfer at secondary level.

Obtaining recognition. Data revealed that many case study schools were unlikely to meet official recognition criteria. These schools seemed to have used unstated but commonly understood procedures to obtain recognition by bribing local officials (similar to Tooley & Dixon, 2003, 2005a; Srivastava, 2007, 2008). Managers of Schools A, C and D, which obtained recognition during fieldwork, were unwilling to answer questions on this with reference to their schools. However, they agreed that political connections and bribes were important factors in schools obtaining recognition, claiming that such practices were common. School A disclosed that its infrastructure was improved by a local political leader who provided windows in all classrooms and built a new classroom, but noted that teacher salary and qualifications did not meet norms even after receiving recognition. School D explained that there had been no fundamental change at his school since obtaining recognition. Noting such discrepancies, School C's manager had explained before his school acquired recognition that

> there are recognised schools whose school conditions are similar to our school as per the norms of the DSEAR. But we are not able to get the recognition. There must have been some mutual understanding between the government and the owners of these schools. (Interview with manager, School C)

These observations suggest the existence of falsely recognised schools, and that the difference between recognised and unrecognised low-fee private schools may not be great (see also Tooley & Dixon 2005a; Srivastava, 2008; Sharma & Ramachandran, 2009). In Srivastava's (2007, 2008) study, all low-fee private schools were single-operation schools. Thus, for the unrecognised schools in her study, affiliation with recognised private schools was seen as part of the external institutions necessary for them to manipulate the formal framework. This was also the case for Schools A and D in this study, and for most of the other case study schools. However, the study indicates that low-fee private schools that are part of a chain may have different mechanisms, as outlined below in the case of School G.

Institutional arrangements of running a chain with an unrecognised school: the case of School G. The group which ran School G, an unrecognised low-fee private school, operated two other schools in a chain – one, a recognised English-medium higher-fee school (nursery through to Class XII), and the other, a Hindi-medium private-aided school (Class I to X). On the face of it, the three schools had little in common except that they were run by members of the same family. Similar to Kingdon's (1996) older study of private schools in Uttar Pradesh, the aided school's funding structure was subsidised at 95% from government funds. The remaining 5%, on the other hand, was generated by unrecognised School G's surplus.[10]

While School G financially supported the chain's private aided school by providing its surplus, the former's popularity was maintained by the strong reputation of the chain, confirmed by parent interviews. Most parents claimed that they were generally satisfied with sending their children to School G because it was under the umbrella of the larger group with a long history of providing education in the local area, because they trusted the 'brand', and additionally, because it was an English-medium and low-fee school.

School G seemed to further increase its desirability by providing a potential transition route to a recognised private school, primarily to the recognised higher-fee school in the chain. As with other case study schools, School G's students were overwhelmingly from poorer backgrounds. Most transferred to state government secondary schools because of financial constraints. However, School G's manager explained that approximately 10% of students at the school could afford to transfer to the higher-fee chain school, where the fee was five times greater (Rs. 1500/month at primary and up to Rs. 2200/month at senior secondary), showing the potential heterogeneity of low-fee private school clients.

While the higher-fee recognised school and the unrecognised school were run by members of the same family and both were meant to be English-medium, there were marked differences in teacher qualifications and infrastructure. The majority of School G's teachers were unqualified, while those at the high-fee recognised school were all qualified. School G was created in the manager's old house and had no playground or library, but the higher-fee school had two acres of land and facilities, such as physics and chemistry laboratories and computers. Despite these differences, according to the manager of the higher-fee recognised school, students transferred from School G managed to continue their education at the higher-fee school because of teachers' efforts. In any case, the arrangement was beneficial for both schools:

> Students from School G have difficulty in the beginning of their study, but they gradually catch up with our students who have been studying at our recognised school from Class I because our teachers make effort to cope with their problem by paying more attention ... We receive many students from neighbouring private schools from secondary class because most of them only provide elementary education. But the strength [i.e. enrolment] of our school in the elementary level is less, so, we are happy to receive students from School G at upper primary class level. We need more strength. (Manager of recognised high-fee chain school)

In effect, the chain's management succeeded in securing the operation of all three of its schools. The chaining arrangement helped meet the aided school's expenses by operating the unrecognised school, reinforced the reputation of the low-fee school (School G) by affiliating it with the higher-fee school, and secured some enrolment for the higher-fee school by establishing a direct transition route from School G. This shows the dependency, in certain cases, of recognised schools and unrecognised low-fee private schools on securing enrolments and finances. Thus, the case of School G illustrates that the growth of small-scale unrecognised schools may contribute to the growth of recognised schools, and vice versa.

The following sections turn to an analysis of how unrecognised schools in Delhi were challenged by state law in the Delhi High Court preceding the implementation of the RTE Act, and during its early mandate.

Disputing the Regulation of Unrecognised Schools Pre-RTE Act: Delhi High Court and Supreme Court orders on unrecognised schools

Pfeffer and Salancik (1978) argue that organisations are 'likely to become involved in political activity when governmental intervention begins to affect their economic well-being and certainty' (p. 222). The findings of this study were in line with this. In 2006, Social Jurist, an NGO comprising a group of lawyers and social activists who had worked on children's rights to education for more than 10 years, filed a PIL to the Delhi High Court triggering a dispute regarding the legitimacy of the growing number of unrecognised schools. The NGO insisted that unrecognised school standards were dismal, with unqualified and underpaid teachers, arguing in the proceedings that their students are often denied admission to the next level at government and recognised schools since they do not possess a transfer certificate. However, as the data above show, while this may officially have been the case, unrecognised schools used other informal procedures to enable transition at higher levels.

Social Jurist further argued that the fees and other demands were exorbitant and unjustified, particularly in relation to poor facilities at unrecognised schools, stressing that under the DSEAR, only recognised schools should be operational. It also claimed that unrecognised schools exploit children and teachers because they do not conform to requirements regarding equipment, teacher qualifications, or salary as stipulated in the Delhi Act. Hence, the NGO argued, unrecognised schools should either apply for recognition or be closed down. In February 2008, the Delhi High Court ruled that if schools did not apply for recognition they would have to close down, or the authorities should institute school closures.

In response to the High Court's ruling, the Co-ordination Committee of Public Schools in Delhi, with recognised and unrecognised school members, filed a special leave petition in August 2008 seeking permission to appeal to the Supreme Court, and requesting a stay against the High Court decision. Contrary to Social Jurist's position, the Co-ordination Committee insisted that unrecognised schools protected children's rights by providing education to students in areas where appropriate facilities and quality education were unavailable at an affordable cost.

The committee further argued that parents in these areas were not interested in sending their children to government schools because teachers there tended not to be committed even if they were qualified. Referring to Tooley and Dixon's (2005b) work on low-fee private schooling in India, the committee stated that unrecognised school students achieve higher marks than government school students. Thus, the committee contended that parents sending their children to unrecognised schools were happy and willing to access them regardless of recognition status since they could not afford recognised private school fees.

Most relevant to the discussion here, the Co-ordination Committee argued that the DSEAR itself originally envisaged two types of schools – namely, recognised and unrecognised schools – thus claiming that it is not mandatory for schools to seek recognition. This claim is based on Rule 141 of the DSEAR outlining the admission procedure for children who had not previously attended a recognised school:

> Parent of guardian to submit an affidavit. (1) Where a candidate who had not previously attended any recognised school applies for admission to class II or to any higher class up to class VIII of a recognised school, the parent or guardian of such candidate shall give full history of the previous education of such candidate and furnish an affidavit on a non-judicial stamp paper duly attested to the effect that such candidate for admission had not attended any recognised school. (Government of NCT of Delhi, 1977)

The committee interpreted Rule 141 to mean that if a child who had not previously attended a recognised school was eligible to enrol in a recognised school, it should follow that unrecognised schools can be allowed to function. Following from this interpretation, the committee also suggested that instituting unrecognised school closure or compelling recognition through established certification procedures and norms were not the only options available for regulating unrecognised schools, arguing instead that unrecognised schools could also be regulated by creating new criteria or mechanisms.

In February 2009, the Directorate of Education submitted an affidavit to the Supreme Court admitting that Rule 141 provided for the existence of unrecognised schools, and further, that there were no norms or regulations in the DSEAR for such schools. The Directorate of Education also reported that a government committee consisting of concerned authorities (i.e. the Directorate of Education, the Municipal Corporation of Delhi and the New Delhi Municipal Corporation) had been set up to formulate guidelines for unrecognised schools with respect to the land, infrastructure and facilities, and teachers' qualifications. As a result, the Supreme Court handed down a judgment in April 2009 to dispose of the High Court's order, and gave directions to the concerned authorities not to institute school closures until a report on the status of unrecognised schools was submitted by the government committee, and a final decision taken.

Although it was argued that unrecognised schools were legal under the DSEAR, the government committee and Supreme Court agreed on the necessity of state regulation for unrecognised schools. However, the government committee did not supply a report or issue guidelines, and none of the concerned parties, including Social Jurist, which started the proceedings, approached government authorities to act. Consequently, unrecognised schools in Delhi remained functional outside the bounds of government regulation. During the course of this study, there was no evidence that unrecognised schools were closed. However, these schools are now challenged by the RTE Act, owing to Section 18(1) compelling schools to be recognised or face closure.

The analysis drew this study to focus on the potential impact of recognised schools on the existence and expansion of the unrecognised low-fee private sector. It is interesting to note that the membership of the Co-ordination Committee, the lead actor contesting the High Court order, comprised both unrecognised and recognised schools, two-thirds of which were low-fee. Interview data confirmed that many recognised member schools owned unrecognised schools. This finding suggests that recognised member schools opposed the High Court ruling because they sought to expand their operations by chaining or branching, initially by running unrecognised schools. There was evidence that the interests of unrecognised schools were also linked with recognised schools for reasons of legitimacy and lobbying. As one manager of a single-operation unrecognised school and member of the Co-ordination Committee stressed:

> It was important for us to appeal to the court not as a group of unrecognised schools, but as a group of private schools including both recognised and unrecognised schools. The latter has more power when faced with official issues. (Interview, unrecognised school manager)

The RTE Act and Regulating Unrecognised Low-fee Private Schools: potential options

The scenario for unrecognised schools in Delhi has changed since the RTE Act was passed, and the discussion above must be viewed in this light by anticipating changes in the institutional context and for unrecognised schools. As the act is in the early stages of implementation, implications are not yet fully clear (see Noronha & Srivastava, 2012 for an initial study on Delhi). Nonetheless, some options can be considered, given the institutional arrangements between unrecognised and recognised private schools, and the broader policy context. Despite the previous ruling, unrecognised schools now are compelled to apply for recognition under the RTE Act since, as central government law, it supersedes state legislation. This section explores potential alternatives by which unrecognised schools in Delhi may be regulated under the RTE Act - namely: (1) standardised regulation; (2) non-state- or self-regulation; and (3) classified regulation.

Standardised Regulation

The first option, standardised state regulation of unrecognised schools, refers to certifying schools that abide by norms and standards prescribed in the act, similar to the recognition process that was already in place. However, as our data indicate, this option seems unrealistic owing to financial implications, particularly for low-fee schools. As a result, if standardised regulation is enforced, many unrecognised schools will likely face closure. Ostensibly, their students will need to be accommodated in government schools, insufficient in number to meet demand. Moreover, as data indicate, given the de facto mode of falsely recognising schools, standardised regulation may result in increased numbers of recognised schools that do not actually meet norms, aggravating quality issues.

Non-state- or Self-regulation

The second option, non-state- or self-regulation, draws on Harriss-White's (2003) and Tooley and Dixon's (2005a) previous work. Harriss-White (2003) argues that 'the fact it [informal economy] is not regulated by the State does not mean that it is not regulated at all, for there are many non-state means for regulation' (p. 4). She describes non-state regulation as involving 'the use of trusted family labour; bilateral and multilateral contracts, especially repeated and interlocked contracts, usually through networks; the importance of individual or collective reputation; regulation through collective institutions' (Harriss-White, 2003, pp. 74-75). These appear to correspond to the informal set of norms and procedures that was employed by case study schools to function. However, as we have seen in the discussion thus far, these informal arrangements may not necessarily ensure education quality.

Conversely, Tooley and Dixon's (2005a) notion of 'self-regulation' focuses on the quality issue, maintaining that a private accreditation service that evaluates the quality of schools may take the place of conventional state regulation. According to Tooley and Dixon (2005a), 'accreditation criteria could focus on outcomes, particularly those that are of concern to parents, such as teacher and student proficiency in English, and measures such as pupil improvement and progress' (p. 283) in addition to basic facilities, such as separate toilets for boys and girls and provisions for extra-curricular activities (p. 283). They contend that the credibility of accredited low-fee private schools would increase, and maintain that accreditation would provide information on school quality, minimising the awareness/information gap among parents. As parents' lack of information about or experience with the formal schooling system, particularly for those from lower socio-economic groups, is seen as rendering them susceptible to exploitation by private schools, accreditation may be effective in eliciting more informed demand, leading to improvements in school quality.[11]

As found in the larger study, even when school choice is made with some knowledge about low-fee private school quality, economic or geographic constraints could be obstacles to choosing higher quality schools. In addition, low-fee private schools, particularly those considered 'good', may not have the capacity to accommodate all students wishing to access them. Moreover, considering the scarcity of qualified teachers generally available to low-fee private schools, 'good' schools may still not be able to meet the RTE Act's teacher qualification norms, and may nevertheless face closure because, ultimately, they cannot meet the state's stringent requirements, let alone cope with competition from other low-fee private schools.[12]

Classified Regulation

The third option, termed 'classified regulation', was proposed by the Co-ordination Committee, which claimed that current recognition criteria are too stringent for unrecognised schools catering to lower-income groups. Noting teacher salaries as a major recognition obstacle for low-fee private schools in particular, the Co-ordination Committee suggested that rather than having a standardised norm across all private schools, teachers' salaries should be classified according to schools' fee structures.[13] Section 23(3) of the RTE Act stipulates that teacher 'salary and allowances payable ... shall be such as may be prescribed' (Government of India, 2009). As there is no further specification, state law prevails according to legislative procedure – that is, the DSEAR, which mandates salaries in line with the Sixth Pay Commission. Relaxing this criterion would allow some unrecognised low-fee schools to gain some form of recognition status under a certain 'class' and operate legally.

The Co-ordination Committee has undertaken much political advocacy in this regard, succeeding in attracting the state's attention. There were media reports that the Minister of Human Resource Development, Kapil Sibal, requested the Delhi Chief Minister to review the DSEAR regarding teachers' salaries (*Times of India*, 2010). According to reports, although the minister seemed to be against private schools operating for a profit, he was keen to ensure that unrecognised schools do not face financial obstacles in obtaining recognition. The Co-ordination Committee described its efforts in facilitating negotiations with the state government to ward off policy that may threaten unrecognised schools:

> We first approached the MHRD Minister Sibal, to review the criteria for teachers' salary as prescribed by the DSEAR. Sibal recommended us to consult with the Chief Minister of Delhi, because it [the rules and regulations regarding teachers' salary in Delhi] is a state matter. After that we held a meeting with the Chief Minister and DoE [Directorate of Education] officers to relax the criteria for teachers' salary. (Co-ordination Committee Interviewee)

At the time of writing, a final ruling had not been made. However, the Co-ordination Committee claimed that, in response to its request, the Delhi government had established a committee to review the DSEAR. There are of course many other requirements in the act which it may not be feasible for unrecognised low-fee private schools to implement at once. Considering the constraints and context within which unrecognised schools in Delhi are operating, classified regulation seems to be the most appropriate and realistic form of regulation for them.

Concluding Remarks

The analysis in this chapter of the legal disputes regarding the regulation of unrecognised schools and the examination of the way these schools operate reveal that the existence and expansion of unrecognised schools in Delhi is partially supported by recognised schools at the level of policy and practice. At the level of practice, unrecognised low-fee private schools were affiliated with recognised private schools (including low-fee and higher-fee schools) to secure their operation. Both unrecognised and recognised schools benefited from these informal arrangements (i.e. through financial gain, increasing student numbers, and establishing a transition route from unrecognised low-fee private schools to recognised schools).

At the level of policy, the Co-ordination Committee, with a membership of unrecognised and recognised schools, played an important role in fighting a Delhi High Court ruling ordering the closure of unrecognised schools pre-RTE. It also facilitated negotiations with the state regarding the potential implementation of certain provisions of the RTE Act. Data also indicate that it was difficult for unrecognised low-fee private schools to comply with the formal rules and policy framework. As such, they actively engaged in employing shadow rules in collusion with state officials, particularly with a view to obtaining recognition. Within this context, it is reasonable to assume that introducing new or further regulatory compulsions may result in creating new opportunities for informal regulation by private schools and state actors.

In her conceptual framing, Harriss-White (2003) also refers to this point in the following contexts: 'instead of being merely bypassed or ignored, formal state law and institutions ... form the basis for a regime of private extortion' (p. 80). She even states that in such cases, 'there will be no change in corruption under a regime of privatization if the State continues to regulate market structure and conduct directly or indirectly through quasi-state organizations' (Harriss-White, 2003, p. 92). Similarly, Sharma and Ramachandran (2009) note that, in India, institutionally, 'given the present mode of functioning, the government's capacity to regulate the private sector is very limited and as in the government system, the emergence of a patronage-based, rent-seeking nexus is very likely' (p. 192).

These concerns notwithstanding, education provision cannot be achieved without the state's initiative. This is highlighted by Kumar (2008), who states that 'nowhere in the world has a national system of education evolved without the state playing the lead role' (p. 8). Thus, the biggest challenge for the RTE Act in assuring the right to access quality education appears to lie in solving institutional inconsistencies caused by uneven state application of regulation. Perhaps the first step can be for the state to institute effective monitoring mechanisms and increase the quality of state schools, cementing its commitment to the right to education, and rendering redundant the existence of unrecognised schools.

Acknowledgements

This study was funded by the Japan Society for the Promotion of Science when the author was pursuing a PhD at the Graduate School of Education, Kyoto University. Thanks are due to Hitoshi Sugimoto, Nalini Juneja and J.B.G. Tilak for their constructive comments on this study. I am grateful to Varsha Anand for her support and commitment to translating interviews. I would also like to express my sincere gratitude to Prachi Srivastava and the reviewer for their insightful comments.

Notes

[1] This chapter draws on a previous article (Ohara, 2012). Earlier versions of this article were presented at the International Workshop of South Asian Education in Kyoto (February 2011).

[2] The purpose of the RTE Act is to secure free and compulsory education for all the children in the 6-14-year age range. The act stipulates the main roles for concerned agencies such as the state, school managers, teachers, parents, civil societies, etc.

[3] Interviews with CCS staff indicated the monthly fee for what they called 'budget schools', to range from Rs. 300 to Rs. 800. The Co-ordination Committee noted that private schools with fees below Rs. 800 would be classified as low-fee private schools in Delhi. It should be noted, however, that fee ranges of low-fee private schools may depend on the distribution of private schools available in the areas where studies are conducted.

[4] Calculations are based on official published minimum wages rates for Delhi (see Government of NCT of Delhi, 2012). At the time of the fieldwork, $USD 1= Rs. 45.

[5] Under the act, a group of seven or more persons can form societies for the promotion of any literary, scientific or charitable purpose by a memorandum of association and registration (Government of India, 1860).

[6] 'Public' here is being used in the classical British sense to refer to non-state, independent schools. 'Private' and 'public' are sometimes used interchangeably in India in this sense.

[7] Political advocacy is explained as coalition formation and efforts at collective action. Organisational legitimation refers to efforts at identifying with highly legitimate community and/or societal symbols.

[8] In all cases, owners, managers and principals were the same individual.

[9] Some of these practices have changed since the passing of the RTE Act, though the impact of the full implementation of the RTE Act on these procedures is unclear.

[10] Kingdon explains that many aided schools run unrecognised schools at primary sections to generate surpluses in order to cross-subsidise their government-funded, tuition-free junior and secondary sections.

[11] Parents in this study were not provided with sufficient or complete information about the schools they accessed, and even when they were, they were often unable to evaluate what constituted a 'good education' or 'good schooling'.

[12] In accordance with Section 23(1) of the RTE Act, in a notification dated 23 August 2010, the National Council for Teacher Education declared professional qualifications (Diploma or Bachelor of Education) as the minimum qualifications required for teachers of Classes I to VIII (Government of India, 2010).

[13] The Co-ordination Committee categorises private schools in Delhi into five groups according to fee structure: (1) below Rs. 500; (2) Rs. 501-1000; (3) Rs. 1001-1500; (4) Rs. 1501-2000; and (5) above Rs. 2000 per month.

References

Aggarwal, Y. (2000) *Public and Private Partnership in Primary Education in India: a study of unrecognised schools in Haryana*. New Delhi: National Institute for Educational Planning and Administration. http://www.dise.in/Downloads/Reports&Studies/Public%20Private%20Partnership%20in%20India.pdf

De, A., Majumdar, M., Noronha, C. & Samson, M. (2002) Private Schools and Universal Elementary Education, in R. Govinda (Ed.) *India Education Report: a profile of basic education*, pp. 131-150. New Delhi: Oxford University Press.

Galaskiewicz, J. (1985) Interorganizational Relations, *Annual Review of Sociology*, 11, 281-304.

Government of India (1860) The Societies Registration Act, 1860 (Act No. 21 of 1860) http://www.usig.org/countryinfo/laws/India/India%20Societies%20Registration%20Act.pdf

Government of India (2009) The Right of Children to Free and Compulsory Education Act, 2009. No. 35 of 2009, 26 August 2009. The Gazette of India: Extraordinary, Part II–Section I. New Delhi. http://www.education.nic.in/elementary/free%20and%20compulsory.pdf

Government of India (2010) National Council for Teacher Education Notification. F. No. 61-03/20/201/NCTE/(N&S), 23 August 2010. The Gazette of India: Extraordinary, Part III–Section 4. New Delhi. http://www.ncte-india.org/publicnotice/NOTIFICATION0001%2023%20August%202010.pdf

Government of National Capital Territory (NCT) of Delhi (1977) The Delhi School Education Act, 1973 and the Delhi School Education Rules, 1973. Delhi: Akalank.

Government of National Capital Territory (NCT) of Delhi (2008) *Status of Education and Major Achievements in Delhi: a quick report.* New Delhi: Directorate of Education, Government of NCT of Delhi. http://edudel.nic.in/a_quick_report__2008.htm

Government of National Capital Territory (NCT) of Delhi (2011) Delhi School Education (Free Seats for Students Belonging to Economically Weaker Sections and Disadvantaged Group) Order 2011. Notification, No. 15 (172)/DE/Act/2010/69. Delhi: Education Department, Government of NCT of Delhi. http://edudel.nic.in/mis/misadmin/DoeNewPublicCircular.htm

Government of National Capital Territory (NCT) of Delhi (2012) Minimum Wages Rates at a Glance [webpage]. New Delhi: Labour Department, Government of NCT of Delhi. http://delhi.gov.in/wps/wcm/connect/doit_labour/Labour/Home/Minimum+Wages/Rates+at+a+glance

Government of National Capital Territory (NCT) of Delhi (n.d.) About the Directorate of Education [webpage]. New Delhi: Directorate of Education, Government of NCT of Delhi. http://www.edudel.nic.in/welcome_folder/aboutdep.htm

Härmä, J. (2009) Can Choice Promote Education for All? Evidence from Growth in Private Primary Schooling in India, *Compare*, 39(2), 151-165.

Harriss-White, B. (2003) *India Working: essays on society and economy.* Cambridge: Cambridge University Press.

Higgins, M.C. & Gulati, R. (2003) Getting off to a Good Start: the effects of upper echelon affiliations on underwriter prestige, *Organization Science*, 14(3), 244-263.

High Court of Delhi (2008a) The Proceedings and Relevant Documents of the Writ Petition, No. 43 of 2006. Collected from the High Court of Delhi.

High Court of Delhi (2008b) Special Leave Petition (Civil) No. 21952 of 2008. Collected from the High Court of Delhi.

Juneja, N. (2010) *Access to What? Access, Diversity and Participation in India's Schools.* Create Pathways to Access Research Monograph, No. 32. Brighton: Centre for International Education, University of Sussex. http://www.Create-rpc.org/pdf_documents/PTA32.pdf

Kingdon, G.G. (1996) Private Schooling in India: size, nature, and equity-effects, *Economic and Political Weekly*, 31(51), 3306-3314.

Kumar, K. (2008) Partners in Education? *Economic and Political Weekly*, 43(3), 8-11.

Lambsdorff, J.G. (2002) Corruption and Rent-seeking, *Public Choice*, 113(1/2), 97-125.

Mehta, A.C. (2008) Elementary Education in India: progress towards UEE. Analytical tables 2006-07. New Delhi: NUEPA. http://dise.in/Downloads/Publications/Publication%202006-07/AR0607/Analytical%20Tables%202006-07.pdf (accessed 5 November 2011).

National Commission for Protection of Child Rights (2010) *Infocus*, 3(2) (August), 1-12. http://www.ncpcr.gov.in/Infocus/Infocus_Aug_2010.pdf

Noronha, C. & Srivastava, P. (2012) The Right to Education Act in India: focuses on early implementation issues and the private sector. Report submitted to the

Privatisation in Education Research Initiative (PERI), Open Society Foundation. Ottawa/New Delhi: University of Ottawa/CORD.

NUEPA (2011a) Education in India under Government Managements 2009-10 (selected tables based on DISE data). New Delhi: Department of EMIS, NUEPA. http://www.dise.in/Downloads/Publications/Publications%202009-10/Elementary%20Education%20under%20Government%20Managements%202009-10.pdf

NUEPA (2011b) Elementary Education in India Progress towards UEE: flash statistics 2009-10 (selected tables based on DISE data). New Delhi: Department of EMIS, NUEPA. http://www.dise.in/Downloads/Publications/Publications%202009-10/Flash%20Statistics%202009-10.pdf

Ohara, Y. (2012) Examining the Legitimacy of Unrecognised Low-fee Private Schools in India: comparing different perspectives, *Compare*, 42(1), 69-90.

Oliver, A.L. (2001) Strategic Alliances and the Learning Life-cycle of Biotechnology Firms, *Organization Studies*, 22(3), 467-489.

Pfeffer, J. & Salancik, G.R. (1978) *The External Control of Organizations: a resource dependence perspective*. New York: Harper & Row.

Puri, V.K. (2010) *Revised Compilation of Sixth Pay Commission Acceptance Orders for Central Govt. Employees*. New Delhi: Jain Book Agency.

Sharma, R. & Ramachandran, V. (Eds) (2009) *The Elementary Education System in India: exploring institutional structures, processes and dynamics*. New Delhi: Routledge.

Srivastava, P. (2007) For Philanthropy or Profit? The Management and Operation of Low-fee Private Schools in India, in P. Srivastava & G. Walford (Eds) *Private Schooling in Less Economically Developed Countries: Asian and African perspectives*, pp. 153-186. Oxford: Symposium Books.

Srivastava, P. (2008) The Shadow Institutional Framework: towards a new institutional understanding of an emerging private school sector in India, *Research Papers in Education*, 23(4), 451-475.

Times of India (2010) Sibal for Easing Norms to Let Small Schools Stay, *Times of India*, 21 February. http://articles.timesofindia.indiatimes.com/2010-02-21/india/28125850_1_Delhi-School-Education-Act-Small-Schools-Kapil-sibal

Tooley, J. & Dixon, P. (2003) *Private Schools for the Poor: a case study from India*. Reading: CfBT. http://cfbtstaging.cfbt.com/cfbt/PDF/91001.pdf

Tooley, J. & Dixon, P. (2005a) An Inspector Calls: the regulation of 'budget' private schools in Hyderabad, Andhra Pradesh, India, *International Journal of Educational Development*, 25(3), 269-285.

Tooley, J. & Dixon, P. (2005b) Private Schools Serving the Poor. Working paper: a study from Delhi, India. CCS Viewpoint, No. 8. New Delhi: Centre for Civil Society. http://schoolchoice.in/research/viewpoint8.pdf

CHAPTER 8

Regulating Low-fee Private Schools in Islamabad: a study in policy and practice

SALMAN HUMAYUN, RIZWANA SHAHZAD & ROGER CUNNINGHAM

Education regulation in Pakistan is a complicated endeavour. As education is a provincial subject supported by federal government efforts, different provinces have taken various approaches to regulating the private education sector with varying scope and implementation procedures. Under a presidential ordinance in 2006, the federal government, responding to a number of writ petitions in the High Court and Supreme Court of Pakistan (e.g. *Sardar Muhammad Farooq Abbasi v. Federation of Pakistan*, Writ Petition No 2601, 2004 CLC 1704), established a regulatory regime and authority for private schools in the Islamabad Capital Territory (ICT) known as the Private Educational Institutions Regulatory Authority (PEIRA).

According to the Islamabad Capital Territory Private Educational Institutions (Regulation and Promotion) Ordinance, 2006 (2006 PEIRA Ordinance), PEIRA was established for three key functions: to register, regulate, and promote private education institutions in the ICT (Preamble; Section 4, Government of Pakistan, 2006). The impetus for this study was PEIRA's potentially conflicting roles as both the *regulator* and the *promoter* of private education institutions according to the mandate. This chapter analyses PEIRA's regulatory framework for private education in ICT, PEIRA's role in principle and in practice, its interactions with low-fee private schools, and the understandings and experiences of low-fee private schools regarding PEIRA.

PEIRA's establishment can be attributed to the rapid but haphazard growth of private schools in the country that led to a number of concerns, including excessive fees, varying degrees of adherence to the curriculum, quality of teaching, and failure to provide adequate infrastructure and equipment, among others. Such issues were presented as justifications for a regulatory framework at the time that the PEIRA bill was submitted in the National Assembly by the then Minister for Education (see Government of Pakistan, 2007c). As such, the 2006 PEIRA Ordinance was promulgated with the express objectives of registering, regulating and promoting 'private education institutions' in the ICT. This experiment with regulating private education in ICT is unique in Pakistan as it marks the establishment of a separate authority dedicated to private schools, in contrast with the other provinces, where responsibility for the regulation of private and public schools is conferred upon existing government education departments.

This chapter begins with an introduction to the private schooling context in Pakistan, with a focus on low-fee private schools, before turning to a brief conceptual discussion on arguments surrounding the need for regulation. The chapter then presents the research methods used, along with a profile of the low-fee private schools in the study. The bulk of the chapter focuses on presenting data regarding the differences in policy and practice in relation to PEIRA's operations.

Background to Private Schooling in Pakistan

Pakistan has witnessed a steady and rapid growth of private schools over the last two decades. This phenomenon is seen as a response to the persistent failure of the public sector to provide sufficient access to basic schooling at both the primary and secondary levels. Private sector growth was initially concentrated in urban areas, and it was generally held that private schools catered only to the needs of the elite and affluent (Jimenez & Tan, 1987).

However, more recent studies have established that private schools in Pakistan cater to a far wider clientele than the urban elite (Alderman et al, 2001; Andrabi et al, 2002, 2008; Alderman et al, 2003; Aslam, 2007; Asadullah, 2009). Education census data tell us that private for-profit schools are now also prevalent in rural areas, and are affordable to middle- and even some lower-income groups (Andrabi et al, 2002). Despite the overall lower education levels of their teachers who are paid, on average, far less than their government counterparts, these private schools have lower student-teacher ratios and less teacher absenteeism than public schools, both of which have been major contributing factors in increasing the enrolment in and expansion of low-fee private schools (Banerjee & Esther, 2005; Andrabi et al, 2007).

The growth pattern of private education over the past decades indicates that as the demand for education increased, the existing mechanisms of public sector supply failed to respond accordingly. The inability of the public sector to match increasing demand, as well as to provide quality education, contributed largely to the rise and growth of private education enterprises (Shami & Hussain, 2005; Andrabi et al, 2008). An important trend evident from both National Education Census and National Education Management Information System (NEMIS) data is that private primary and secondary institutions are expanding at a much faster rate than those in the public sector. Between 1999-2000 and 2007-2008, the number of these private education institutions increased by 69%, compared with a mere 8% increase in government institutions – that is, more than eight times the public sector (I-SAPS, 2010).

A quick mapping of growth in the private education sector in Pakistan shows that in 1983 the total number of private primary and secondary education institutions was only 3343, which grew tenfold to 33,645 by 2000 (I-SAPS, 2010). According to National Education Census data, the comparative rate of growth over the next five years (from 2000 to 2005) increased, and this number reached 56,360 (Government of Pakistan, 2005). The total share of private sector enrolment in 2007-2008 was estimated at around 33%, with an annual growth rate of 25% (I-SAPS, 2008).

For Islamabad, according to official data sources, the total number of education institutions at all levels in the ICT saw a 63% increase between 2000 and 2007-2008, with the highest increases at the higher secondary (193%) and high school (163%) levels (see Table I). Out of the 487 total private institutions in the ICT in 2007-2008, the share of private primary schools was the highest, claiming 33%, followed by private high schools (29%), middle schools (21%), and higher secondary schools (8%). The remaining 8% of private education institutions included pre-primary schools, *deni madaris* (Islamic religious schools/seminaries), and degree-level institutes.

Education level/(grades)	2000	2005	2007-2008	% change since 2000
Pre-primary	n/a	30	31	N/A
Primary (I-V)	149	156	160	7
Middle (VI-VIII)	73	100	103	41
High school (grades IX-X)	54	136	142	163
Higher secondary (XI-XII)	14	30	41	193
Degree level (XIII-XIV)	8	10	10	25
Total	298	462	487	63

Table I. Private education institutions in Islamabad.
Source: Compiled by I-SAPS from Census of Private Educational Institutions 1999-2000, National Education Census 2005 (Government of Pakistan, 2005), and NEMIS reports for 2000 and 2007-2008

According to 2007-2008 NEMIS data, out of 81,982 students enrolled in private institutions of the ICT that academic year, 40% were enrolled at primary level and 28% at pre-primary level, followed by 14% in middle school, 8% in high school, 4% in higher secondary, and 7% in degree-granting institutions.[1] It is important to note that, contrary to the trend of growth in enrolment at all other levels, enrolments at primary-level private institutions in Islamabad witnessed a decline of 7.42% between 2000 and 2007-2008 (Ministry of Education, 2009), whereas at the middle, high school and higher levels, there was more than 100% growth during the same period. Overall, private sector enrolment in Islamabad has seen a growth of 69% between 2000 and 2008 (Ministry of Education, 2009).

Heterogeneity of the Private Sector

Analysis of the expansion patterns of for-profit private schools in Pakistan has challenged assumptions of a homogeneous sector. Closer examination shows a wide diversity of private schools based on income, faith, gender, medium of instruction, and religion, reflecting the varied demand for education. This is seen in the emergence of a heterogeneous, diverse and complex private education market in Pakistan (I-SAPS, 2010), catering to diverse sets of parental preferences (CRCP/CCP, 2010). While 'not-for-profit' private schools – that is, schools run by trusts or voluntary organisations, or organised along religious denominations or ideological lines - also exist, they do not figure prominently in the literature on private schooling. The spectrum of private schools falling outside this category in Pakistan serves both the rich and some of the poor, and is the focus of the analysis here.

At one end, high-fee elite private schools are considered to be providing a high quality school experience resulting in high learning outcomes, but they perpetuate 'education apartheid' (Najam, 1998) and exacerbate inequalities in the country. The continuing expansion of such schools has major implications for social cohesion and nationhood, where education is used as a means to retain power and influence among existing social and economic elites. At the other end of this spectrum, the literature shows that the performance and outcomes of low-fee private schools in some cases are not necessarily better than those of public sector schools (Batley et al, 2004) which perform below standard. This raises serious questions about the benefits of private schools in general and low-fee private schools in particular, and about whether they provide a better deal for those who access them.

The expansion of low-fee private schools has generated a significant and unsettled debate, particularly on the role of such schools in developing countries. Supporters, most notably James Tooley, advocate that private schools are the way forward, given persistent dysfunctional public sectors in many countries and increasing demand (Tooley & Dixon, 20003; Tooley, 2009). Some critics consider private schooling inimical to the public good, arguing that education is a basic right and therefore that it is a duty of the state to provide it free of cost to all (Watkins, 2004; Lewin, 2007). The middle ground in the debate is occupied by those who maintain that the function of the state is to ensure provision, which may entail delegating actual provision to other, non-state actors and upholding the principle of the right to education for all through regulation to ensure quality and equity, introducing, for example, subsidies to cover costs for the poorest.

There is growing evidence of, and debate on, this middle way being introduced in Pakistan through partnership arrangements. For example, the Punjab Education Foundation, which operates on a non-commercial/non-profit basis, was established as an autonomous statutory body in 1991 to encourage and promote education in the private sector.[2] The importance of the role of the state as regulator to ensure that all schools, irrespective of management, orientation and funding source, maintain commonly agreed minimum standards emerges from this debate. However, in the Pakistani context, the difficulty arises when the state is unable to ensure basic standards in government-run schools. This has become the major driver behind the expansion of private schools. In such a context, one might expect private schools to resist any interference by the state given its inability to effectively regulate public schools already within its jurisdiction.

The Need for Regulation

The debate on private schools inevitably encompasses both comparative advantages and disadvantages of regulation. In addition to the state's responsibility to ensure minimum levels of education quality (Randall, 1992; Watkins, 2004; Lewin, 2007; Rashid, 2007), researchers have also argued that education, being a public good, cannot be left to the mercy of the private sector, and requires state regulation (e.g. Randall, 1992; Ravitch, 2010). In earlier research on Pakistan, Jimenez and Tan (1985, 1987) identified that despite the growth in private schools, large sections of the population, especially girls in rural areas, were not served by them. In the current context, given the less than satisfactory performance of some private schools in Pakistan, some researchers advocate robust regulation by government authorities (Batley et al, 2004).

While there seems to be general agreement on the need to regulate the private sector, a wide variety of opinions exists concerning the nature, scope, mandate and implementation procedures of such regulation. In the case of Pakistan, the diversity and complexity of the private education sector has posed serious challenges for the state in terms of articulating a coherent response to regulation that can balance concerns of equity and public good. The rigorous application of standards to private schools which, it is generally accepted, are frequently not maintained in public schools, would threaten the existence of many low-fee private schools as it would necessitate increases in fees to cover the costs of adhering to regulatory compulsions. This runs the risk of driving away parents who cannot afford to absorb fee increases, further excluding their children from school, though in the absence of such standards, issues of uneven quality persist.

Research on regulation in the current context is severely limited. Available literature on private education in Pakistan focuses mainly on the growth and expansion of the sector, with very little on its regulation and ensuing impacts on low-fee private schools. Despite the fact that initiatives to develop regulatory frameworks for private schools in some provinces, regions, and the federal area have been under way since 2001 (if not before) – such as the NWFP Registration and Functions of Private Educational Institutions (Amendment) Ordinance, 2002; the Sindh Educational Institutions (Regulation & Control) Ordinance, 2001 and Amended Act 2003; and the Islamabad Capital Territory Educational Institution (Regulation & Promotion) Ordinance XXII of 2006 – there is no documented work exploring their efficacy and impact on private schools.

An important exception in this regard is a study by Kardar (2001) on Punjab, the only province to have addressed the issue of regulating private schools as early as 1984, with the Punjab Private Educational Institutions (Promotion & Regulation) Ordinance, 1984. According to the study, Punjab's complex regulatory requirements focused on facilities and equipment rather than on the quality of education and teaching standards. In the case of PEIRA, except for some reports of policy dialogues (I-SAPS, 2008), no substantial research has been undertaken that provides evidence regarding its impact. Our study aims to fill this gap. We now turn to the methods used in the study, before going on to a fuller discussion of the results.

Methods and Sample

The focus of this study is on the PEIRA legal and policy framework and its implementation. Besides critically reviewing PEIRA's mandate, we examine the understandings and experiences of low-fee private schools in this regard, presenting evidence seeking to answer the following questions:

- How comprehensive is the scope and mandate of PEIRA in terms of ensuring, as per its mandate, fair and healthy competition in the marketplace of private schools?
- How far has PEIRA been able to put into practice its twin mandates of 'regulation' and 'promotion' of private schools?
- What is the nature of the relationship between PEIRA and low-fee private schools, and what impact is it having?

The study was conducted between January and March 2011. Our approach has benefited from Srivastava's (2008) work on a new institutional understanding of an emerging model of private schooling in India, as well as from Tooley and Dixon's (2005) research focusing on the regulation of 'budget private schools', also in India. Though both groups of researchers use different approaches and are known to draw different conclusions, they analysed the rules and regulations on paper and in practice to draw inferences. We used the following methods: document analysis of the regulations and the 2006 PEIRA Ordinance; a school survey; focus group discussions; and key informant interviews.

The review of the PEIRA framework and its rules was carried out with two objectives. The first was to identify salient issues and gaps in PEIRA's scope and mandate in a number of areas, including: the promotion of competition; registration procedures; whether the opening and general operation of private schools was encouraged; the financing and governance of PEIRA; and provisions to ensure equity. The second was to develop an inventory of the key relevant legal provisions and clauses of the 2006 PEIRA Ordinance that directly relate to the functioning of private schools in order to examine the extent to which these were being implemented.

Interviews with PEIRA officials, representatives of the Private Schools Network (an organisation established in 1996 to serve the interests of private schools in the ICT), low-fee private school owners, and researchers were conducted to collect data from the field on PEIRA's governance, financing and operations. Separate focus group discussions were conducted with teachers, owners and parents from the 21 low-fee private schools in our study to gather views from all main stakeholders. The teachers and owners of low-fee private schools were invited through the Private Schools Network, whereas parents of the children were invited from the school neighbourhood with the help of teachers and through school visits.

Eighteen owners and teachers from the 21 low-fee private schools in our study participated in the focus group discussions and raised issues such as: regulatory mechanisms and barriers; PEIRA's dual mandate and self-financing status; the penal nature of the regulatory framework; PEIRA's performance vis-à-vis mandated functions; and areas for improvement. The second focus group discussion was attended by 16 parents to get a sense of their opinions on the private schools, and on the regulatory authority and its mandate. Parents' data are not presented here in the interest of space and relevance.

A survey was conducted with 21 low-fee private schools (selection method described below), followed by school visits by key researchers. The survey was designed to capture data relevant to providing insight on the research questions, and focused on such topics as: the implications of PEIRA's self-financing status; the impact of recovering PEIRA's costs from fees paid by schools; opinions on PEIRA's effectiveness as a regulator and promoter of private education; and opinions on whether PEIRA could maintain and increase state authority while recognising the role of low-fee schools in increasing access. Six schools were selected out of the original sample for additional school visits and to gather qualitative data to further contextualise survey responses.

Finally, a comprehensive review and analysis of available statistical data was undertaken to provide an overview of the private education sector in Islamabad. These data included those available from the Ministry of Education, the Academy of Education Planning and Management (AEPAM), NEMIS, and published reports such as the Federal Bureau of Statistics' Census of Private Schools 1999-2000, the Ministry of Education's

National Education Census 2005, and Pakistan Education Statistics for 2000 and 2007-2008, among others.

Specification on Selection of Low-fee Private Schools

For this study, we used the definition of low-fee private schools that PEIRA uses for registration purposes. Low-fee private schools are defined by PEIRA as charging a monthly fee not exceeding Rs. 500, and that do not receive any government funding, are not managed or financed by the state or local body, and additionally, are not operated by a trust, voluntary organisation or NGO.

Somewhat surprisingly, despite being the regulatory authority, PEIRA has no database of schools. Information on schools for sampling purposes was gathered by interviewing PEIRA officials, who stated that, according to the number of private schools registered with PEIRA until 2011, there were 665 registered private schools in the ICT, including low-, medium- and high-fee private schools.[3] Further discussion with PEIRA officials provided an estimated number of about 250 schools falling in the low-fee category. More accurate figures regarding the number of low-fee private schools in the ICT were not available.

The sample of 21 schools was drawn by randomly selecting from all private schools registered with PEIRA that fell within its low-fee category. Sample schools were from rural and urban areas of the ICT. For this study, and consistent with PEIRA's definition, low-fee private schools did not include not-for-profit or charitable institutions and academies, or schools established by NGOs. The low-fee private schools in our study were generally single schools, managed by an owner who usually also acted as the principal, and who drew a salary from school revenue. For the most part, we characterised these schools as managed for commercial purposes and 'for-profit', in contrast to the former category of private schools. The study also did not include private academies, tuition centres or coaching institutions.

Low-fee Private School Profiles

Most (56%) of the low-fee private schools in our study were established during the 1990s, half of which were registered with PEIRA during 2007, the first year of PEIRA's operation. Schools from rural areas comprised 40% of the sample, and the remaining 60% were located in urban areas. The share of primary schools (Grades I to V) in the sample was 24%, with 33% being middle schools, and 43% high schools.[4]

School size ranged between 30 and 750 students, with a mean enrolment of 208. All schools were co-ed. The total number of students enrolled in the study schools was 4360, 65% of whom were male and 35% female. Of the head teachers, 52% possessed a master's degree, and 33% had a bachelor's degree. Just over three-quarters (76%) of the schools had their own library, and 62% possessed a playground. Toilet facilities and electricity were available in all schools. Observations during schools visits found that all schools had separate toilets for girls and boys.

Despite the fact that these schools were registered in the low-fee category, the actual monthly fees of primary schools ranged between Rs. 200 and Rs. 2000, representing 2.9% to 28.6% of the minimum wage for unskilled workers, with fees varying between different grades and increasing at different levels.[5] Around 29% of primary schools in the sample charged a monthly fee below Rs. 500, and 5% charged fees above Rs. 1501. At high school level, the maximum fee range went up to Rs. 2500, with 10% at the higher secondary level charging fees above Rs. 1501 per month. This indicates that a number of the schools registered with PEIRA claiming to be 'low-fee' (i.e. charging Rs. 500 or less) later increased their fees without informing PEIRA. This highlights a serious issue of poor, nearly non-existent monitoring by PEIRA after schools were registered.

PEIRA Regulations: issues of policy and practice

This section presents our analysis of PEIRA's statutory provisions, its Rules of Business, 2007 (Government of Pakistan, 2007b), and its practices, with an aim to identify how they were applied and implemented, and any issues thus arising. As mandated by the 2006 PEIRA Ordinance, PEIRA formulated the Rules of Business, which define and explain the different functions and duties to be performed by PEIRA and its personnel. Together, the statutory provisions and Rules of Business relate to the private education sector in general, and to low-fee private schools in particular. The results of our analysis identify four major themes of interest in this regard: definitional deficits and general institutional issues arising; issues regarding PEIRA's role as promoter and facilitator and, in particular, challenges in upholding curricular uniformity and quality and evaluation standards; issues regarding registration, monitoring and inspection of private schools, and complications arising from PEIRA's self-financing status; and the penal nature of the regulation and its application in practice. These are presented in detail below.

Definitional Deficits and Institutional Issues

As highlighted in the chapter's introduction, the 2006 PEIRA Ordinance mandated three key functions for PEIRA: to register, regulate and promote private education institutions in the ICT (Preamble; Section 4, Government of Pakistan, 2006). Our analysis of the 2006 PEIRA Ordinance and 2007 Rules of Business highlights some definitional deficits in the regulation, and ensuing institutional issues emerging mainly from PEIRA's simultaneous roles as both the regulator *and* promoter of private education institutions. These were shown to be problematic in our study, both in principle institutionally, and in practice.

First, the key roles of regulation and promotion are neither defined nor clearly delineated. This has significant implications for PEIRA in defining its scope and developing mechanisms to achieve its objectives, leaving both functions open to multiple interpretations by various actors. In the absence of articulated definitions of these two roles, it is particularly difficult to arrive at a legally binding consensus of PEIRA's scope of functions. This concern was echoed in our focus group discussions with low-fee private school owners/ managers, who stated that they were unclear about the nature and extent of PEIRA's mandate.

Our data also revealed that while mandated to register, regulate and promote private schools, in practice PEIRA concerned itself primarily with registration from its inception. As a result, there was a lack of understanding among the low-fee private schools in our study about PEIRA's full role, as reflected in our data. Table II presents key aspects of PEIRA's mandate and the proportion of schools in our study that were aware of the different functions. Only 57% of schools were aware of PEIRA's full role. About half (53%) of the sample schools were of the view that PEIRA had not been performing the roles of regulation and promotion effectively, and 95% believed that PEIRA's key role was to register private schools.

Aspects of PEIRA's Mandate	Awareness (%)
Registration of private schools	95
Promote private schools	57
Ensure uniform policy in schools	24
Promotion of curricular and co-curricular activities	33
Check qualifications and service terms of the teaching staff	43
Make related rules and policies	62
Provision of finance to newly established schools	29

Table II. Proportion of schools aware of the different aspects of PEIRA's mandate.

Second, we found the definition of 'private institutions' as stated in the law to be deficient. Section 2(h) of the ordinance defines a privately managed institution as an 'institution which is not *owned or managed* by a government, local body or a body set up or controlled by the Government' (Government of Pakistan, 2006, emphasis added). However, interviews with PEIRA officials revealed that for the purposes of regulation, PEIRA defines private institutions as including all those institutions *not receiving finances* from government budgets. The difference between the two raises an important definitional issue, which is particularly problematic for schools that operate in more hybridised management and financing arrangements.

Third are broader institutional issues emerging from the laws governing regulators in Pakistan, and PEIRA's positioning within them. Regulators are generally meant to promote competition in order to protect consumers from monopoly prices, poor quality services and cartel behaviour. Moreover, unlike PEIRA's mandate, while regulators are generally mandated to promote 'competition' in the market, they do not usually provide support services (i.e. the provision of textbooks and training) to the 'service providers' or 'enterprises' – in this case, private schools – being regulated.

Some researchers believe that effective competition can be maintained in the market by using effective national competition laws rather than dedicated industry-level regulatory offices (e.g. see Parker, 2001). However, contrary to these views, according to Pakistan's legal framework for competition and regulation, sectors with dedicated regulators do not come under the purview of competition laws of the country. Instead, the dedicated regulators of particular sectors, such as the National Electric Power Regulatory Authority for the electricity sector and the Pakistan Telecommunication Authority for telecommunications, are responsible for the regulation and promotion of competition among private enterprises.

Thus, in accordance with the institutional structure of dedicated regulators in Pakistan, the regulation and promotion of competition among private education providers in Islamabad is PEIRA's responsibility. However, data from our study found that, thus far, PEIRA had not provided service standards for private education providers. This, according to the devised institutional framework, can hinder competition among different education provide providers, which goes against PEIRA's mandate under the ordinance.

Fourth, as PEIRA is under the administrative control of the Federal Ministry of Education and the Secretary is also given appellate authority, our analysis revealed potential complications in rejecting or suspending private school registration and other functions due to its limited authority. Section 17 of the ordinance states: 'Where the regulatory authority rejects an application for registration or suspends or cancels registration the aggrieved person may ... prefer an application to the Secretary, Ministry of Education and the order passed by him shall be final and given effect to by the Regulatory Authority' (Government of Pakistan, 2006).

However, literature on the regulation of private education and research conducted elsewhere (e.g. OECD, 2005) establishes that the regulator should remain independent of line agencies. Furthermore, even in Pakistan, all other regulators (with the exception of the Pakistan Electronic Media Regulatory Authority) are under the control of the Cabinet Division and not their respective ministries. The intention is to allow the regulator clear autonomy to perform its functions without hindrance or undue influence of the ministry. The current arrangement, whereby the Ministry of Education exerts control over PEIRA, seriously constrains its independence and neutrality in arbitrating potential conflicts between private schools and government.

Finally, the absence of an appropriate lead-in period led to institutional drawbacks. Section 1(3) mandates the 2006 PEIRA Ordinance to 'come into force at once' (Government of Pakistan, 2006), thus providing no gestation period for either PEIRA or affected private schools in which to develop an appropriate understanding of the processes and instruments available to carry out the mandate. The opportunity for PEIRA to collectively examine, among stakeholders, the relative merits and challenges of the statute prior to its enforcement was not provided. A lead-in period for the enforcement of the ordinance might not only have helped PEIRA to equip itself, but might also have enabled the private education sector to prepare for its compliance with new regulations.

Our analysis suggests that PEIRA began its functions under the burden of quick compliance, affecting its performance. Immediate compliance also resulted in institutional limitations faced by PEIRA, which was not able to train its staff and officials, develop a database of private schools, or develop a clear communication strategy to engage with them. This had profound implications for the desired relationship with low-fee private schools in our study from the outset.

Role as Promoter and Facilitator: challenges in upholding uniformity in curricula, standards and evaluation

Although the ordinance empowers PEIRA to promote the private education sector, 'promotion' in the context of the present law is unclear and not fully defined. However, two provisions, Sections 4(d) and 5(d) of the ordinance, outline two main areas in this regard: (1) the promotion of students' physical and moral well-being; and (2) the promotion of inter-institution curricular and co-curricular activities. These are under Sections 4 and 5 of the 2006 PEIRA Ordinance with the aim of ensuring a uniform policy regarding curricula, teaching staff and service conditions, and academic standards and evaluation. Section 5 empowers PEIRA to ensure that standards of facilities and services provided by private schools are commensurate with fees charged.

Our field observations and interviews suggest that PEIRA did not undertake effective action to ensure consistent policy across schools, and there were no identifiable actions or measures that related to the quality of services being provided by private schools in relation to their fees. Furthermore, we did not find evidence to suggest that substantial work had been done at the levels of policy or practice to fulfil this mandate. The ordinance does not clearly state whether the standards used to register and regulate private schools are those used in the public sector, or whether PEIRA has the authority to set alternative criteria, though Section 5(l) empowers it to develop policy. In any case, PEIRA had not yet done this, nor had it established clear rules establishing what was expected of private schools.

This highlights a serious policy and practice gap as the National Education Policy 2009 aimed to establish clear and universal standards for schools (Government of Pakistan, 2009), but this provision had not yet been implemented. In the absence of such standards, expecting PEIRA to perform the function of upholding standards seems impractical and unrealistic. Furthermore, according to the National Education Policy, it is the responsibility of the government to ensure that all children attend schools that conform to basic minimum standards. Potentially mandating PEIRA to develop these common standards instead of implementing national standards itself seemed, to some private school interviewees, an example of the state relinquishing its responsibilities in education.

Interviews with owners of low-fee private schools revealed that, in practice, owing to a diverse client base for different types of low-fee schools (i.e. Urdu-medium, English-medium, co-ed, single-sex, etc.), each school uses different textbooks to respond to parents' demands or expectations for a particular curriculum in line with the school's set-up (see also I-SAPS, 2010 for a discussion of differences between textbooks in faith-based and English-medium schools). In 2009, PEIRA launched an initiative for low-fee schools in this regard to distribute a total of 56,000 books worth Rs. 10 million. Due to financial constraints, PEIRA set an eligibility criterion for the scheme, including only schools charging a maximum of Rs. 300 per month.

However, as data from our small sample of schools indicate, it is likely that not all schools in this sub-category received the free books. In our sample, 29% of primary schools charged fees below Rs. 500, and out of these, 48% charged Rs. 300 or less and thus were eligible for the scheme, but many of them did not receive the free textbooks. Interviews with the Private Schools Network reported a similar lack of coverage. Private school owners felt that the inconsistent manner in which this support was provided did not adequately address curricular issues, and in any case, providing free textbooks to a few schools would not have addressed equity between schools or bring about uniformity in the curricula. They proposed waiving registration fees for the lowest fee-charging schools to lessen their financial burden, and establishing/implementing quality standards as more effective strategies.

PEIRA officials, on the other hand, highlighted its role as a promoter and facilitator by claiming to have organised teacher training to improve education quality, and also referred to the free textbook scheme. Our school-level data indicate that PEIRA's teacher training activities were seen as ineffective. All school respondents were of the opinion that PEIRA did not provide incentives to teachers, only 24% felt that adequate support for teacher training was provided, and only 10% of school owners agreed that PEIRA organised co-curricular activities. In interviews, school owners/managers stated that, given high levels of teacher turnover in low-fee private schools, PEIRA's provision of in-service training is not a viable strategy for improving standards. Somewhat surprisingly, it seemed that teacher training further contributed to the problem of teacher retention at low-fee private schools – that is, once teachers were trained, they had options for upward mobility in other (better paying) schools, and thus sought other jobs.

Registration, Monitoring and Inspection: PEIRA's self-financing status and private school registration

In principle, private schools are interested in registering with PEIRA for two reasons: (1) registration with the government authority signals quality to parents; and (2) non-compliance with PEIRA registration rules might result in punitive penalties. Registration, monitoring and inspection are fundamental to PEIRA's functions (Sections 5(c) and 15, Government of Pakistan, 2006). Crucially, in this regard, PEIRA is mandated to fix, demand and receive fees for registration and inspection under Section 5(f) of the ordinance, established in the 2007 Rules of Business. Furthermore, Section 9(2) of the ordinance states: 'The Regulatory Authority shall have a fund to which shall be credited all income including income from inspection fee, registration fee, other sources, etc. and account shall be maintained in a scheduled bank of Pakistan approved by the Government' (Government of Pakistan, 2006).

PEIRA's fee structure divides schools into three tiers based on the monthly tuition fee per student. Schools charging up to Rs. 500 per month are categorised as low-fee schools; those charging from Rs. 501 to Rs. 2000 are categorised as medium-fee; and schools charging more than Rs. 2000 are high-fee. Furthermore, PEIRA levies a security fee based on the different tuition-fee brackets, but the sliding scale is not accurately matched to different categories of schools. For example, elite schools charging more than Rs. 10,000 per month paid a security fee of Rs. 25,000, whereas low-fee schools charging below Rs. 500 were required to pay Rs. 5000. In addition, there is a separate inspection fee (Rs. 2500 for low-fee schools), and, according to school interviewees in our study, a request for the schools to provide PEIRA with logistical support and transport for the inspection, placing an additional financial burden on them which is particularly difficult for low-fee schools to cope with compared with their higher-fee counterparts.

Section 5(r) of the 2007 Rules of Business outlining registration, inspection and security fees (Government of Pakistan, 2007b) has been revised twice since its formulation in January 2007. Significantly, no other provision has been subject to change since PEIRA's inception. Our data revealed that the revisions were undertaken as a result of private school pressure. The first was a revision downwards to Rs. 2500 for the registration fee, and it was instituted in February 2007, just one month after the official formulation. The next revision was in April 2008, amending the prescribed inspection fee for registration or registration renewal.

The establishment of PEIRA as a self-financing regulatory authority may initially seem novel and cost-effective on the part of the government. However, it raises a series of concerns linked to the current practice of charging fees to providers that are to be regulated by the same authority. First, how autonomous and independent can PEIRA actually remain, given the influence of private schools and their associations, when it is financially reliant on their fees? Second, if schools are required to pay for their own regulation, the burden will eventually be passed on to parents and/or students through fee increases. Interviews and focus group discussions during this study suggest that due to financial and logistical constraints PEIRA may further curtail mandatory monitoring visits to schools.

In our study, two-thirds of the low-fee private schools perceived PEIRA's self-financing status as a challenge, hindering its effective functioning, particularly regarding its duties in conferring registration and subsequent monitoring. According to interview data, over the past four years PEIRA did not refuse registration to any private school, nor was registration cancelled on account of non-compliance. Some high-performing schools expressed concern, viewing PEIRA's need to generate income from school registration fees as superseding its duty to confer registration as a benchmark of schools having met minimum quality standards. The majority of low-fee private school owners in focus group discussions felt that registration and security fees led to a perception that the process was mainly a means to generate revenue for PEIRA. They claimed that officials only visited schools at the time of registration or renewal, and that schools were rarely inspected otherwise. Indeed, interviews with PEIRA officials revealed that they had no set schedule for monitoring and inspection after registration.

Schools claimed that the self-financing status created problems for private school owners, forcing them to pass costs on to parents. The implications are serious for low-fee schools where revenue margins are much tighter and the affordability of parents is low. Thus levying extra charges was seen as inimical to their interests, which is not the case for high-fee schools.

Almost half (48%) of the head teachers in our survey believed that the regulatory system had not improved their schools. However, more than a third (35%) believed that PEIRA registration had improved the reputation of their schools as quality and certified service providers. When asked to rate PEIRA's performance, 52% of low-fee schools in the study rated it as 'average', and 24% believed that PEIRA's performance was 'good'. No owner/manager rated it as 'very good', whereas 10% and 14% rated PEIRA'S performance as 'poor' and 'very poor', respectively.

When low-fee private school owners were asked if they were satisfied with the registration system, 62% expressed their satisfaction. The remaining 38% who were not satisfied wanted to see improvement in the system, especially for registration renewal and school inspection. Nonetheless, 81% of schools claimed that there were no delays to first-time registration. However, owners felt that the monitoring and renewal of registration process was inefficient, particularly the compulsion to renew registration every two years. It is noteworthy that registration renewal in other provinces is usually after a minimum of four years.

Finally, some private school owners/managers felt that PEIRA's self-financing status established the state's unwillingness to pay the bill to regulate private schools, which they felt was the least that should be expected as, in their opinion, these schools fill the gap of the state's failure to provide education for all. To some of our interviewees, not financing such an important function confirmed that the state relinquished its responsibilities in education and abdicated the interests of citizens. However, interviews with PEIRA officials revealed that they did not view the self-financing status as a major challenge. Officials held the view that charging fees for PEIRA's services instils a sense of responsibility and accountability in private schools.

Penal Nature of the Regulation

Another feature of the regulatory framework is the uncharacteristically strict nature of penalties to be imposed, in principle, on private school owners in contravention of the ordinance. Section 19 states: 'whoever runs an institution in contravention of the provisions... shall be punished with imprisonment which may extend to one year or with fine which may extend to five hundred rupees for each day during the period [the] offence continues, or with both' (Government of Pakistan, 2006). This contradicts the principles of the administration of justice, which generally provide for civil penalties for offences that are not of a criminal nature. The set penalties for private schools are unnecessarily strict and, if rigidly enforced, would significantly compromise existing grievance redressal systems dealing with the mediation of disputes between private providers and the authorities. Thus, it appears that state regulation of private schools is focused on penalising providers rather than on providing compensation to or redressing grievances of clients accessing private education services.

Evidence from our study shows that PEIRA has used discretion and has not exercised its full powers under this provision, preferring instead to develop positive relationships with private providers and avoiding resistance to regulation. On the implementation side, PEIRA officials informed us that instead of penalising education institutions in cases of non-compliance, they preferred to issue a notice to the school administration and involve local Islamabad district administration to ensure compliance.

However, school owners in our study claimed that many private education institutions that did not meet norms obtained registration anyway, and were not monitored by the district education administration. This led to a feeling among many low-fee private school owners and managers in our study that the ordinance and its rules were selectively implemented and had the potential to give way to corrupt practices, thus making the regulation counterproductive to the healthy functioning, promotion and growth of the private sector. Our analysis indicates that instead of applying or changing procedures at its discretion and causing a policy–practice disconnect, PEIRA should initiate a process to amend the penalties and enable better private school performance by instituting a timely grievance redressal mechanism.

Conclusions

Our analysis of the 2006 PEIRA Ordinance and Rules of Business, PEIRA's practices, and its interactions with and experiences of low-fee private schools indicates a number of deficiencies that have serious implications for the healthy functioning and growth of low-fee private schools in the ICT. The main issues are summarised below.

First, the relationship between PEIRA and low-fee schools can be best described as cautious and complicated. Shortcomings in PEIRA's legal and policy framework as well as definitional deficits and lack of clarity on PEIRA's many functions have led to the selective implementation of various provisions of the 2006 PEIRA Ordinance, and to a lack of awareness of PEIRA's full role among low-fee private schools. Revisions of the Rules of Business in the area of fees due to pressure from private schools, unclear definitions of 'private schools', and PEIRA's simultaneous roles as regulator and promoter are some examples of this. Likewise, low-fee private schools tread carefully in interactions and remain apprehensive about the full extent of PEIRA's mandate, given the risk of strict penalties for non-compliance.

Second, the analysis showed that PEIRA's self-financing status posed fundamental problems for it and for low-fee private schools. The financing of monitoring and inspection, which is down to the private schools themselves, raises serious questions about how consistently quality standards are applied, and about the impartiality of PEIRA as a regulator. Third, the administrative control of the Ministry of Education over PEIRA further compromises its status as an independent regulator. This led to the low-fee private schools in our study viewing PEIRA as a de facto subordinate department of the Ministry. Schools rightly pointed out that independent adjudication against PEIRA's decisions is not possible, since the appellate authority rests with the Ministry of Education instead of with an independent judicial process.

According to our analysis, increased autonomy from the government and financial support independent from private schools would increase PEIRA's chances of performing more optimally. Additionally, serious consideration should be paid to revisiting PEIRA's dual mandate in order to preserve its neutrality as regulator. The draconian nature of some of the regulation contributes to a policy–practice disconnect, and complicates the functioning of low-fee private schools, in particular. This has serious implications on the quality of the low-fee private sector as a whole, which is an important consideration, given its contribution to Pakistan's broader national 'education for all' goals. Thus, there is a strong case for keeping the regulatory requirements minimal *and* realistic. This will help improve competition in the private sector and limit difficulties faced by this sector that is catering to some of the poor, a group that the public sector is currently failing to fulfil in terms of providing access and quality.

Acknowledgements

The authors gratefully acknowledge the invaluable comments and support of Ahmad Ali, Research Fellow, Institute of Social and Policy Sciences (I-SAPS), Pakistan.

Notes

[1] The number of pre-primary schools indicates those schools which were registered in kindergarten classes only. However, primary and some middle schools also have pre-primary classes. Therefore, the actual percentage of students enrolled at the pre-primary level is likely to be higher than that reported in pre-primary schools only.

[2] The Punjab Education Foundation has been restructured under the Punjab Education Foundation Act-XII of 2004 for the promotion of education, especially encouraging and supporting the efforts of the private sector in providing education to the poor, through public-private partnership.

[3] Note that data presented in Table I represent the number of private schools as reported in the Private Education Census and NEMIS database until 2007-2008; hence, there may be discrepancies.

[4] The middle and high schools were all-through schools and offered classes from Grade I to middle (I to VIII) and high school (I to X).

[5] The 2010 labour policy set the minimum wage for unskilled workers in Pakistan at Rs. 7000/month.

References

Alderman, H., Kim, J. & Orazem, P.F. (2003) Design, Evaluation, and Sustainability of Private Schools for the Poor: the Pakistan urban and rural fellowship school experiments, *Economics of Education Review*, 22(3), 265-274.

Alderman, H., Orazem, P.F. & Paterno, E.M. (2001) School Quality, School Cost, and the Public-Private Choices of Low-income Households in Pakistan, *Journal of Human Resources*, 36(2), 304-326.

Andrabi, T., Das, J. & Khwaja, A.I. (2002) The Rise of Private Schooling in Pakistan: catering to the urban elite or educating the rural poor? Working paper. http://economics-files.pomona.edu/andrabi/research/pakschool%20march29.pdf

Andrabi, T., Das, J. & Khwaja, A.I. (2008) A Dime a Day: the possibilities and limits of private schooling in Pakistan, *Comparative Education Review*, 52(3), 329-355.

Andrabi, T., Das, J., Khwaja, A.I., Vishwanath, T., Zajonc, T. & LEAPS Team (2007) Pakistan Learning and Educational Achievement in Punjab Schools (LEAPS): insights to inform the education policy debate. http://leapsproject.org/assets/publications/LEAPS_report.pdf

Asadullah, M.N. (2009) Returns to Private and Public Education in Bangladesh and Pakistan: a comparative analysis, *Journal of Asian Economics*, 20(1), 77-86.

Aslam, M. (2007) The Relative Effectiveness of Government and Private Schools in Pakistan: are girls worse off? Research Consortium on Education Outcomes and Poverty (RECOUP), Working Paper No. 4. Cambridge: Faculty of Education, University of Cambridge. http://recoup.educ.cam.ac.uk/publications/Wp4-mas.pdf

Banerjee, A. & Esther, D. (2005) Addressing Absence, *Journal of Economic Perspectives*, 20 (1), 117-132.

Batley, R., Hussein, M., Khan, A., Mumtaz, Z., Palmer, N. & Sanson, K. (2004) Pakistan: non-state providers of basic services. Country study commissioned by Policy Division, Department for International Development (DFID), UK. Birmingham: International Development Department, School of Public Policy, University of Birmingham. http://www.birmingham.ac.uk/Documents/College-Social-sciences/Government-society/idd/research/Non-State-providers/Pakistan-Report-24march05.pdf

Consumer Rights Commission of Pakistan (CRCP)/Competition Commission of Pakistan (CCP) (2010) Competition Assessment Study of the Private Education Sector in Pakistan. Draft report. Islamabad: Competition Commission of Pakistan.

Government of Pakistan (2005) National Education Census. Islamabad: Ministry of Education.

Government of Pakistan (2006) The Islamabad Capital Territory Private Educational Institutions (Regulation and Promotion) Ordinance, 2006. *Gazette of Pakistan*, Extraordinary, Part I. Islamabad: Government of Pakistan.

Government of Pakistan (2007b) PEIRA Rules of Business, 2007. Islamabad: Private Education Institutions Regulatory Authority.

Government of Pakistan (2007c) Statement of Objects and Reasons, Islamabad Capital Territory Educational Institution (Regulation & Promotion) Ordinance 2007. Ordinance No. LV of 2007, P 09. *Gazette of Pakistan*, Extraordinary, Part I, 3 October 2007.

Government of Pakistan (2009) National Education Policy, 2009. Islamabad: Ministry of Education.

Institute of Social and Policy Sciences (I-SAPS) (2008) Report on Policy Dialogue: private sector education: policy and regulatory issues. Islamabad: I-SAPS/ Campaign for Quality Education. http://I-saps.org/Publications/Info/PolicyDialogueonPrivateSectorEducation290808.pdf

Institute of Social and Policy Sciences (I-SAPS) (2010) Private Education Sector in Pakistan: mapping and musing. Islamabad: I-SAPS. http://I-saps.org/publication.html#

Jimenez, E. & Tan, J.P. (1985) Educational Development in Pakistan: the role of user charges and private education. Discussion paper, Education and Training Series, Report No. EDT 16. Washington, DC: World Bank. http://www-wds.worldbank.org/servlet/WDSContentServer/IW3P/IB/1985/12/01/000009265_3980623151351/Rendered/PDF/multi_page.pdf

Jimenez, E. & Tan, J.P. (1987) Decentralized and Private Education: the case of Pakistan, *Comparative Education*, 23(2), 173-190.

Kardar, S.H. (2001) Private Sector in Education. Report commissioned by the World Bank. Lahore: Systems (Private) Ltd.

Lewin, K. (2007) The Limits of Growth to Non-government Private Schooling in Sub-Saharan Africa, in P. Srivastava & G. Walford (Eds) *Private Schooling in Less Economically Developed Countries: Asian and African perspectives*, pp. 41-65. Oxford: Symposium Books.

Ministry of Education (2009) *Pakistan Education Statistics 2007-08.* Islamabad: Academy of Education Planning and Management.

Najam, A. (1998) Educational Apartheid, *The News* (daily, Pakistan), January, 11.

Organisation for Economic Cooperation and Development (OECD) (2005) Designing Independent and Accountable Regulatory Authorities for High Quality Regulation. Proceedings of an experts' meeting in London. http://www.oecd.org/dataoecd/15/28/35028836.pdf

Parker, D. (2001) Economic Regulation: a preliminary literature review and summary of research questions arising. Working Paper Series, Paper No. 6. Manchester: Centre on Regulation and Competition, Institute for Development Policy and Management, University of Manchester. http://www.Competition-regulation.org.uk/publications/working_papers/wp6.pdf

Randall, E.V. (1992) Private Schools and State Regulation, *Urban Lawyer*, 24, 341.

Rashid, A. (Ed.) (2007) *Engaging with Basic Education in Pakistan.* Education Watch study. Lahore: SAHE.

Ravitch, D. (2010) *The Death and Life of the Great American School System: how testing and choice are undermining education.* New York: Basic Books.

Shami, P.A. & Hussain, K.S. (2005) Basic Education in Pakistan. Research Study No. 181. Islamabad: Academy of Educational Planning and Management (AEPAM), Ministry of Education.

Srivastava, P. (2008) The Shadow Institutional Framework: towards a new institutional understanding of an emerging model of private schooling in India, *Research Papers in Education*, 23(4), 451-475.

Tooley, J. & Dixon, P. (2003) *Private Schools for the Poor: a case study from India.* Reading: Centre for British Teachers. http://cfbtstaging.cfbt.com/cfbt/PDF/91001.pdf

Tooley, J. & Dixon, P. (2005) An Inspector Calls: the regulation of 'budget' private schools in Hyderabad, Andhra Pradesh, India, *International Journal of Educational Development*, 25(3), 269-285.

Tooley, James (2009) *The Beautiful Tree: a personal journey into how the world's poorest people are educating themselves.* New Delhi: Penguin; Washington, DC: Cato Institute.

Watkins, K. (2004) Private Education and 'Education for All' or How Not to Construct an Evidence-based Argument: a reply to Tooley, *Economic Affairs*, 24(4), 8-11.

CHAPTER 9

Low-fee Private Schools: a methodological and political debate

GEOFFREY WALFORD

Low-fee private schools are at the centre of a debate about the role that the private sector might have in achieving the Millennium Development Goal of universal primary education and beyond. A growing number of research reports exist dealing with the extent and nature of low-fee private schools, as well as a few reports which attempt to assess their quality. However, there is little agreement, and contradictions and conflicts of interpretation abound.

In this chapter, I will examine one particular academic paper and the debate to which it gave rise. The study is important in itself because it reports an early attempt to describe the extent of low-fee schooling in particular areas, and because it gave rise to a debate in an academic journal (which has since continued). It was the result of a large-scale survey of schools, which had not been attempted elsewhere at the time.

In examining this article and debate, I will apply a framework for the reading and assessment of research put forward by Martyn Hammersley (1990, 1994) which stresses the need to identify various aspects of the research and the research publication – in particular, the focus of the research, the cases investigated, the main arguments and evidence (identifying in particular the definitions, descriptive and explanatory factual claims, and the value claims), and the theoretical inferences and empirical generalisations made in conclusion about the focus. It is argued that by going through this process (or one very similar), the logic of published papers can be clearly laid out and identified. Then, of course, the validity of the arguments and claims need to be assessed against the evidence provided.

My model of empirical research is that each piece of research can be seen as a brick in a wall. The 'brick' represents the individual piece of empirical research and the associated academic paper or other output. The 'wall' represents the wider argument that might be made using this particular brick. In the best possible case, high quality bricks are added to firm foundations and further high quality bricks are added on top. There will always be several different walls into which a single brick might be incorporated, and some of these walls will eventually be stronger and more fit for purpose than others.

However, the first objective in assessing the validity and reliability of a particular piece of research is to examine it as it exists. Is this a solid brick that can be used within a wall? What are its size, weight and dimensions? What is it made of? What are its limitations? This is not to deny that all empirical work builds in part on previous work – both in terms of the research tradition and theoretical and practical knowledge that previous work has produced. But it seems advisable to me to try to see what is being said in *each particular piece* of reported research work. For even bricks that might be incorporated within unstable walls might themselves be sturdy and actually worth using somewhere.

An Empirical Study of Schools in Hyderabad, India

In November 2007, James Tooley, Pauline Dixon and S.V. Gomathi published an article in the *Oxford Review of Education* that presented the results of a study of 918 schools in slum areas within three zones in the District of Hyderabad. As I was editor of the *Oxford Review of Education* at the time, I know that the article had been originally submitted for consideration for publication in November 2005, and had been through the normal refereeing process, with two independent referees producing reports and asking for revisions. After publication of this article, I was asked by Christopher Winch whether the *Review* might be interested in publishing a *Reply* to the article. The editorial board of the journal encourages such debate, so I replied that such a response would be welcome, subject, of course, to the normal refereeing process. The *Reply* was submitted in October 2008 and, following revisions, published in August 2010. I had sent a copy of this article to James Tooley, asking if he wished to write a short *Rejoinder to the Reply*. Both the *Reply* and *Rejoinder* were published in the same issue (Sarangapani & Winch, 2010; Tooley, Dixon & Gomathi, 2010).

The original article resulted from a study, funded by the John Templeton Foundation, which 'aimed to contribute to the understanding of private school provision for the poor, its relative quality *vis-à-vis* government provision, and its potential role in meeting the Millennium Development Goal of universal basic education' (Tooley, Dixon & Gomathi, 2007, p. 541). The authors do not explicitly state why the three particular zones within Hyderabad (or indeed Hyderabad itself) were selected for study, but it is implicit that these three zones of Bandlaguda, Bhadurpura and Charminar are amongst the poorer zones in the District (stated in the linked article; see Tooley, Dixon, Shamsan et al, 2010). In practice, the study excluded schools in the three zones that were not found in 'notified slums', so the focus is meant to be on schools available to the 'poor'.

The study consists of two parts: a census of schools, and what Tooley, Dixon and Gomathi (2007) call a survey of inputs. However, such a census was far from straightforward, as many of these schools were unrecognised, and thus their names did not appear on any official lists. Four types of school are considered: government, private aided, recognised private unaided, and unrecognised private unaided. In order to conduct a full census of the schools in the chosen areas (including the unrecognised schools), it was necessary for the trained researchers to visit 'every street and alley' in the area to find all schools. Each of the schools was individually visited and an interview was conducted with the head teacher or school manager exploring such issues as school enrolment, pupil fees and gender balance. Registration documentation was viewed where possible, and the researcher then visited the school itself, checked facilities against a given list, and observed the classroom activities of a chosen Class 4 teacher.

Most of the data in the article were derived from the 918 schools found in that census, but a stratified random sample of 153 schools was studied in more depth. While some of these data are reported in the article, most of the data on academic performance, background variables and satisfaction levels are said to be reported elsewhere (see Schagen & Shamsan, 2007; Tooley, Dixon, Shamsan et al, 2010), but these are not specified in the article. These sample schools were visited several times so that more data could be generated.

All empirical research involves compromises, and some of these are noted (Tooley, Dixon & Gomathi, 2007, p. 543). In particular, a physical count of the number of children in each school would have been desirable, and more than one visit to each school would have produced greater validity in the data on teacher activity. Further limitations as to how the statistics should be interpreted are also noted (Tooley, Dixon & Gomathi, 2007, p. 544). However, the methodology followed and the data presented in the article seemed sufficiently robust to warrant publication. In particular, as very little was known at the time about low-fee private schools, a study that examined their extent and nature was timely.

The majority of the article presents simple descriptive claims about results of the census and survey. To a very high degree, these descriptive claims are made specifically and only about the particular schools that were found in these slum areas in three zones of Hyderabad. The article reports the number of schools in each category, and the proportion of pupils in each category. Thus, 24% of pupils were found to be in government schools, 11.4% in private aided schools, 41.5% in recognised private unaided schools, and 23.1% in unrecognised private unaided schools. A whole host of other data are presented in the article about, for example, the gender balance of the schools (where it was found that girls were more likely to attend government schools than boys), the pupil-teacher ratios (where unrecognised private unaided schools had the most favourable average figures), the age range of the schools, the average time since establishment of the schools (where unaided private schools were newest), the claimed medium of instruction, fees, concessionary places available in unaided schools, and teacher salaries. In all of this, the article presents the evidence that has come from the empirical work, with very little interpretation.

The second part of the presentation of results deals with 'inputs' into the schools in terms of the observed teaching activity and available facilities. Tooley, Dixon and Gomathi (2007) state:

> The majority of these indicators were those explored in other research ... as important proxies for the quality of learning experience, such as those vital for basic health and hygiene (e.g. drinking water and toilets), for safety, comfort and ease of learning (e.g. 'pucca' buildings, electricity in the classrooms, fans, desks, chairs and blackboards), and the activity of the teacher. Other indicators focussed on input signalling investment in educational provision (library, tape-recorders, television and computers for teaching purposes), all of which are seen as important by the Government of Andhra Pradesh for improving educational quality. (p. 550)

Most of these data were also derived from the census of schools and relate solely to the particular schools surveyed. The comparisons drawn relate to averages for the particular schools of each type found in the census. The nature of teaching activity is described within three categories – teaching, non-teaching, and absent – according to what was observed in the chosen class during the single visit to each school. All of these are simple descriptive claims. Tooley, Dixon and Gomathi (2007) recognise that more valid measures could have been achieved through more than one observation per school, but there were more than 900 schools in the census (p. 543). Given the resources available for any empirical research, there is a need to make compromises. In this case, a compromise was made between the number of observations that could be made in each school and the number of schools that could be visited. To me, this seems reasonable.

Tooley, Dixon and Gomathi (2007) report that for government schools, nearly 20% of activities were of the non-teaching variety (compared with 2 to 5.5% for each of the other three categories), and that government schools had the highest proportion of absent teachers. Various tables then present details of the data found for each of the four categories of school, and a final table provides a comparison between government and unrecognised private schools only. Several of these tables use a chi-squared significance test to highlight those differences that are deemed to be of greatest importance.

This is technically an inappropriate use of significance tests, since these data relate to a census and not a random sample drawn from a wider population (see Gorard, 2001, 2010a, b). However, this type of test is widely used with such data and reported in the educational and social science literature. It is sufficient to note that there are considerable differences on average between the types of school in terms of the provision of drinking water, toilets, libraries, computers, television, desks, chairs or benches for children, and electric lights. On all of the indicators, except for provision of a playground and of a television or video, private unaided schools had better (usually far better) provision than government schools.

In the bulk of the article, the descriptive claims are clearly related to the particular cases studied, but in the conclusion, the discussion moves from the cases to the focus of the study, which is on the potential role of private schools in meeting Millennium Development Goals. However, even here, the article only makes cautious claims and there are no explanatory statements. Tooley, Dixon and Gomathi (2007) state, 'Our study suggests that the private sector is certainly a significant provider for the poor' (p. 557), and then return to a brief summary of the specific evidence from their study. The word 'suggests' indicates the cautious nature of the claim. No explicit generalisation is made, and it is correct that it has been shown that the private sector is a significant provider for the poor (but not necessarily the poorest) in their study zones.

The article then returns to two objections that are made to private schools being seen as a possible help towards the achievement of universal primary education: (1) that, as private schools charge fees, they are not available to the very poorest families; and (2) that the quality of private schools for the poor is low and thus cheating parents of their money. To the first objection, the authors argue that some schools offer scholarships to poor families and that targeted vouchers could be used to support the very poor. To the second, they argue that these concerns about low quality 'may be somewhat misplaced' (Tooley, Dixon & Gomathi, 2007, p. 558), since in their study, private schools fared better than government schools on all but two of their indicators. This claim is still cautious, in that it states 'may be somewhat misplaced'.

However, they then imply a prescriptive claim that support should be given to private schools to improve them further because they are starting at a higher level than government schools. One might have wished for some recognition that there could be negative aspects of such support, but it could be argued that this was not the purpose of the article, which was to challenge existing academic literature, which had hardly recognised potential positive roles for private schools until that point. In summary, this is fundamentally a descriptive article based on empirical work in three case tudy zones in Hyderabad.

Sarangapani and Winch's Reply

Sarangapani and Winch's (2010) *Reply* is lengthy and divided into two main parts. In the first part, they take issue with the extent to which education should be seen as a public as well as a private good, and also with what they take to be Tooley's conceptualisation of that good. The second part deals with some of the details of the empirical work.

The first part of their critique does not bear scrutiny, for it only loosely relates to the original article and, in my opinion, has misunderstood Tooley's wider position. It is an attempt to contextualise the article within earlier writings by Tooley, but fails to do so adequately. It does not, in fact, quote sufficiently from these earlier writings and seems to rely on a broad memory of previous work. Sarangapani and Winch (2010) claim that Tooley has 'mistakenly conceptualised education as a commodity, namely as educational opportunities' (p. 502). They state that Tooley takes 'the term "education" to mean "opportunities to become educated"', which 'is not only to offer a circular definition of a key term, but [also] to depart radically from normal usage' (Sarangapani & Winch, 2010, p. 502). In the *Rejoinder*, Tooley, Dixon and Gomathi (2010) state the following:

> Indeed it [education] is and does. But where did Tooley ever say such a bizarre thing? ... Tooley's position is completely at odds with Sarangapani and Winch's reporting: to spell it out, for Tooley, education is *not* defined as educational opportunities, and education is *not* a commodity (although the delivery of educational opportunities may be). (p. 517)

Tooley, Dixon and Gomathi (2010) then provide quotations from Tooley's earlier work where his view is stated.

Sarangapani and Winch (2010) also imply that Tooley is advocating here the benefits of unregulated private schools as such (p. 501). While in some of his most extreme writings he does advocate that there should be no state regulation for schools beyond those that control any business (e.g. Tooley, 2000), he has been inconsistent in his writing on this issue. In this article and elsewhere, Tooley recognises the need for 'the establishment of improved regulatory environments' (Tooley & Dixon, 2005; Tooley, Dixon & Gomathi, 2010, p. 558), although not necessarily from the state as such. These schools may be unregulated at the moment because they are unrecognised, although Indian laws still apply, but in this article this is not put forward as an ideal. What the article indicates is that, even in this unregulated condition, these unrecognised private schools seemed to do better than government schools on a range of indicators.

In the second part of their *Reply*, Sarangapani and Winch (2010) move on to a critique of the empirical study itself. This part is divided into eight sub-sections. Space limitations make it impossible to discuss each of the many points in detail (and, indeed, this is not the purpose of this chapter), but, in amongst much that is irrelevant to the claims being made in the Tooley, Dixon and Gomathi (2007) article, Sarangapani and Winch do make some worthwhile points.

The first worthwhile point is that the characterisation of the sample as being simply from the slum areas of three zones in Hyderabad is inadequate because it highlights only the variable of economic status. They argue that this group is not just 'poor' but also a religious minority – specifically, an Urdu-speaking Muslim population. Here we have a definitional claim from Tooley, Dixon and Gomathi (2007) that is suspect. In the *Rejoinder*, Tooley, Dixon and Gomathi (2010) admit that this should have been clearer (p. 519).

As it was not even mentioned in the first article, this is certainly correct. The fact that many of these children were from religious and linguistic minorities is a necessary contextualising feature that should have been included in the original article. It may well have affected parents' motivations for sending their children to private schools and, importantly, it may also mean that there is some domestic advantage to these children, since they are more likely to have their mother at home. In the later linked article (Tooley, Dixon, Shamsan et al, 2010), the authors actually show that there is an advantage to the group in private schools in that the *fathers* of these children had longer formal educations than the fathers of children in government schools.

But it is also important to recognise that the 2007 article, which is the subject of the *Reply*, is not about motivations, and no descriptive or explanatory claims are made about them; nor is it about a wider Indian population. It is about the schooling of 262,000 children in the three zones, about three-quarters of whom were in private schools. These figures show that 'the private sector is certainly a significant provider for the poor' (Tooley, Dixon & Gomathi, 2007, p. 557) in this context, although not necessarily the very poorest. There is no need to state that Tooley, Dixon and Gomathi are trying to imply that 'the findings of the experiences of this group vis-à-vis education providers is representative in general of the urban poor' (Sarangapani & Winch, 2010, p. 505). This is not what they stated in that article.

Indeed, Tooley, Dixon and Gomathi (2007) indicate that '[p]arallel research was undertaken in selected low-income areas of India, China, Ghana, Nigeria and Kenya' (p. 541). Tooley and Dixon (2007a) had already published a somewhat similar study of schools in East Delhi; Tooley, Dixon and Amuah (2007) had published one on the District of Ga, Ghana; and Tooley et al (2005) had published one on Lagos State, Nigeria. These three publications follow a similar structure to the Hyderabad article under critique and result from very similarly conducted empirical work. A further chapter on the wider study was also available in 2007 in an edited book by Srivastava and Walford (2007) (Tooley & Dixon, 2007b).

The article on schooling in the slums of East Delhi (Tooley & Dixon, 2007a) is based on a census of 265 schools providing for 137,000 children. In this case, while only about one-quarter of schools were government schools, they provided schooling for 60% of the children in the census. Here, teacher absence rates were lowest in government schools, but the percentage of teachers actually teaching when researchers visited classrooms was only 38%, compared with an average of 61% overall, and 72% in unregistered private schools. That study also found that there was gender inequity, with considerably more girls in government schools than boys (60.4% and 39.6%).

The study in the District of Ga, Ghana (Tooley, Dixon & Amuah 2007) had a slightly different method of locating schools, but a total of 161,000 students were found in 779 schools, of which 64% were in private schools. There was little gender imbalance. The study in Nigeria found 540 schools in the selected areas. The authors calculated that about three-quarters of the more than one million children in Lagos State were in private schools. More results from the wider project have been published since the time of the original article (e.g. Tooley, 2009; Tooley, Dixon, Shamsan et al, 2010). The various studies (and those by other researchers) show that in many different areas and countries, low-fee private schools are certainly providing education for many children from poor families. Again, there are no claims that these areas are representative of the countries studied – indeed, most of the study sites were chosen specifically because they were *not* representative.

The second main area of critique by Sarangapani and Winch (2010) is that of the quality indicators used in the original article. They state: 'Tooley et al have chosen a new set of very unusual metrics as proxies for "quality" of educational opportunities' (Sarangapani & Winch, 2010, p. 511). Yet, Tooley, Dixon and Gomathi (2007) argue that these indicators have already been widely used in previous research, and many have. Most are straightforward variables that relate to the quality of infrastructure, such as having a playground, desks, library, access to a computer, toilets, and drinking water.

This is not to argue that they are ideal indicators of quality. Indeed, there are wide-ranging debates about what quality education would actually constitute. However, the compromises that are inherent to empirical work often demand that less-than-ideal indicators are used simply because they can be readily measured. In a survey of more than 900 schools, it may simply not be possible to undertake a full analysis of the curriculum as presented in the classroom. Such a study would certainly be worth doing, but it could not possibly be conducted as part of a survey of 900-plus schools.

What is worrying about Sarangapani and Winch's *Reply* is that there are several indications that they do not seem to have read the detail of the original article. They claim, for example, that Tooley, Dixon and Gomathi (2007) have missed results from their earlier research which showed that schools can give free places for instrumental self-interested reasons rather than philanthropic ones. In fact, Tooley, Dixon and Gomathi (2007) claim that 'the reasons for offering these [free and concessionary seats] may be a mixture of philanthropy and self-interest' (p. 579). There is no attempt to suggest that the majority of these schools are not profit-making concerns, but they do suggest that some, on occasion, act philanthropically.

Similarly, Sarangapani and Winch (2010) state that the original study 'does not contain even a mention of tuition centres, tuition classes or tutorials' and that 'given the total absence of any mention of the tuition centres in this otherwise detailed survey, we cannot be sure that their researchers did not classify tuition centres as "schools", thereby leading to over-reporting' (p. 506). However, the original article shows that Tooley, Dixon and Gomathi (2007) were well aware of learning centres and other forms of part-time additional schooling, and have explicitly excluded them from the study (p. 542). Another example is Sarangapani and Winch's (2010) statement that Tooley, Dixon and Gomathi claim that 'provision of English is 'an additional reason' why parents choose to send their children to these schools' (p. 509). In fact, they claim nothing of the sort, but say that the literature suggests this. They then present data showing the percentages with English provision for the different types of school.

In places, Sarangapani and Winch's logic is somewhat convoluted. They argue, for example, that it would have been useful to sub-divide the government schools in a similar way to the private schools and, in particular, to 'identify the very large number of schools created under Sarva Siksha Abhiyan [SSA] (1998 ongoing) and the District Primary Education Project [DPEP] (1992-1998)' (Sarangapani & Winch, 2010, p. 508), which resulted from foreign aid and loan driven programmes, and where there was a very significant lowering of standards in basic school requirements. They later state that 'it is not surprising that the government schools come out worse than the private schools [on various proxies for quality], given that a large majority were opened under the SSA and DPEP[,] programmes that deliberately downgraded the resources available relative to other government schools' (Sarangapani & Winch, 2010, p. 512).

The division into two groups might, indeed, have been informative. But if SSA and DPEP schools really are a 'large majority' (Sarangapani & Winch, 2010, p. 512) of schools in census zones, then these *are* a good representation of available government schools. Sarangapani and Winch seem to admit that the majority of government schools have been downgraded and have poor facilities, yet cling to an ideal of a government school that may hardly still exist.

Sarangapani and Winch's (2010) discussion of pupil-teacher ratios is similarly muddled (p. 507). They seem to accept that the 1:25 ratio found by Tooley, Dixon and Gomathi (2007) for the unrecognised unaided private schools in their sample is actually better than that found in government schools, but they then seem to advocate that multi-grade classes and unfilled vacancies should be seen as an acceptable part of schooling. Sarangapani and Winch conclude their *Reply* by applying the criteria used by Tooley with Darby (1998) in assessing the conduct of educational research. They recommended that research reports should be judged against the following four questions:

> 1. Does the research involve triangulation in order to establish its trustworthiness?
> 2. Does the research avoid sample bias?
> 3. Does the research use primary sources in the literature review?
> 4. Does the research avoid partisanship in the way it is carried out, and the interpretation of the data? (Tooley with Darby, 1998, quoted in Sarangapani & Winch, 2010, p. 513)

Sarangapani and Winch (2010) indicate their belief that questions 1, 2 and 4 are not respected in Tooley, Dixon and Gomathi's (2007) work (p. 513). They believe that the lack of triangulation is evident in the failure to obtain parents' perceptions on why private schooling is thought to be desirable. But this is irrelevant as there are no claims made about motivations. While it is actually difficult to use triangulation in a survey of this type, the researchers tried using it by checking easily available documentation against what was said by principals. As the study is a census of a particular group, sample bias is not a consideration. No claims are made about the representativeness of the census group. Indeed, it is evident that they are an unusual group, being from the poor areas of three particular zones in Hyderabad.

Sarangapani and Winch (2010) claim that the most glaring violation is that of question 4 (p. 513). Tooley, Dixon and Gomathi (2010) admit that explaining the religious composition of the census group would have been preferable (p. 519). This would have allowed a greater contextualisation of the particular group within the wider Indian context. It needs to be stressed, however, that no claims are made in the article about generalisation or motivations for using private schools. My evaluation of the original article is thus more positive than that of Sarangapani and Winch. It does have limitations, as does all published research.

My criticisms of the *Reply* are *not* to be read as saying that there is nothing of value in what Saragapani and Winch (2010) have written. There are several points that are central to a wider debate about the possible effects of supporting such private schools, but these are lost within a critique that misreads what has been said in the article, and over-interprets the actual claims made. One of the problems is that the critique is partly about a 'wall' that Saragapani and Winch (2010) believe Tooley, Dixon and Gomathi are building (which may be a valid concern), and they do not look carefully enough at the structure and nature of this particular single brick.

The Personal and the Political

In his book *The Beautiful Tree*, Tooley (2009) writes about the reception that his work has often had at conferences, where he claims to have often come under sustained attack from academics and those involved in aid and development work (p. 198). He claims that results of his empirical research are ignored or dismissed because of a widely held ideological belief that schools that make a profit could never be 'pro-poor'. It is undoubtedly true that much of Tooley's work has been controversial, though it is certainly not marginalised.

He is considered a right-wing academic, and for a long time was Director of the Education and Training Unit at the Institute for Economic Affairs, London. He established the E.G. West Centre at the University of Newcastle (where he is Professor of Education Policy), named after a historian who argued that universal primary education in the West had been achieved predominately by private provision, not through public intervention (Tooley, 2008).

Tooley's position (and that of his colleagues) on private schooling and privatisation is well known. Tooley has championed the role of the market in the provision of education with titles such as *Disestablishing the School* (1995), *Education without the State* (1996) and *Reclaiming Education* (2000) (see also Tooley, 1997, 2001b; Tooley et al, 2003). He edited a 25-year celebratory volume on the University of Buckingham, the UK's first private university (Tooley, 2001a), and wrote a controversial book on women and education provocatively titled *The Miseducation of Women* (2002). More influentially, he was the main author of a highly critical report for the Office for Standards in Education (Ofsted) on the quality of educational research (Tooley with Darby, 1998). Chris Woodhead, the then Director of Ofsted, further exaggerated the trenchant criticism in the report. More recently, Tooley has been President of the Orient Global Education Fund, which was designed to invest in low-fee schools in developing countries, and in Hyderabad he created a chain of low-fee private schools.

My own position on private schools, privatisation and the market is also well known. I am a long-time supporter of comprehensive education (Walford, 1997). I wrote a book on the relationships between private schools and privilege in 1990, and researched the first City Technology College (Walford & Miller, 1991) where we saw the potentially negative effects of the school on other neighbouring schools. I have investigated the problematic nature of markets in education and firmly critiqued the pro-market position (Walford, 1990, 1994, 1996, 2006).

But what do either of these records imply for the assessment that should be made of a particular piece of research? Surely, each piece of research and the report of that research should be examined on its own terms? We should, of course, be critical of all research, but we should also be open to new research from wherever it comes.

My own view follows that of Hammersley (2005) in his response to an editorial in the first issue of the *International Journal of Research & Method in Education*, where it was argued that there was a 'duty of doubt', and that the function of academic work was iconoclasm – the attacking of cherished beliefs. Hammersley (2005) argues that 'a willingness to be sceptical is a very important element of the process of enquiry, but the *purpose* of research is to pursue knowledge' (p. 106, emphasis in original). The purpose of academic work is for a community of researchers to gradually build new knowledge. It is not helpful if critics are over-critical – that is, if they do not take into account the limitations that are inherent in all empirical research, or if they draw upon elements that are not relevant to the actual contribution in their criticism.

Thus, the key aspects that have to be judged of any academic contribution are the plausibility and credibility of any claims made by researchers. This is a matter of degree, but there comes a point when, based on the evidence presented, the knowledge claims must become sufficiently plausible and credible to be accepted as true. There is, of course, no foundation of absolutely valid knowledge, but researchers within a research community need to take note of what their colleagues are likely to accept as beyond reasonable doubt. As Foster et al (1996) argue, agreement is likely to be greater, and the resulting consensus likely to be closer to the truth, to the extent that the research community is guided by the following norms:

> 1. The overriding concern of researchers is the truth of claims, not their political or practical implications.
> 2. Arguments are not judged on the basis of the personal and/or social characteristics of the person advancing them, but in terms of their plausibility and credibility.
> 3. Researchers are willing to change their views if arguments from common ground suggest those views are false; and, equally important, they assume (and behave as if) fellow researchers have the same attitude.
> 4. The research community is open to participation by anyone able and willing to operate on the basis of these first three rules. In particular, there must be no restriction of participation on the grounds of political or religious beliefs and attitudes.
> 5. Where substantial agreement does not result, all parties must recognise that there remains some reasonable doubt about the validity of their own positions, so that whenever these are presented they must be accompanied by supporting argument or reference to where such argument can be found. (p. 39)

The examination of a single academic study or 'brick' is merely the first step. No action should be based on the results of a single study. One must examine the much larger growing 'wall' of research and determine how well the new brick fits with existing ones. In various writings, academics will try to build substantial arguments out of the bricks. These 'walls' may well be unstable if the new brick is of a different structure, size or shape to the other bricks, but by examining each brick for what it is, we may be able to find a use for well-made bricks even if they come from an unexpected manufacturer.

Meanwhile, the problems in developing countries remain, and simple solutions to the provision of high quality schooling in situations of endemic poverty and corruption are not possible. Tooley, Dixon and Gomathi (2007) record just how common low-fee private schools were in the particular poorer areas in Hyderabad, and how (on some simple indicators) the quality of what they offer seemed to be higher than that of comparable government schools. There is obviously a need for further research and the development of better quality indicators, but there is also a need to take this message seriously and to study low-fee private schools for what they are. In so doing, we add a small brick to our knowledge and, with the results of other studies, we can try to evaluate how developing countries might, or might not, be able to use these schools in their attempts to reach Millennium Development Goals and goals beyond 2015.

References

Foster, P., Gomm, R. & Hammersley, M. (1996) *Constructing Educational Inequality: an assessment of research on school processes*. London: Falmer Press.

Gorard, S. (2001) *Quantitative Methods in Educational Research: the role of numbers made easy*. London: Continuum.

Gorard, S. (2010a) Measuring is More than Assigning Numbers, in G. Walford, E. Tucker & M. Viswanathan (Eds) *The Sage Handbook of Measurement*. London: Sage.

Gorard, S. (2010b) All Evidence is Equal: the flaw in statistical reasoning, *Oxford Review of Education*, 36(1), 63-77.

Hammersley, M. (1990) *Reading Ethnographic Research*. London: Longman.

Hammersley, M. (1994) Approaches to Educational Research and its Assessment, in *Study Guide: MA in education. Educational research methods*. Milton Keynes: Open University Press.

Hammersley, M. (2005) A Brief Response about Dissent, the 'Duty of Doubt', etc, *International Journal of Research & Method in Education*, 28(2), 105-108.

Sarangapani, P.M. & Winch, C. (2010) Tooley, Dixon and Gomathi on Private Education in Hyderabad: a reply, *Oxford Review of Education*, 36(4), 499-515.

Schagen, I. & Shamsan, Y. (2007) Analysis of International Data on the Impact of Private Schooling – Hyderabad, India. Statistics Research and Analysis Group, National Foundation for Educational Research, UK. http://www.nfer.ac.uk/nfer/publications/SJT02/SJT02.pdf

Tooley, J. (1995) *Disestablishing the School*. Aldershot: Avebury.

Tooley, J. (1996) *Education without the State*. London: Institute of Economic Affairs.

Tooley, J. (1997) Choice and Diversity in Education: a defence, *Oxford Review of Education*, 23(1), 113-116.

Tooley, J. (2000) *Reclaiming Education*. London: Cassell.

Tooley, J. (Ed.) (2001a) *Buckingham at 25: freeing the universities from state control.* London: Institute for Economic Affairs.

Tooley, J. (2001b) *The Global Education Industry: lessons from private education in developing countries* (2nd edn.). London: Institute of Economic Affairs in association with the International Finance Corporation.

Tooley, J. (2002) *The Miseducation of Women.* London: Continuum.

Tooley, J. (2008) *E.G. West. Economic Liberalism and the Role of Government in Education.* London: Continuum.

Tooley, J. (2009) *The Beautiful Tree: a personal journey into how the world's poorest people are educating themselves.* New Delhi: Penguin.

Tooley, J., with Darby, D. (1998) *Educational Research: a critique.* London: Office for Standards in Education.

Tooley, J. & Dixon, P. (2005) An Inspector Calls: the regulation of 'budget' private schools in Hyderabad, Andhra Pradesh, India, *International Journal of Educational Development*, 25(3), 269-285.

Tooley, J. & Dixon, P. (2007a) Private Schooling for Low-income Families: a census and comparative survey in East Delhi, India, *International Journal of Educational Development*, 27(2), 205-219.

Tooley, J. & Dixon, P. (2007b) Private Education for Low-income Families: results from a global research project, in P. Srivastava & G. Walford (Eds) *Private Schooling in Less Economically Developed Counties: Asian and African perspectives.* Oxford: Symposium Books.

Tooley, J., Dixon, P. & Amuah, I (2007) Private and Public Schooling in Ghana: a census and comparative survey, *International Review of Education*, 53(4), 389-415.

Tooley, J., Dixon, P. & Gomathi, S.V. (2007) Private Schools and the Millennium Development Goal of Universal Primary Education: a census and comparative survey in Hyderabad, India, *Oxford Review of Education*, 33(5), 539-560.

Tooley, J., Dixon, P. & Gomathi, S.V. (2010) A Rejoinder to Sarangapani and Winch, *Oxford Review of Education*, 36(4), 517-520.

Tooley, J., Dixon, P. & Olaniyan, O. (2005) Private and Public Schooling in Low-income Areas of Lagos State, Nigeria: a census and comparative survey, *International Journal of Educational Research*, 43(3), 125-146.

Tooley, J., Dixon, P., Shamsan, Y. & Schagen, I. (2010) The Relative Quality and Cost-effectiveness of Private and Public Schools for Low-income Families: a case study in a developing country, *School Effectiveness and School Improvement*, 21(2), 117-144.

Tooley, J., Dixon, P. & Stanfield, J. (2003) *Delivering Better Education: market solutions to education.* London: Adam Smith Institute.

Walford, G. (1990) *Privatization and Privilege in Education.* London: Routledge.

Walford, G. (1994) *Choice and Equity in Education.* London: Cassell.

Walford, G. (1996) Diversity and Choice in School Education: an alternative view, *Oxford Review of Education*, 22(2), 143-154.

Walford, G. (1997) Privatization and Selection, in R. Pring & G. Walford (Eds) *Affirming the Comprehensive Ideal.* London: Falmer.

Walford, G. (2006) *Markets and Equity in Education.* London: Continuum.

Walford, G. & Miller, H. (1991) *City Technology College*. Milton Keynes: Open University Press.

Notes on Contributors

Folasade Adefisayo is Director, Corona Secondary School, Lagos, Nigeria, the only secondary school in the group of schools owned by the Corona Schools Trust Council. Prior to this appointment, Ms Adefisayo was Executive Director of the Corona Schools Trust Council, a position from which she retired after eight years. A committed educationist, she has also been involved in research and education reforms and, for over six years, was consultant to the Education Policy Group of the Nigerian Economic Summit Group (NESG), a private sector-public sector think tank. In 2008, Ms Adefisayo was commissioned by the World Bank to conduct a survey of private secondary schools in Lagos State. A seminal experience, this led to another survey, this time on private primary schools in Lagos State commissioned by DFID. Ms Adefisayo holds an MBA and, before becoming an educationist, was a banker for over 16 years.

Kwame Akyeampong is Reader, Sussex School of Education and Social Work, University of Sussex, UK, and as of 2012, Senior Policy Analyst, Education for All Global Monitoring Report Team, UNESCO, Paris, France. From 2010-2012 he was Director, Centre for International Education, University of Sussex. Dr Akyeampong's research interests include teacher education policy and practice, access and quality issues in basic education, and education system and programme evaluation in low-income countries, and he has conducted research on teacher education in sub-Saharan Africa, education access, and decentralisation with a special focus on Ghana, Kenya, and Rwanda. He has published widely on the topics, and co-edited a special issue on 'Educational Access in Sub-Sahara Africa' for the journal *Comparative Education* (2009). His most recent research is an impact evaluation of the 'Speed School' accelerated learning programme for school dropouts in Ethiopia.

Roger Cunningham is Senior Education Adviser with Cambridge Education, Cambridge, UK. He was formerly Senior Education Adviser with the UK Department for International Development (DFID) (1997-2010). In the latter capacity he worked in Pakistan (2008-2010), India (2002-2005), and the Caribbean (1997-2002), and was on secondment to the European Union (2005-2008) as Regional Education Adviser to Southern Africa. In a career spanning work in over 25 countries, he has also worked for non-government organisations, the British Council, and private-sector companies.

His experience ranges across a number of areas in education and development, including education policy and strategic planning, aid programme design and management, and monitoring and evaluation. He is also a qualified primary teacher, and has worked in both public and private schools.

Pauline Dixon is Senior Lecturer in Development and Education, Newcastle University, UK, where she gained her PhD in 2003. For the last ten years her research has focused specifically on private and government schools that cater for low-income families living in the slums of Asia and Africa. Her work is published widely in books and academic journals, including *School Effectiveness and School Improvement*. She is currently acting as a consultant for the London-based charity Absolute Return for Kids (ARK), and is working with their team in Delhi to provide a framework and working model for a targeted education voucher scheme. Her doctoral research considered the regulations that private unaided schools in India had to abide by in order to gain recognition, from an Austrian economic perspective. She is author of *International Aid and Private Schools for the Poor: smiles, miracles and markets* (Edward Elgar, 2013).

Shailaja Fennell is a university lecturer in Development Studies, a Fellow, Jesus College, University of Cambridge, UK, and Director of Research, Cambridge Central Asia Forum. Dr Fennell was an international team leader on the project on public-private partnerships in education for the DFID-funded Research Consortium on Educational Outcomes and Poverty (RECOUP). She was a member of the team commissioned by the EU to bring about the first European Report on Development (2008-2009), *Overcoming Fragility in Africa: forging a new approach forward*. Dr Fennell has been appointed Visiting Professor at the Kazakh National University in Almaty (2008), and had a professorship conferred by the Kazakh-Turk University (2009). She holds BA, MA and MPhil degrees in Economics from the University of Delhi, and MPhil and PhD degrees from the University of Cambridge.

Joanna Härmä is Research Officer, Education for All Global Monitoring Report Team based in UNESCO, Paris, France, and Research Associate with the DFID-funded Consortium on Educational Access, Transitions and Equity (CREATE), University of Sussex, UK. Until October 2011, she was the private education specialist for the DFID-funded Education Sector Support Programme in Nigeria (ESSPIN), and had worked on the education management information system for three of ESSPIN's six states since April 2009. Before this, she was Visiting Scholar at Columbia University from 2008 to 2009, based in the National Center for the Study of Privatization in Education. She earned her doctorate at the Centre for International Education, University of Sussex. Her thesis investigated the school choice decisions of parents in remote rural Uttar Pradesh, India. She has authored several papers on the topic. While working for an anti-child-labour NGO, she started a girls' school with her husband in the same part of Uttar Pradesh. The school is funded through charitable contributions, and continues to thrive. Dr Härmä's writing is unconnected to her current work at UNESCO.

Stephen Heyneman is Professor of International Educational Policy, Vanderbilt University, USA, where he has been since 2000. He spent 22 years working on education at the World Bank. He received his PhD in Comparative Education at the University of Chicago.

Salman Humayun is Executive Director, Institute of Social and Policy Sciences (I-SAPS), Islamabad, Pakistan, and previously worked with the Education Sector Reforms Assistance (ESRA) Programme in Pakistan. He has substantial experience in the areas of strengthening policy and planning capacities of the Federal and Provincial Ministries of Education in Pakistan, and improving education governance through increased use of evidence-based decision making at national, provincial and district levels. Dr Humayun's range of experience spans public policy, public finance and governance reform, particularly with respect to sector financing and decentralisation and accountability mechanisms.

Yuki Ohara has been awarded a Japan Society for the Promotion of Science (JSPS) Postdoctoral Research Fellowship, Graduate School of Asia-Pacific Studies, Waseda University, Tokyo, Japan (2011~). She was previously awarded a JSPS doctoral research fellowship, which she held at the Department of Education, Kyoto University (2008-2010), and was also a research intern at the National University of Educational Planning and Administration (NUEPA), New Delhi (2008-2009). She completed her doctoral thesis on low-fee private schooling in India based on fieldwork conducted in Delhi, and recently obtained her PhD from the Department of Education, Kyoto University, Japan. Her work on low-fee private schools has been published in several Japanese journals, including *Comparative Education*, *South Asian Studies* and *Educational System and Organization*, and in the British Association for International and Comparative Education's journal, *Compare* (2012).

Caine Rolleston is Education Research Officer for Young Lives, Department of International Development, University of Oxford, UK. Previously, he worked as a researcher for the Consortium on Educational Access, Transitions and Equity (CREATE), University of Sussex, while conducting doctoral research at the Institute of Education, University of London, focused on issues of access to and the economic benefits of education in sub-Saharan Africa. Dr Rolleston's background is in economics and education, but he has experience working across a variety of disciplinary approaches, and on issues of education access and poverty reduction. This includes research on the growth of the low-fee private sector in Ghana and Nigeria, as part of the Soros Open Society Institute Privatisation in Education Research Initiative (PERI), and on financing the education MDGs for UNESCO's Education for All Global Monitoring Report.

Ian Schagen is currently working as a freelance analyst with particular interests in education in developing countries. He was, for many years, Head of the Statistics Research and Analysis Group at the National Foundation for Educational Research (NFER), leading the largest group of statisticians in the UK on education research. His particular interests are on value-added analysis and multilevel modelling. Following his retirement in April 2008, he worked for a year with the Research Division of the Ministry of Education of New Zealand as Chief Research Analyst. He is the author of numerous academic papers and technical reports, and the co-editor of *But What Does It Mean? The use of effect sizes in educational research* (2004).

Rizwana Shahzad is Research Fellow, Institute of Social and Policy Sciences (I-SAPS), Islamabad, Pakistan, where she has been conducting various studies and assessments on education financing, governance, and service delivery systems. Ms Shahzad holds a master's degree in Social Sciences from the Quaid-i-Azam University, Islamabad.

Prachi Srivastava is Associate Professor, School of International Development and Global Studies, University of Ottawa, Canada. Her research interests include the privatisation of education and private schooling in developing countries, in particular low-fee private schooling; non-state and private actors in international education and development; and global education policy and the right to education. She has been working on low-fee private schooling with a focus on India for more than a decade. She has published widely on the topics. Her works have appeared in *Compare*, *Development*, *Development in Practice*, the *International Journal of Educational Development*, among others. She co-edited *Private Schooling in Less Economically Developed Countries: Asian and African perspectives* (2007, with Geoffrey Walford). Dr Srivastava has recently been awarded a major grant as Principal Investigator by the Social Sciences and Humanities Research Council (SSHRC) of Canada to investigate the emergence of new non-state private actors in education and the right to education, and has recently completed a project (with CORD) on the early implementation of India's Right to Education Act and the role of the private sector in Delhi, funded by the Soros Open Society Institute's Privatisation in Education Research Initiative (PERI). She earned her doctorate from the University of Oxford.

Jonathan Stern is a doctoral student in International Education Policy and Management at Vanderbilt University, USA. He is a participant in the Experimental Education Research Training (ExpERT) program sponsored by the US Department of Education. He is also a sponsored Fellow of the Institute of Education Sciences, and recipient of a Peabody Graduate Honor Scholarship.

James Tooley is Professor of Education Policy, Newcastle University, UK. He has been working in the field of low-cost private schools in Asia and Africa for over a decade. His book documenting this work, *The Beautiful Tree* (2009), won the 2010 Sir Antony Fisher Memorial Prize. He was founding president of the education fund Orient Global, and lived in Hyderabad, India for two years, where he created a chain of low-cost private schools. Since then he has helped set up educational companies in China and Ghana, with a further company in India.

Geoffrey Walford is Emeritus Professor of Education Policy and Emeritus Fellow of Green Templeton College, University of Oxford, UK. He was joint editor of the *British Journal of Educational Studies* (1999 to 2002), and editor of the *Oxford Review of Education* (2004 to 2010). His books include: *Privatization and Privilege in Education* (1990); *Choice and Equity in Education* (1994); *Policy, Politics and Education: sponsored grant-maintained schools and religious diversity* (2000); *Private Education: tradition and continuity* (2005); and *Markets and Equity in Education* (2006). He has also edited many books, including: *Private Schools in Ten Countries: policy and practice* (1989); *Private Schooling: tradition, change and diversity* (1991); *The Private Schooling of Girls: past and present* (1993); *Private Schooling in Less Economically Developed Countries: Asian and African perspectives* (2007, with Prachi Srivastava); and *Blair's Educational Legacy?* (2010).